The Secret
Code
of
Revelation

The Secret Code

of

Revelation

With the Keys to Genesis and the Rest of the Bible

by
Daniel R. Condron
D.M., D.D., M.S.

Library of Congress Control Number: 2006905885

Library of Congress Cataloging in Publication Data
Condron, Daniel R.
   The Secret Code of Revelation
   With the Keys to Genesis and the Rest of the Bible
   Summary: Revelation and explanation of the secret code and meaning
of the *Book of Revelation* based upon a lifetime of intuitive insight, study, effort
and investigation. Includes insights into earlier scriptures and their modern
application for enlightenment of consciousness.

ISBN: 0-944386-37-7

If you desire to learn more about the research and teachings in this book,
write to School of Metaphysics World Headquarters,
163 Moon Valley Road
Windyville, Missouri 65783
Or call us at 417-345-8411.

Visit us on the Internet at:
www.som.org or
www.dreamschool.org

The Bible is: The book of the Whole Structure of Mind

Thank you to Karen Mosby who with devotion and perseverance, aided in the preparation of the manuscript.

Thanks also to my wife Barbara for her support and encouragement.

Table of Contents

Introduction

This I know.

At the age of 10 I realized the Bible was written in pictures. I thought, "It would be great to have the whole Bible in pictures." I began to look for and read Bible stories with pictures. I began to collect pictures of Bible stories, putting them in a spiral notebook.

In the 1970's I began to understand that the word 'symbols' is a way to describe this idea of pictures. Metaphor, allegory and pictures are all ways of describing a story.

When a story is read to you, your mind begins to form pictures from the words spoken. Thus, words are a symbolic or abstract representation of an idea or mental picture being conveyed by an author.

In 1978, during one weekend, I read and interpreted the entire book of Revelation into the language of pictures, which is the Universal Language of Mind.

The Mind thinks in pictures. The physical brain thinks in abstractions based on separation. The mind thinks in pictures based upon connectedness.

Connectedness is the true reality. Separateness is the illusion. Separateness is the false, kind of physical way of thinking that is totally based on sensory experience. The true reality is known by the conscious, subconscious and superconscious minds, not the physical brain.

In 1980, I read the Bible from cover to cover.

I wrote this book after writing a book entitled <u>Permanent Healing</u> that explains and reveals how thought-image-pictures affect one's physical health and how to change mental pictures to achieve health.

I wrote this book in 1992. It is a book I was born to write in partial fulfillment of my requirements for this lifetime. My soul came into this lifetime to teach the Universal Language of Mind, the Universal Principles and the Universal Structure of Creation. I am here to teach Universals.

The book of Revelation is the Universal story of the evolution of humanity. This is a book about Revelation and its secret or inner meaning. So why cover the first three chapters of Genesis? Genesis is the first book of the Bible and Revelation is the last book of the Bible. In order to understand Revelation it is necessary to know something of the deeper meaning of Genesis.

I have also included the part of the book of Matthew that explains Jesus' discipline in the wilderness and his encounter with the devil-Satan. The conscious-serpent-devil-Satan-dragon must be mastered in order for the Real Self, I AM, to manifest as the Christ within. Those who read this entire book will find their understanding of the whole Mind, the whole Self and the Purpose of Life magnified.

We are here on this planet Earth, in physical bodies, for the purpose of receiving and achieving enlightenment, which is Christ consciousness which is the second coming of Christ. The second coming of Christ is meant to happen in each individual. It does not happen by chance or accident. It must be caused.

Christ consciousness must be brought about by the conscious will and the imaging faculty of the individual. Then the Self must surrender the conscious ego to the High Self-I AM. Only then can and will the second coming of Christ be received into one's full conscious awareness.

Within these pages are the step-by-step instructions for enlightenment. Revelation has given these coded instructions. In this book are the keys to unlocking the secret code of the Revelation.

Now the door lies open to anyone who would consciously choose to receive, use, apply and practice the truth herein.

Let those with eyes see. Let those with ears hear, as the Bible says.

May Christ consciousness be yours. May the second coming of Christ be within you.

In love and truth——Daniel R. Condron

"Truly, truly, I say to you,
He who believes in me shall do
the works which I do; and even
greater than these things he
shall do, because I am going
to my Father."

John 14:12

Keys to Genesis

Chapter 1 of Genesis

Few Word Essence of Chapter 1
of the Book of Genesis

Beginning
The Plan of Creation is designed

Brief and More Expanded Essence of Chapter 1
of the Book of Genesis

From stillness comes a thought. This thought is the beginning of
creation. All creation begins with thought. The details of the
Plan of Creation are imaged with thought. The Plan includes
creating beings that will become like the Creator.

Chapter 1 of Genesis

New Symbols & The Interpretation of Chapter 1 of Genesis

1. heavens - Superconscious Mind

2. earth - Subconscious Mind

3. void - empty

4. spirit - breath

5. LIGHT - awareness

6. darkness - receptivity

7. water - conscious life experience

8. trees and vegetation - subconscious existence and experience

9. living creatures - habits, compulsion

10. day - a cycle of aggressive and receptive, giving and receiving

11. image - imagination, visualization

12. likeness - with similar attributes

The Book of Genesis

The book of Genesis can be physically interpreted as a history book concerning the past, or mentally interpreted about the individual in the present moment.

The mental interpretation for the individual, the soul, in the present moment is the approach I have taken. Why?

Because only in the present moment may one grow in soul awareness and gain enlightenment. The present moment, the ever-present now is the only reality. The past is over. The future is yet to come. The present is all we have.

Most people live in memories of the past whether conscious or unconscious. Some exist in their thoughts about imagined fantasies of the future. However, I AM, the Real Self, exists in the ever present now.

I AM is present.

I was is past.

I will be is future.

Therefore, to gain the Christ consciousness we must practice being in the present moment.

A physical interpretation of Genesis as history can be stated thusly:

A Creator perceived from the vantage point of a still and empty mind, the need to create.

This perception created an awareness of a need to create with form. This awareness we call LIGHT.

This LIGHT was separated from darkness which created the Aggressive and Receptive Principles of creation.

The Creator, by whatever name you choose to call him, breathed life-spirit-cosmic energy into this thought form of creation. The Old Testament book of Genesis in the original Hebrew language uses the word Elohim to indicate God.

The Creator then created Mind. From Mind the Creator created three divisions of Mind. The Conscious Mind, the Subconscious Mind and the Superconscious Mind.

Heaven - Superconscious Mind

Earth - Subconscious Mind

Sea - Conscious Mind

The Creator then created the root races of:
> gas
> mineral
> plant
> animal
> and the beginning of human or reasoning man.

The Creator created beings with the capability of being like the Creator (gods). These capabilities may be described as image and likeness.

The rest of the Old Testament of the **Bible** is the history of humanity striving to be like our Maker. At this point in the **Bible** the name of God shifts from Elohim to Yahweh or Jehovah, which is translated as Lord. Elohim Yahweh is translated as Lord God in Genesis 2:5.

This is the historical interpretation of Genesis.

Next you will find out the mental, present time interpretation. This interpretation will tell you how the Creator creates so you can create your own enlightenment in the present moment.

Book of Genesis
The Book of the Whole Plan and Beginning of Creation

Chapter 1

1 God created the heavens and the earth in the very beginning.

A creator creates. All creation begins with an idea. The word for God in Hebrew is Elohim. Elohim is a plural word. Thus the creator has both the aggressive and receptive principles of creation and of being.

In order for a creation and a creator to succeed there needs to be a plan. There also needs to be created the field of experience or place of activity in order to fully manifest the plan.

Heaven is that plan. Earth is the field of experience.

2 And the earth was without form and void; and darkness was upon the face of the deep; And the Spirit of God moved upon the face of the water.

The earth, the field of experience, is without form until some experience is gained. An idea doesn't begin to take on form until something, some movement or action, is taken on the idea.

Void means to be empty and without matter.

Before creation can begin the mind must be empty.

Before the mind can be empty the mind must be still.

The earth was empty and formless because the first action had yet to be taken on the idea.

Darkness is the lack of awareness that exists when there is no experience.

The face symbolizes identity. Darkness was upon the face of the deep because the one whose identity has developed an empty mind is capable of thinking deep thoughts.

Spirit means and is breath.

0 = zero = stillness = void or empty

1 = moved = aggressive

2 = water = receptive

Once a thought of creation begins to move in the Self the breath is employed to move an idea into existence.

Thought and breath together bring an idea into existence.

The spirit of God is the breath of the one creating.

Anytime anyone is creating, that one needs to breathe. To breathe is the intake and outflow of life force. Life force or cosmic energy provides the energy, the fuel, for creation to occur.

Water is conscious life or conscious life experience, or conscious experience.

The face of the water symbolizes one's identity in the experience.

That the spirit of God moved upon the face of the water indicates that the breath of a creator is necessary to add experience to the identity.

Breath or breathing is the inflow and outflow of life force.

The steps of Creation:
1. **First comes the still mind.**
2. **Then comes the empty mind.**
3. **Then the mind is ready to be filled.**
4. **Then a formless thought is chosen.**
5. **Then the breath moves the idea into form.**
6. **From this there is an addition to the identity and awareness.**
7. **Then one builds on and creates details and specifics from the Light of awareness.**

3 And God said, Let there be light; and there was light.

LIGHT is awareness.

To state, "let there be LIGHT," indicates one has a greater awareness and intends to use that greater awareness to create in a greater way. When one experiences a growth in consciousness one never goes back to the old way of being. From then on the life takes on greater meaning. When one says let there be LIGHT-awareness and there is LIGHT-awareness, the ability to cause permanent learning has been achieved. LIGHT is the only begotten son of the Creator.

The keys to creation, given in the commentary of verse 2, indicate the steps a creator causes, receives and achieves in order to learn how to cause awareness.

4 And God saw that the light was good; and God separated the light from the darkness.

A creator recognizes and identifies that greater awareness is productive.

To be good is to be useful, purposeful, serviceable, advantageous, beneficial and wholesome.

Therefore, a creator identifies the awareness as being useful and beneficial for adding to the whole Self. This separation of LIGHT from darkness is our movement away from our source or beginning as LIGHT through the levels of Mind until the final descent into the physical world, the level of Mind with the most darkness.

The one creating learns to separate what produces awareness from what is lacking awareness. Such a one separates and identifies what needs to occur in order for greater awareness and understanding to occur. There is an admitting of what one needs to do and produce in order to connect with greater and more expanded LIGHT-awareness.

One needs to learn what produces permanent learning and what leaves one unchanged.

5 And God called the light Day, and the darkness he called Night. And there was evening and there was morning, the first day.

In order to call the LIGHT day, one must identify awareness and what produces awareness.

In order to call or name anything one must identify that thing. Once something is identified by using one's awareness, that thing, situation or circumstance can usually be repeated over and over. A creator identifies awareness as productive and beneficial and therefore continues to produce greater awarenesses. A creator also identifies the lack of awareness in Self and the need to assimilate the learning. This produces a cycle of learning. The new awareness and assimilation of the new awareness produce a cycle of learning.

This completes the first step of the Plan of Creation.

The first step of any conscious, productive creation is to separate what produces awareness-day from what gives assimilation of the learning-night.

**6 And God said, Let there be a firmament in the midst of
the waters, and let it divide the waters from the waters.**

A firmament is firm. A firmament is the region of the air, sky or
heavens. The firmament is the Dome in Mind that separates the
Superconscious Mind from the conscious Mind.

The firmament in the midst of the waters is the Creator separating
the Plan of Creation from the action-activity of creation, the field of
experience.

Water is conscious life experience. Conscious life experience is
caused learning of Self and creation through and in one's life experiences of which one is consciously aware.

Some people sit around and daydream all day without taking action on their ideas. This does not produce permanent learning for the
Self. Other people work hard day after day yet fail to create and bring
greater awareness and understanding to the Self. The one who would
become an enlightened Christ brings the thoughts, plans, and ideals
into physical manifestation.

The firmament divides the plan and the life force-breath from the
activity and experience.

**7 And God made the firmament, and divided the
waters that were under the firmament from the
waters that were above the firmament; and it was so.**

A creator divides the plan from the experience, the idea from the
activity.

Before one manifests or makes a creation occur, the thought image
must be clear enough in the mind that one can speak it. Speaking an
idea or thought is the first step of understanding and manifesting a
thought. Until a thought is spoken it is an idea. To speak a thought
requires action. To understand an idea and to include it in one's experience requires action.

Speaking, to say an idea, a thought, is the firmament. Speaking is
the separating point or the middle step between thinking a thought or
idea and fully manifesting or creating it as part of one's experience.

In order to know your thoughts it is important to speak them aloud.

**8 And God called the firmament Sky. And there
was evening and there was morning, the second day.**

The firmament is when the idea becomes more firm in your consciousness. Writing also can be a way to make the idea more firm in one's consciousness.

Making the idea firm in one's consciousness is called sky in this verse. Sky comes from the word for cloud. Jesus, the Christ said, "See I come amidst the clouds." Sky is also related to the word for shade. Sky is the apparent vault or arch of heaven. To call something is to give it a name. To name something is to identify it. A creator must identify the thoughts of Self by speaking and secondarily writing them.

The second step or day of any and all creation is to be used in separating and identifying the thought-idea from the experience.

> **9 And God said, Let the waters that are under the sky be gathered together in one place, and let the dry land appear; and it was so.**

Water symbolizes conscious, life experience. To gather the waters into one place one must identify one's experiences and begin to see how to use them productively.

Land represents subconscious mind substance that prepares the way for subconscious life experience.

The subconscious mind's duty is to store one's permanent understandings.

This separation of the land from the water represents a creator's ability to begin to plan to store one's understood experiences, one's understandings, permanently.

This design creates a place and way for temporary experiences and a place for storing permanent learning received from those temporary experiences.

> **10 And God called the dry land Earth; and the gathering together of the waters he called Seas; and God saw that it was good.**

Calling the dry land Earth shows identification. Calling the gathered water seas indicates a creator has identified the conscious life experiences.

Earth means soil and dwelling. Soil symbolizes subconscious mind substance. The Universal Subconscious Mind is the dwelling, the abode of the soul.

To be good is to be productive and beneficial. It is productive and beneficial to have both a mental, idea plan and a plan of action. One needs to learn and one needs a way to remember what has been learned. The brain serves as a temporary memory storage device for the physical body. However, you are not just a temporary physical body. You are an eternal soul. One's subconscious or soul therefore, was created with the ability to store permanent understandings of Self and Creation.

> 11 And God said, Let the earth bring forth vegeta-
> tion, the herb yielding seed after its kind, and the
> fruit tree yielding fruit after its kind, wherein is
> their seed, upon the earth; and it was so. 12 And the
> earth brought forth vegetation, the herb yielding
> seed after its kind, and the tree bearing fruit,
> wherein is its seed, after its kind; and God saw that
> it was good. 13 And there was evening and there
> was morning, the third day.

Then a creator creates a way to produce and reproduce knowledge and permanent understanding from every creation. This ability to produce permanent knowledge, termed understandings, is symbolized by fruit and seeds. Food symbolizes knowledge.

It is productive and beneficial to be able to reproduce success. It is also productive and beneficial to be able to remember, use, and apply all the learning one has received.

The third day of creation involves imaging a plan that enables one to:

1. have experiences,
2. receive the learning in the experiences,
3. store the permanent learning received from those experiences.

> 14 Then God said, Let there be lights in the firma-
> ment of the heaven to separate the day from the
> night; and let them be for signs, and for seasons, and
> for days, and years.

Light symbolizes awareness.

The plan a creator designs must have a way to involve learning. There also needs to be a way to record one's progress. One needs to learn when to be receptive and when to be aggressive, when to be in an experience and when to assimilate that experience.

A creator also needs to be able to determine progress and the rate of progress. All creations are and need to be for the learning of all those involved. The greatest learning, the true learning is permanent and eternal. When one has added to one's consciousness, the quality and aspects and details need to be identified and understood in the conscious mind. Then this understanding may be given as permanent knowledge and understanding to the soul, one's subconscious mind.

The Four steps or stages of growth are:
1. infancy
2. adolescence
3. adulthood
4. and wisdom

These four stages can be practiced with the following four qualities:
1. separate
2. identify
3. admit
4. connect

The word separate, as given in verse 14, indicates the ability to divide, set out or keep apart and determine the details of this Plan of Creation.

> **15 And let them be for lights in the firmament of the heaven to give light upon the earth; and it was so.**
> **16 And God made two great lights, the greater light to rule the day, and the smaller light to rule the night; and the stars also.**

The light in the firmament of Heaven is the LIGHT and life force that descends from Superconscious Mind. This LIGHT and Life Force from Superconscious Mind lights and enlivens all of the Subconscious Mind and the Conscious Mind or physical universe.

The greater light is the sun that symbolizes superconscious awareness.

The smaller or lesser light is the moon that symbolizes subconscious awareness.

Just as the moon reflects the sun's light, so the subconscious mind receives and reflects the Superconscious Mind Plan and Life Force. The stars symbolize awareness in the conscious mind. Therefore, each individual needs to learn to receive and use superconscious, subconscious and conscious Light, Life Force and Energy.

> **17 And God set them in the firmament of the heavens to give light upon the earth, 18 And to rule over the day and over the night, and to separate the light from the darkness; and God saw that it was good.**

The Superconscious Mind provides LIGHT for all of Mind. The LIGHT of Superconscious Mind flows down and into the Subconscious and Conscious Minds. This gives energy and motion to all life. This gives awareness and the possibility of greater awareness and high consciousness to all beings.

The cosmic energy of Superconscious Mind manifests as life force through all of Mind.

The greater light, the sun, is Superconscious Mind.

The lesser or smaller light, the moon, symbolizes Subconscious Mind.

The superconscious-sun rules over awareness gained through the aggressive quality of conscious experience.

The subconscious-moon rules over awareness gained through the receptive quality of conscious experience.

A creator's plan is the infancy stage of creation. This is why the word 'separate' is used so often in this, the first chapter of the first book of the **Bible**. To separate things out is a quality of infancy.

The first chapter of Genesis, the first book of the Bible, presents the quality of infancy.

Creating a plan for one's creation is the infancy stage of a creation. In a similar way, drawing up a blueprint, a plan for the construction of a building, is the infancy stage of that creation.

Darkness receives light. Light aggressively moves into and illuminates darkness. In a similar way, an enlightened being brings the light of awareness to the darkness of the people's ignorance.

> **19 And there was evening and there was morning, the fourth day.**

The quality of the number one is the aggressive and initiating factor.

The quality of the number two is the receptive nurturing, receiving factor.

The symbolic quality of the number three is creation. Bringing together the aggressive and receptive qualities creates a third factor. The Father and Mother together create a child.

The symbolic quality of the number four is stability. Once a new quality or understanding has been created in the Self, there is the need to stabilize at a higher or greater level.

Evening symbolizes the end or completion of one stage of awareness.

Morning represents the beginning of a new opportunity to learn and grow in awareness.

> **20 And God said, Let the waters bring forth swarms of living creatures, and let fowl fly above the earth in the open firmament of the heaven. 21 And God created great sea monsters, and every living creature that moves, which the waters brought forth abundantly after their kind, and every winged fowl after its kind; and God saw that it was good.**

Animals symbolize habits and brain pathways. Animals represent the way memories are stored in the brain and the need to learn to use these memories consciously and productively.

Water symbolizes conscious life experience. Our waking conscious life brings experiences. In order to add to one's creation there must be a memory bank installed. Without memory there can be no adding to or building upon what previously existed. Therefore, the quality of memory, of record keeping, must be factored into any plan.

Flying fowl, birds, symbolize subconscious thoughts. Flying fowl indicate the need for a capacity to transfer temporary memory and temporary experiences to permanent and lasting memory. The temporary memory is in the brain and conscious mind. The permanent memory is in the subconscious mind, the soul. Permanent memory is stored as understandings of Self and Creation. Thus, the Plan of Creation contained within chapter one of Genesis includes both short term and long term memory. Long term memory is permanent understandings of Self and Creation that last throughout eternity.

First God says something and then God creates what he just said. This occurs because stating aloud one's mental images is the first step to creating that mental image in a more solid, lasting or dense form. The stated mental image may be a goal, a desire, a need, or an ideal.

Then the next stage of a creation is the first action or activity such as speaking aloud one's ideas or writing one's ideas on paper or other method of bringing the idea more firmly into one's experience.

Verse 21 offers the first time since verse one in the **Bible** where it is stated that God created:

Verse 1-God created
Verse 2-The spirit of God moved

Verse 3-God said
Verse 4-God saw
Verse 5-God called

Verse 6-God said
Verse 7-God made
Verse 8-God called

Verse 9-God said
Verse 10-God called

Verse 11-God said
Verse 12-God saw

Verse 14-God said
Verse 16-God made
Verse 17-God set them
Verse 18-God saw

Verse 20-God said
Verse 21-God created

Therefore, memory is necessary to be a conscious creator. In previous verses the keys of attention and imagination have been presented. Now memory is added.

In order for full reasoning to occur and develop, one must employ the three factors of memory, attention and imagination. Thinking that lacks any of these three factors is not reasoning. Therefore, verses 20 and 21 show the incorporation of reasoning into the Plan of Creation.

In order to create and be a creator, one must have memory and use that memory with attention and imagination in order to create a more enlightened Self. Also, in order to create, one must initiate action on the thought, ideal, or goal.

22 And God blessed them, saying, Be fruitful and multiply, and fill the waters in the seas, and let fowl multiply on the earth.

To bless is to sanctify and to make holy with truth and life force.
To be holy is to be whole and complete.
Therefore, when God blessed them, it is to say, "This is a whole and complete idea."

In order to create the reasoner needs a whole plan and each part of the plan needs to be whole.

Fruit symbolizes knowledge. To multiply is to grow and to add to what already exists. Adding to what already exists is the mark of a reasoner.

This whole part of the Plan of Creation includes adding the productive use of memory and memory storage, both temporary and permanent.

The statement, "fill the water in the seas," means to fill the conscious mind with temporary memory capacity that can be used productively. Let the fowl multiply on the earth means to fill the subconscious mind with permanent memory called understandings.

23 And there was evening and there was morning, the fifth day.

Five is the number of reasoning. This is appropriate, for with the addition of memory we have the three factors necessary for reasoning in place.

The three factors of reasoning are attention, imagination and memory.

Attention-keeps one in the present moment.
Memory-allows one to draw upon the experiences of the past.
Imagination-enables one to direct the mind to create a
productive future.

The fifth day of creation adds animals in the water and air. Animals have memory. Now memory can be used and developed enabling the Self and mind to develop enough to enable reasoning.

All productive plans of creation need a way for one to learn and grow in consciousness.

> **24 Then God said, Let the earth bring forth living creatures after their kind, cattle, and creeping things, and beasts of the earth after their kind; and it was so. 25 And God made the beasts of the earth after their kind, and the cattle after their kind, and everything that creeps upon the earth after its kind; and God saw that it was good.**

The sixth day of creation begins by adding living creatures of the earth.

The creatures created during the fifth day were of the water and that fly above the earth.

The next part of the Plan of Creation is the opportunity to use the memory together with imagination and attention to grow in conscious. The creatures in the water are the way consciousness interacts with the physical body. In order to fulfill creations one must value and use the physical body, the highly developed animal body. The fowl of the air symbolize the deeper levels of Subconscious Mind. Cattle and beasts of the earth symbolize the ability to move one's thoughts through the lower levels of Subconscious Mind into the conscious, waking Mind.

The word 'saw' indicates perception. Good indicates what is useful, productive, and beneficial. When the productiveness of a plan is identified, then it is good. When the plan is seen to be beneficial to the whole Self and useful, then it is good.

Reasoning is good for the whole Self. Reasoning is the power of the conscious mind. Jesus who became the Christ reasoned better than the devil in the book of Matthew, chapter 4.

Reasoning enables individuals to build permanent understandings of Self and Creation.

> **26 Then God said, Let us make man in our image, after our likeness; and let them have dominion over the fish of the sea, and over the fowl of the air, and**

over the cattle, and over all the wild beasts of the earth, and over every creeping thing that creeps upon the earth.

Said, or to say aloud, is the first step of making an idea, a plan more real and solid in one's consciousness.

The words "us" and "our" indicate a plural creator or more than one creator.

The use of the word "them" indicates there is more than one man.

An image is a representation of any person or thing.

When the Creator said, "Let us make man in our image," there is the representation of the creator in the thinker-man. Therefore, each individual, each soul, each person has the potential of becoming an enlightened creator. To accomplish this we must learn to use the image making faculty correctly. The image making faculty is something called imagination or visualization.

Each I AM, each individual was created with two free gifts. Those two gifts are or were individuality and choice.

To image is to conceive in thought. To image is to form an idea in the mind. In order to image or imagine, one first must choose or make a choice of what to imagine.

To be like, as in the word likeness, means to be similar or of the same kind. To be like is to be equal and exactly corresponding of the same kind. To be like is to develop the understanding of one's individuality.

So when the plural or multiple Creator creates "after our likeness" the Creation takes on the qualities, traits, abilities and potentialities of the Creator. This means we have the potentiality and destiny as those that created us. This destiny or potentiality is in the Divine Plan of Creation. To have dominion is to have sovereign or supreme authority. It is the power of governing. Therefore, the individual, the I AM, reasoner is to gain understanding and full use of all the learning that came before or earlier.

This, the use of temporary and permanent memory, proves effective in enabling the reasoner to build upon the learning in the Self that has come before. Whatever is built or added to the Self in terms of mobility, stability, sensitivity, reproducibility and memory finds fulfillment in the mastery of the attention and imagination.

Choice is one of the gifts we were given when we were created. To choose is to image, to create a mental image or picture of what one wants to move to, achieve, possess or attain. To direct the mind repeatedly toward a given image or ideal is the development of the will. With the development of the will and reasoning comes conscious choice.

> **27 So God created man in his own image, in the image of God he created him; male and female he created them.**

In verse 26 God is talking to his friends who he calls, us and our.

Yet in verse 27 God creates in his own image. The word 'his' is singular. The word 'he' is singular.

In verse 26 the Creator is conversing with all aspects of Self to gain consensus.

In verse 27 a creator uses the consensus to initiate the creation. A creator, an individual who creates, must gain the full commitment, in all aspects of Self in order to fulfill the plan one has created. Each I AM is created in the image of the Creator. Each individual, each I AM, has intrinsic within its being both the aggressive-male and receptive-female principles.

Thus, we create with our imager and through using the aggressive and receptive principles of creation.

> **28 And God blessed them, and God said to them, Be fruitful, and multiply, and fill the earth, and subdue it; and have dominion over the fish of the sea, and over the fowl of the air, and over the cattle, and over all the wild beasts that move upon the earth.**

1. First one has an idea.
2. Then one images the idea more clearly with the will.
3. Then one states the imaged thought-idea aloud.
4. Then one initiates greater activity on the imaged-idea-plan, causing it to be fruitful.

Verse 28 is the commitment to continue exercising choice and will to cause the plan to manifest fully.

When a creator blesses a plan it means there is the full commitment given to the fulfillment of that plan. Such a one will give all the life force and truth available in order to cause it to manifest.

The reasoning process together with choice, imaging, will and the Aggressive and Receptive principles is the key to fulfilling the plan.

29 And God said, behold, I have given you every herb yielding seed, which is upon the face of all the earth, and every tree which bears fruit yielding seed; to you it shall be for food. 30 And to every beast of the earth, and to every fowl of the air, and to everything that creeps upon the earth, wherein there is life, I have given every green herb for food; and it was so.

The creator gives all the earlier learning, all the earlier experiences to the present creation.

The creator gives dominion over all the animals, fish, fowl, cattle and beast. This signifies that the individual will be able to use the physical brain, the conscious mind and the subconscious mind and the memory capacity of all three.

The food for man, the thinker, is to be seeds and fruit. This indicates the thinker, as a part of the plan, will be able to create seed ideas for greater enlightenment. The use of memory will allow one to use previous subconscious experience only. In order to cause a quickening of one's soul growth and spiritual development, one must exercise the imagination - seed idea as well as the memory - animals.

The key is the choice to be in the present moment.

31 And God saw everything that he had made, and, behold, it was very good. And there was evening and there was morning, the sixth day.

A creator looks to see if a plan is whole and complete and if all the factors and details have been given attention. When this is so a creator recognizes or identifies this plan as being whole and complete. Therefore, this plan is good. Therefore the plan is sanctified and sacred.

First God saw everything that he had made. Full attention in the present moment was given to the plan. A new awareness has come into being. It will be fully assimilated into one's consciousness. Six is the number of service and intuition. Once one has mastered reasoning, the next step is intuition. Intuition draws upon the understandings stored in one's subconscious mind, soul.

Service is a necessary practice in order for the reasoner to progress to the next level of awareness and understanding that is the intuitive being. The highest form of service is teaching and the highest form of teaching is of the Self and Creation. Service is the practice needed to understand connectedness. Connectedness is the true nature of reality.

This plan of six days of creation will give each individual, each I AM, the opportunity to become enlightened.

Summary of the Inner Meaning of Chapter 1 of the Book of Genesis
From the emptiness of a still mind comes a creative thought.

Chapter 2 of Genesis

Few Word Essence of Chapter 2
of the Book of Genesis

Conscious and Subconscious Minds
Life Force and Movement to fulfill the Plan of Creation

Brief and More Expanded Essence of Chapter 2
of the Book of Genesis

The Plan of Creation includes the steps necessary for each
individual, each I AM, to become a Christ, an enlightened
being. The energy driving this creation is life force or
cosmic energy accessed by the individual through the
medulla oblongata while in a physical body.

Chapter 2 of Genesis

New Symbols & The Interpretation of Chapter 2 of Genesis

1. rest - assimilation, creating a space
2. Tree of Life - ability to access life force through the medulla oblongata
3. Tree of the knowledge of good and evil - ability to develop the high reasoning of universal connectedness
4. Pishon - third level of Mind that flows into the acupuncture meridians
5. Havilah - the physical body
6. Gihon - fourth level of Mind that flows into the parasympathetic nervous system
7. Ethiopia - spinal column
8. Tigris - fifth level of Mind that flows into the sympathetic nervous system
9. Euphrates - sixth and seventh level of Mind that flows into the Kundalini energy, the creative energy
10. Eden - Superconscious and Subconscious Mind
11. a garden - the highest levels of Subconscious Mind
12. Lord God - I AM
13. animals, beasts - brain pathways of memories, habits
14. fowl of the air - subconscious thoughts
15. Adam's rib - 6th level of Mind, the emotional level
16. woman - the conscious mind
17. bones - structure
18. naked - without experience in the outer world, the outer levels of Mind.

Chapter 2

1 Thus the heavens and the earth were finished, and all the host of them. 2 And on the sixth day God finished his works which he had made; and he rested on the seventh day from all his works which he had made.

The Plan of Creation is completed.

The different aspects or parts of the Plan have been designed.

This Plan requires six days. The number six symbolizes service.

A creator rests on the seventh day. Rest symbolizes the assimilation of the plan or seed idea into one's consciousness and the preparation to implement the plan.

The number six is represented two dimensionally by the hexagon. The hexagon is the shape of the sections or cells in a bee hive. The six sided hexagon is a very strong and stable shape. The number six is also symbolized by the six pointed star that is sometimes known as the Star of David. The stability that service creates in the Self is indicated three dimensionally by the cube which has six sides.

The number seven represents the seven levels of Mind. The number seven represents the stability of the number four plus the creative power of the number three.

3 So God blessed the seventh day, and sanctified it; because in it he had rested from all his works which God created and made.

To sanctify is to make holy. A creator identifies a plan that has been constructed and is complete. When the plan is complete it is whole and therefore, holy.

In resting, as on the seventh day, one is preparing to act on the plan. Once the plan is complete, a creator has a detailed, mental image such as a blueprint. From this plan, ideal, or blueprint one can initiate regular, consistent action to fully manifest or achieve or receive this ideal.

The number six is half the number twelve. Twelve is a master number and symbolizes the twelve apostles and the mastery of the Aggressive and Receptive Principles of Creation. The number 13 symbolizes the Christ consciousness and the cosmic Christ, which is the ideal of enlightenment. The number six as given in the first six days of creation, indicates that creating a mental plan, a mental image of what one wants to achieve and become, is one half of becoming and achieving. The other one half is fulfilled through activity, action, work, or effort expended.

The plan is a creation. A plan is made. Activity fulfills the creation made in the plan. The plan is a creation because thoughts are things. Thoughts are real. Thought is cause.

> **4 These are the generations of the heavens and of the earth when they were created, in the day that the Lord God made the heavens and the earth.**

Generations means to generate. To generate is to produce, to procreate, to cause to be or to bring into existence. A day is a space of time in which there continues to be light. A day is a space of time.

Before this verse the word God is used. This is the first time the word Lord is used.

God is a Creator. God is Elohim.

Lord God is a son of the Creator.

Lord God is generated from a Creator.

Lord God is I AM. Lord is Yahweh or Jehovah.

In order for I AM to come into being a space needed to be created in order to receive. That space was created on the seventh day and is signified with the words, "God rested." A space is empty. Emptiness is a space. Emptiness is a space to receive.

Creation is now set into motion. It is the responsibility of each I AM, each individual, to use creation to become enlightened. Mind is the vehicle to know the Self. We are to use the Conscious, Subconscious, and Superconscious Minds to come to know the whole and Real Self.

> **5 And all the trees of the field were not yet in the ground, and every herb of the field had not yet sprung up; for the Lord God had not caused it to rain upon the earth, and there was no man to till the ground.**

Once each individual has a place to create and learn creation, it is our duty to create and learn to be creators. Trees and herbs of the field symbolize permanent understandings of Self and Creation that one can store in one's subconscious mind or soul. Rain symbolizes one's conscious life experiences.

A man to till the ground symbolizes one who uses the waking, conscious life experiences to produce permanent understandings of Self and Creation that are then given to the subconscious mind or soul. This verse symbolizes the point when the individual is just about ready to act on the mental plan, goal, or ideal.

> **6 But a powerful spring gushed out of the earth, and watered all the face of the ground.**

The powerful spring of water that gushes up out of the earth symbolizes the one who begins to act on the idea or plan through experience. Water symbolizes conscious life experience. The phrase, 'watered all the face of the ground,' symbolizes the one whose consciousness is directed toward creating and learning in all areas of the life.

Face indicates identity. The identity of Self needs to be invested in gaining experience. Experience can then be reasoned with until one comes to understand the Universal Laws and Truths.

The earth, subconscious mind substance, brings experiences to the consciousness and conscious mind of the individual in order to gain understanding of all Creation.

> **7 And the Lord God formed Adam out of the soil of the earth, and breathed into his nostrils the breath of life; and man became a living being.**

Lord God symbolizes I AM. I AM forms Adam, the first man, the thinker, out of the soil of the earth. Both the words Adam and man mean thinker.

The soil of the earth symbolizes subconscious mind, the soul. The thinking, conscious mind comes from or is an extension of the subconscious mind.

Breath is the carrier of and symbolizes life force. I AM gives or transfers life force from superconscious mind to subconscious mind. The thinker can exist in the subconscious mind because life force provides the energy and animating factor. In order to manifest any creation and to move it forward one needs energy and life force. Knowing the power of breath is a major key to enlightenment. The breath is the key to cosmic energy, life force or as it is called in India, prana, and in China, chi.

8 And the Lord God planted a garden eastward in Eden; and there he put the man whom he had formed.

I AM provides a way for one to use subconscious mind and subconscious experiences starting with the third level of Mind. The third level is the deepest level of Subconscious Mind.

Each person that desires to create will always need to image their creation. That creative thought moves from the conscious mind to the third level in subconscious mind. From there the thought form moves out through the fourth, fifth, and sixth levels of Mind, finally becoming a manifested creation in one's outer, waking, physical life.

9 And out of the ground the Lord God made to grow every tree that is pleasant to the sight and good for food; the Tree of Life also in the midst of the garden, and the tree of the knowledge of good and evil.

Trees symbolize subconscious experience. Subconscious experience is the permanent learning called understanding of Self and Creation. The Tree of Life is related to or connected with the breath of life given in verse 7.

The breath of life is life force from Superconscious Mind given through the aggressive and receptive principles of creation. The Tree of Life means that you and I or anyone can learn to consciously breath in and out this great life force of eternal life.

The tree of knowledge of good and evil indicates that each person has the capability to learn to live in harmony with the Universal Laws and Universal Truths. Each person can reason and, therefore, learn to discipline the mind to live in greater harmony and peace. The one who would successfully create has developed reasoning and uses life force.

10 And a river flowed out of Eden to water the garden; and from thence it divided and became into four heads.

Eden is the Superconscious Mind. The garden is Universal Subconscious Mind. The river that flows out of Eden is the life force that flows from Superconscious Mind to the Subconscious Mind and from there to the conscious mind.

The four heads symbolize the movement of life force from Subconscious Mind into the physical, the seventh level of Mind and the conscious mind.

The number four symbolizes stability. The number four represents the movement of energies into the physical existence from the inner levels of Subconscious Mind. Energy to produce activity is required to be able to cause a creation to come into being. This energy originates as life force from Superconscious Mind.

> **11 The name of the first is Pishon; it is the one which
> encircles the whole land of Havilah, where there is
> gold; 12 And the gold of that land is good; there is
> also beryllium and the onyx stone. 13 And the name
> of the second river is Gihon, the one which encircles
> the whole land of Ethiopia. 14 And the name of the
> third river is Deklat (Tigris); it is the one which flows
> east of Assyria. And the fourth river is the
> Euphrates.**

The first of the four heads, the Pishon, symbolizes the deepest level of subconscious mind, the third or mental level. It manifests in the physical body as the acupuncture meridians.

The second head or river, the Gihon, is the life force as it moves into the fourth level of mind.

The third head or river, the Tigris is the fifth level of Mind.

The fourth head or river, the Euphrates, is the life force as it moves through the sixth level of mind, the emotional level. From the sixth or emotional level, the life force moves into the seventh level, the physical world where it manifests as Kundalini energy in the physical body. This means that anyone desiring to manifest a goal or ideal must place a clear thought form in the third level of Mind. Then the individual will need to prepare to receive the object of desire.

> **15 And the Lord God took the man, and put him in
> the garden of Eden to till it and to keep it.**

Lord God, I AM, moves into Universal Subconscious Mind and exists there as soul. Now it is up to you to fulfill your soul urge, your soul assignment for this lifetime. The individual subconscious mind or soul's duty is to fulfill the desires and mental images of the conscious mind. The garden is Subconscious Mind.

The conscious mind's duty is to receive those physical manifestations and creations in the life and then to use those experiences to build permanent understandings of Self and Creation. This means that you need to learn and better yourself from every experience. It is each person's duty to grow in awareness, understanding and enlightenment every day. No experience is wasted when Self receives the essence of the universal learning in every experience.

16 And the Lord God commanded the man, saying,
Of every tree of the garden you may freely eat;

Trees indicate subconscious experience. Food symbolizes knowledge. Eating of the nuts or fruit of trees represents the ability to receive knowledge from one's experiences that are then stored as permanent understanding in one's subconscious mind. Therefore, in the present time, in the present moment, it is our duty to receive the learning. If you are not changed by an experience you are either fully enlightened or you missed out on the learning. You may freely eat of every tree in the garden. This means that you can gain permanent soul learning called understanding in every experience by having a disciplined and still mind that is willing to receive.

17 But of the tree of the knowledge of good and evil,
you shall not eat; for in the day that you eat of it you
shall surely die.

The Lord God said, "You may freely eat of every tree in the garden." Then the I AM Lord God said, "But don't eat of the tree of good and evil." How can you eat of every tree of the garden if you don't eat of the tree of good and evil? Unless the tree of good and evil is not in the garden.

What is the tree of good and evil? The tree of good and evil symbolizes the ability to use and develop the reasoning capability in the Self. Reasoning is practiced through the exercise of memory, attention, and imagination in the conscious mind in the present moment.

To die is the second death explained later in this book concerning Revelation.

The meaning is that if any soul in the Universal Subconscious Mind is to try to reason with the physical brain, that soul will become entrapped. This entrapment in a physical body will lead to the cycle of reincarnation and Karma.

> True reasoning begins when one recognizes:
> a) Thought is cause, and therefore,
> b) Self is the cause of one's life, and
> c) Self is not separate from everything and everyone.
>   Instead one is connected with all creation.

The tree of the knowledge of good and evil is not in the garden, it is in the midst of the garden. Therefore, reasoning is the center from which all knowledge and understandings grow.

To die symbolizes change. When you use and apply the knowledge received in each experience, you do change and grow. To be in the present moment, with the still mind and to consciously choose to receive the essence of the universal learning in the present moment, brings about change and transformation within the Self.

18 Then the Lord God said, It is not good that the man should be alone; I will make him a helper who is like him.

Man symbolizes subconscious mind. I AM realizes that something more than just the superconscious and subconscious minds are needed in order for Self to gain enlightenment.

No one becomes enlightened on a desert island. No one becomes enlightened alone because the true nature of reality is connectedness. Therefore, each individual must be connected with others of like mind and others of like ideals. It is in working together with others for the betterment of all and the enlightenment of the planet that we progress most rapidly.

The word "man" comes from the Sanskrit word "manu," which means thinker. In order for one to align conscious and subconscious minds and attune them to superconscious mind, one must discipline the thoughts and mind. One must choose the thoughts consciously. One must choose the thoughts one thinks. The one with a busy, conscious mind is not a thinker. The one with a busy brain, with racing thoughts, is unconscious.

A thinker is not unconscious.

Therefore, be conscious of every thought. Consciously choose every thought.

> **19 And out of the ground the Lord God formed
> every beast of the field, and every fowl of the air; and
> brought them to Adam to see what he would call
> them; and whatever Adam called every living crea-
> ture, that was its name.**

Beasts or animals symbolize habits. Habits are often practiced unconsciously.

Ground symbolizes subconscious mind substance.

All thoughts held in the conscious mind as desires when released travel to one's subconscious mind. Once there the individual subconscious mind or soul goes to extreme lengths to fulfill those desires of the Self. Therefore, it is important to learn to identify all one's thoughts and to be conscious of one's thoughts and desires.

To call something or to name something is to have experience and thereby identify that something. Adam identified his habits and brain pathways. Adam is man, the thinker. It is each person's duty to identify consciously the thoughts, habits, memories and desires of the Self.

> **20 And Adam gave names to all cattle, and to all
> fowl of the air, and to all wild beasts; but for Adam
> there was not found a helper who was equal to him.**

There is no habit that is equal to a thinker or reasoner. Unfortunately, most people are controlled by their habits. In order for one to know and direct one's habits, a disciplined mind is required and needed.

A disciplined mind that has become still is needed in order to know one's thoughts to know all aspects of Self and to attain the highest reasoning capabilities. When the mind has become still then is the Self able to use the mind and reasoning for enlightenment.

> **21 So the Lord God caused a deep sleep to fall upon
> Adam, and he slept; and he took one of his ribs, and
> closed up the place with flesh in its stead;**

Sleep is a time and way of assimilating the previous day's experience and learning. For most people, sleep is also a time of unconsciousness. I AM caused the subconscious mind to extend farther, thereby, creating what we call the conscious mind. The rib, Adam's rib, symbolizes the sixth level of Mind, the emotional level. The emotional level of Mind is the level of Mind closest to the conscious mind, the seventh level. This is why the emotional level or emotions are experienced in our physical experience and in the conscious mind. Therefore, learn to discipline your mind and use your emotions productively. Emotions are always caused by a thought, so choose productive thoughts.

**22 And of the rib which the Lord God had taken
from Adam he made a woman, and brought her to
Adam.**

Woman symbolizes the conscious mind.

I AM-Lord God made a woman-conscious mind out of the rib-emotional level of the Adam-subconscious mind. Man represents the thinker. Adam, being the first man, indicates the first thinker. Wo-man is an extension of the thinker. Wo-man is the extension of the subconscious mind that is extended out to create the conscious mind. *(See diagram 1)*

Only an individual with a disciplined, conscious mind is a thinker. Those with undisciplined minds are re-actors. Those with undisciplined minds are habituators.

I AM, your true individuality that is connected and one with all creation and all beings, draws the conscious mind toward the soul in Universal, Subconscious Mind. Therefore, create productive thoughts and desires in the conscious mind that can be given to subconscious mind, the soul.

**23 And Adam said, This is now bone of my bones,
and flesh of my flesh; she shall be called Woman,
because she was taken out of Man.**

Bones are the framework, the supporting structure for the physical body. The subconscious mind is the supporting structure for the conscious mind, and the conscious mind is the supporting structure for the physical body which includes the brain. The conscious mind supports the thinker's life in the physical world. Flesh enables us to interact

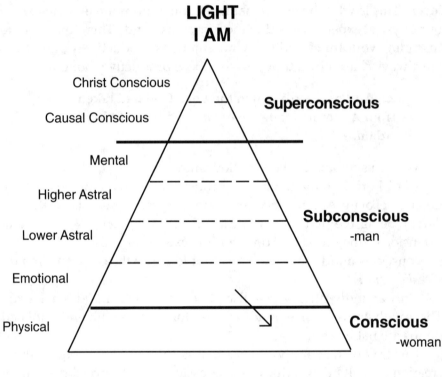

Diagram 1

with the world around us. The world of the Universal Subconscious Mind is extended in order to form the world of the Conscious Mind. Therefore, it is our duty in the present moment to still the mind and receive the learning in the conscious mind. Then this received learning can be reasoned with by the thinker-man in order to be added to the subconscious mind where it is housed as permanent memory called understandings.

Man indicates the aggressive act of thinking and woman indicates the receptive mode of thinking or no thought. The difficulty arises in that most people, while engrossed in a physical body and physical brain, think aggressively, thus maintaining their entrapment.

To overcome entrapment in a physical body, the conscious mind must become still in order that the Self can cause the conscious mind to become receptive. Being receptive, the conscious mind can then receive first the soul and then superconscious awareness. Superconscious awareness develops into Christ consciousness.

> **24 Therefore shall a man leave his father and his**
> **mother, and shall cleave unto his wife, and they shall**
> **be one flesh.**

Man symbolizes subconscious mind. Father and mother symbolize the Aggressive and Receptive Principles of Superconscious Mind. The man's wife symbolizes the conscious mind that is committed to the subconscious mind, the soul. The subconscious mind or soul leaves the Father-Mother-Superconscious Mind and clings-connects with the conscious mind-wife. Thus, it is each person's duty to be committed to knowing the whole Self, to building permanent understandings of Self and Creation, and to align the conscious and subconscious minds. This one does in order to attune the aligned conscious and subconscious minds to superconscious mind.

Through the still mind is the Real Self known.

> **25 And they were both naked, Adam and his wife,**
> **and were not ashamed.**

Clothes symbolize one's outward presentation or expression, based on one's experiences.

Being naked symbolizes one who is without experience and, thereby, is open to receive new learning and new experiences. Shame is distress over guilt or disgrace. A baby is not ashamed of being naked because a baby is without experience. A baby has not been taught guilt or shame. A baby is fully in the present moment. A baby's consciousness is not in the past.

A new conscious mind has no past. Therefore, view each moment in the eternal now, the present. Then you will receive the bountiful knowledge and awareness available. The time of infancy is the period of most rapid learning. Therefore, be in the present moment.

Summary of the Inner Meaning of Chapter 2 of the Book of Genesis
The Plan of Creation is completed. The activity of fulfilling and manifesting that creation begins. The creation has within it the ability to become like the Creator.

Chapter 3 of Genesis

Few Word Essence of Chapter 3
of the Book of Genesis

The ego

Brief and More Expanded Essence of Chapter 3
of the Book of Genesis

The soul becomes intrigued with the animal body and brain. From
this the conscious mind is formed, then the conscious mind meets
and interacts with the conscious ego.

Chapter 3 of Genesis

New Symbols & The Interpretation of Chapter 3 of Genesis

1. serpent - conscious ego

2. gods - having the ability to create

3. fruit - knowledge

4. eyes - perception

5. thistles - doubt

6. cherubim - superconscious thoughts or messengers from I AM

Chapter 3

1 Now the serpent was more subtle than all the wild beasts that the Lord God had made. And the serpent said to the woman, Truly has God said that you shall not eat of any tree of the garden?

The serpent symbolizes the conscious ego in the infancy state.

The **Bible** does not say that the Lord God-I AM created the serpent. It only says that the serpent was more subtle than all the wild beasts the Lord God had made. The **Bible** does not say that the serpent was-is a wild beast.

The wild beasts are animals. Animals symbolize habits. Wild animals or wild beasts symbolize habits that you do not have control of during the day to day experiences. In some cases people are not even aware of their habits. The serpent-ego is even more subtle than this. This means that most people are not even aware of the workings and physical motivations of the conscious ego within the brain and the body.

The New American **Bible** uses the term cunning instead of the word subtle concerning the conscious ego.

The conscious ego is both cunning and subtle.

To be cunning is to be crafty and clever.

To be subtle is to be hardly noticeable and clever.

The conscious ego beguiles. The conscious ego is clever.

Yes, the conscious ego is hardly noticeable and clever and a tempter. Therein lies its power or control. The conscious ego is not a very good reasoner. Therefore, it has to rely on subtlety and guile and craftiness and consciousness rationalization and logic and sensory temptation to be able to control the conscious mind. This is how the serpent-ego controls the conscious mind-woman.

Originally the conscious mind was not designed to be controlled by the conscious ego. Rather the individual was designed to have a disciplined mind and thereby, be in control of Self. With the disciplined mind one knows the thoughts of Self and chooses thoughts consciously.

Notice the way the serpent controls and manipulates and is subtle and crafty in the first sentence spoken by the serpent. The first thing the serpent does is state his question in the negative by using the word, not. If the serpent had not been trying to manipulate and control through subtlety and cunningness the question would have been stated directly. The question would have been, "Did the Lord God tell your husband Adam not to eat of the tree of knowledge of good and evil?" Or the conscious ego might have said, " Is it okay to eat of all the trees in the garden?" The serpent-conscious ego lied and was deceitful by using the word God when, in fact, it was the **Lord** God that spoke and gave the command about the trees in chapter 2, verse 17.

God represents Creator. Lord God is I AM.

Neither God nor the Lord God said, "*you shall not eat of any tree of the garden.*" The Lord God-I AM said, "*of every tree of the garden you may freely eat,*" chapter 2, verse 16. This is a positive statement. The Lord God made a positive statement about the trees in the garden while the serpent-ego made a negative statement about the trees in the garden. Therefore, when you find yourself making a lot of negative statements and using the word 'not' a lot, unconsciously, the serpent, the conscious ego may be controlling or manipulating you. This the ego does by changing the facts through deceit and lies. The Lord God did not even talk to the woman-conscious mind about what trees to eat of or not to eat of. The Lord God talked to the man, Adam, about these things. The conscious ego-serpent knew he couldn't deceive the man-Adam-subconscious mind-soul as easily as he could the woman-conscious mind because the conscious mind is younger and lacks experience.

2 And the woman said to the serpent, We may eat of the fruit of all the trees of the garden;

In response to the serpent's question the woman does not give the whole story, the whole mental picture. Therefore, the woman is not completely honest either. This is why the woman-conscious mind can be deceived.

A more honest statement on the part of the woman would have been that someone, probably the man-subconscious mind, had told the woman-conscious mind that they may not eat of the fruit of all the trees of the garden.

The woman-conscious mind acted like she knew the truth when, in fact, she only believed the truth. The woman's experience was not first hand, it was second hand. The Lord God told the man, not the woman. The **Bible** does not say the Lord God told the woman.

3 But of the fruit of the tree which is in the midst of the garden, God has said, You shall not eat of it, neither shall you touch it, lest you die.

The woman used the name or word "God" concerning the "tree in the midst of the garden." However, it was not God but Lord God-I AM that gave this instruction. Even so, the Lord God did not mention a tree that was in the midst of the garden. Instead in chapter 2, verse 17, the Lord God said, *"But of the tree of the knowledge of good and evil, you shall not eat, for in the day that you eat of it you shall surely die."*

So again the woman has the story wrong. It may be the tree of good and evil is in the midst of the garden, however, that is not the point. The point is, the woman-conscious mind is changing the original instructions, the words and the mental picture.

The Lord God did say *"You shall not eat of the tree of good and evil."* However, the Lord God did not say, *"Neither shall you touch it,"* concerning the tree of good and evil. Again the woman-conscious mind has changed the story. The conscious mind-woman has changed the story, the facts, from not being allowed to eat of the tree of the knowledge of good and evil to not being allowed to eat or touch the tree of the knowledge of good and evil.

The fact is, it was okay to touch the tree of knowledge of good and evil. This tree symbolizes reasoning. Therefore, it was okay to experience reasoning. It was and is not okay to let your desires and craving control you so that you become engrossed and entrapped in physical experiences by eating of the fruit.

Therefore, remain disciplined with a still mind. Recognize all physical life is temporary. Receive situations and circumstances with equanimity.

To die is to change. To become ensnared and engrossed in physical experiences is to change, for the nature of physical life is change. The nature of physical life is change because all that is physical is temporary and impermanent. All physical energy must be recycled into the deeper levels of Mind. Adam and Eve did not physically die on the day they ate of the tree of good and evil. However, death symbolizes and is change. On the day Adam-subconscious mind and Eve-conscious mind ate of the tree of good and evil they changed. They began to be engrossed in the physical, animal-proto-human body and brain. They were changed. This led to entrapment and the cycle of reincarnation.

Therefore, in the present moment, each person must strive to overcome environmental stimulus that leads to desire that leads to attachment.

> **4 And the serpent said to the woman, You shall not surely die; 5 For God knows that in the day you eat of it, your eyes shall be opened, and you shall be like gods, knowing good and evil.**

The serpent contradicts the Lord God-I AM. Because to die is to change. The day or time that you learn how to reason is the day or point in time that you begin to learn to master change-death and the conscious ego.

Eating of the tree of good and evil symbolizes reasoning and the ability to assimilate knowledge through reasoning and thereby begin to learn about caused change.

Again the serpent does not mention Lord God-I AM and instead refers to God-Creator. This is because the conscious ego is only a pale reflection, a shadow of I AM, yet it falsely believes it is the Real Self.

It is true that when reasoning is used and applied one's perception-eye does improve and increase. Eyes symbolize perception.

The tree is called the tree of knowledge of good and evil. So eating of the fruit-knowledge of the tree of good and evil will give one knowledge and the ability to discern what is productive from what is unproductive.

Gods are immortal and live beyond the temporary physical existence. Gods have higher perception and reasoning capability. Therefore, eating of the true knowledge of good and evil enables one to reason. However, in order to live forever, one needs to eat of the tree of life which the man and woman were not allowed to do as they were driven from the garden before they could do so.

The serpent told a truth wrapped around a lie. The truth was by eating of the tree of knowledge of good and evil the man and woman would know good and evil.

The lie was when the serpent said, *"You shall not surely die."* The conscious ego deceives by presenting the conscious mind with a lie wrapped with a lie, or in other words, a partial truth or partial lie. This is why you must diligently strive to reach and receive greater, deeper levels of Truth in your being.

6 So when the woman saw that the tree was good for food, and that it was pleasant to the eyes, and that the tree was delightful to look at, she took of the fruit thereof, and did eat, and she also gave to her husband with her; and he did eat.

The woman-conscious mind perceived an opportunity for learning and was stimulated by the conscious ego-serpent. This stimulus lead to a desire. The woman-conscious mind acted on the desire for knowledge and gave the man-subconscious mind the opportunity for the same knowledge.

The woman's husband is the man. In order to have a husband there must be a marriage. A marriage symbolizes commitment between a man-subconscious mind and a woman-conscious mind.

7 Then the eyes of them both were opened, and they knew that they were naked; and they sewed fig leaves together, and made themselves aprons.

By eating of the tree of knowledge the perception eyes of both conscious-woman and subconscious minds was enhanced. The difficulty with this is that both the man and the woman were still in the infancy stage of learning.

Knowing you are naked represents the recognition that you are without experience. It is like an infant trying to be like an adult. Infants do not know they are naked. Adults or adolescents know this. This is a case of infants having to grow up too quickly. This is like a child who never gets to experience childhood.

Fig leaves come from trees. Trees symbolize subconscious experience. Since the man and woman were in infancy and with little conscious mind experience they relied upon subconscious experience or understandings. Clothing indicates one's outer expression or presentation.

8 And they heard the voice of the Lord God walking in the garden in the cool of the day; and Adam and his

wife hid themselves from the presence of the Lord God among the trees of the garden. 9 And the Lord God called to Adam, and said to him, Where are you, Adam? 10 And he said, I heard thy voice in the garden, and when I saw that I was naked, I hid myself.

A voice is a sound vibration that moves through a medium such as air. Adam, the subconscious mind avoided listening to I AM. When the conscious mind makes a mistake the effect is avoidance of the I AM unless one chooses to be honest and learn from the situation or experience. It was or is the conscious ego-serpent that got and gets the conscious mind in trouble by practicing conscious rationalizations. Instead, the conscious mind needs to be receptive and follow the instructions of I AM in order to gain the necessary knowledge to be able to reason.

The conscious and subconscious minds are designed to follow the instructions of the Lord God - I AM, not those of the conscious ego serpent.

Mind is the vehicle or tool for I AM to experience in and through in order to come to know Self as a creator. Mind is the vehicle for Self. Mind is the vehicle for Self to use to learn to be a Christ, an enlightened being.

The conscious ego-serpent is not the Lord God-I AM. The conscious ego is a temporary, shadow Self, a pale reflection of I AM. Therefore, the conscious ego's power lies in deceit, guile, cunningness and subtlety. The conscious ego does not know truth because truth is eternal and lasting. Whereas, the conscious ego identifies with the temporary experiences of the five senses, the conscious mind and the brain.

In verse 9 the Lord God-I AM asks, *"Where are you, Adam?"* In verse 10 Adam does not answer the question. Adam does not tell I AM where he is. Instead, Adam says what he saw and what he did. Adam saw the nakedness of Self and he hid. Adam is therefore not being completely honest with I AM.

The subconscious mind has begun to reason before gaining experience. This is backwards to the way things are supposed to occur.

1. One is to gather experiences,
2. receive the learning in the experiences and
3. reason with the learning in order to add knowledge, understanding and wisdom to the Self.

When the mind is used incorrectly or the mind is undisciplined then one experiences fear. Fear is the product of an undisciplined mind.

Therefore, practice the disciplined mind and align with the Universal Laws and Universal Truths.

11 And the Lord God said to him, Who told you that you were naked? Have you eaten of the tree of which I commanded you that you should not eat?

I AM-Lord God understands that as soon as the subconscious mind and conscious mind begin to reason they will understand the importance of experience. This is why infancy comes before adolescence and adolescence comes before adulthood and adulthood comes before wisdom.

Infancy is a time of receiving experiences and learning into the Self like a dry sponge absorbs water. When a baby or infant absorbs enough experience and learning from the environment then does reasoning begin. Around the age of seven to eight the infant has gathered enough experience and learning to begin to reason. Then the one in infancy moves to the next stage called adolescence.

Eating of the tree of the knowledge of good and evil robbed the children of their infancy. Since an infant is not yet responsible the infant needs to be kept safe by the parents. It was no longer safe for the infants because the conditions had changed. Therefore, in later verses, the man and woman are commanded to leave the garden.

12 And Adam said, The woman whom thou gavest to be with me, she gave me of the fruit of the tree, and I did eat. 13 And the Lord God said to the woman, What is this that you have done? And the woman said, The serpent beguiled me, and I did eat.

The woman-conscious mind gave the man-subconscious mind the fruit of the tree of knowledge of reasoning-good and evil. The conscious ego-serpent beguiled the conscious mind-woman into premature experiences with reasoning. How did this premature experience with reasoning occur? Originally, as designed, we were not meant to have conscious egos because we were not meant to become engrossed and entrapped in physical, sensory experiences. We were meant to learn from observation. We were meant to receive through observation the learning into ourselves as permanent understandings.

An observer does not try to control what is being observed. When the observer starts to control what is being observed, the observer then becomes part of what was being observed. This is how souls became entrapped in physical bodies and set into motion the cycle of reincarnation and karma. Once the souls observing the physical earth began to control the physical bodies of animal man, that is proto-humans or early humans, at that point the soul's consciousness became entrapped and ensnared in a physical, humanoid body. Thus began the cycle of reincarnation.

Reincarnation or rebirth means that at first you, a soul, move into a physical body. You then reside in that physical body until death. Then, after a period of assimilation of learning in Universal Subconscious Mind, the soul chooses to incarn again into another physical body. Each lifetime you have the opportunity to build permanent learning and soul understandings. Karma keeps the lessons of life coming to you and at you until you understand the essence of the Universal Laws and Universal Truths in those physical experiences.

The ultimate goal or ideal is to progress to full enlightenment. Then the soul no longer needs to reincarn in physical existence because all the spiritual lessons of physical life have been learned or mastered.

Now we learn through activity, action, effort, work or physical experience. Before entrapment in the human or humanoid form, we learned through observation. Because of entrapment in a physical body each person forms a new conscious mind and a conscious ego each lifetime.

The conscious ego forms each lifetime as a reflection of I AM. The word ego means I AM or I.

The serpent-conscious ego beguiles the conscious mind-woman. To beguile is to deceive, delude, to cheat or to trick. To beguile is to divert the mind. The serpent-conscious ego diverted the conscious mind-woman through forming a question that was meant to deceive through changing what the Lord God had said. Therefore, each individual needs to practice mental discipline in order to form clear mental images and thoughts. When you know your own thoughts and have experience, and have learned the truth, you will not be deceived.

14 And the Lord God said to the serpent, Because you have done this thing, cursed are you above all cattle, and above all beasts of the field; on your belly shall you go, and dust shall you eat all the days of your life;

Now for the first time, Lord God-I AM talks to the conscious ego-serpent. This is because there is no conscious ego until the consciousness of the individual becomes engrossed in physical, sensory experiences. There was no serpent until after the woman was created. The thing the serpent-ego did was to tempt and stimulate, by deception, the conscious mind to mature too early. This in turn led to the cycle of reincarnation and Karma.

Have you ever seen someone who had an unpleasant childhood and so they tried to grow up early? People like this usually miss out on the adolescent stage of learning. Therefore, people like this are in adult body while inside, emotionally, they are still like a little child. Sometimes adult people like this have a high pitched voice that sounds like a child. A person like this is in an adult physical body yet has fear thoughts related to childhood. Many of these thoughts are unconscious, some are conscious. People like this re-act often and in the most egotistical ways.

Therefore, the conscious ego that motivates one for physical stimulus and physical experience only is cursed above all the cattle-habits-brain pathways, memories. When one craves physical experiences solely for the sensory experience of pleasure or pain they provide, then one misses out on the true purpose of life. The purpose of life concerns receiving the essence of the learning of Universal Laws and Universal Truths in every experience. This essence is not physical. To miss this essence and settle for the cheap imitation of just sensory experience is to miss the purpose of life. We are here to build permanent understandings of Self and Creation.

The serpent is cursed to go on its belly and eat dust all the days of its life. Dust and dirt symbolize subconscious mind substance. Trees and green plants symbolize subconscious experience. Trees and green grass indicate one who is receiving the essence of the learning in every experience and is adding permanent understandings to the soul, the individual subconscious mind. However, dust symbolizes mind substance that is barren. Dust symbolizes one who is not gaining permanent learning of Self and Creation from the experiences of life. Such a one has settled for the lowly life of physical, sensory experience only without reaching for the higher wisdom and higher knowledge. This is the curse. The curse is that the one who is motivated solely by the conscious ego will miss out on the real learning of life. Such a one sacrifices the permanent for the temporary, the real and lasting for the maya-illusion.

To curse is to call for injury to fall upon. It is very injurious for one to miss the essence of learning the life provides. It causes pain and suffering.

Therefore, cause yourself to learn in every situation, every experience and become a better person. The ego-serpent is cursed above all cattle and all beasts-habits. Therefore, it is better for one to be habitual than egotistical. As long as the conscious ego controls you, you will have low self worth-crawl on your belly. In contrast I AM consciousness is unlimited worth and value.

> **15 And I will put enmity between you and the woman, and between your posterity and her posterity; her posterity shall tread your head under foot, and you shall strike him in his heel.**

Enmity means to be enemies. Enmity is the quality or state of being an enemy, hostile or unfriendly, or to have ill will. Therefore, the conscious mind-woman and the conscious ego-serpent are not friends. The conscious ego strikes at the spiritual foundation of the conscious mind. The conscious ego-serpent will try to make you think you are someone other than the Real You.

If you allow the conscious ego to rule you and your life, you will do so at the expense of your spiritual foundation. The essence and key to a strong spiritual foundation is discipline of the mind. **There is no ego in a still, conscious mind.** In addition, a disciplined, conscious mind is connected to others and all creation, thereby overriding the serpent's efforts at separation, externalization, victimization, stimulation and irresponsibility.

> **16 To the woman he said, I will greatly multiply your pain and your conception; in pain you shall bring forth children, and you shall be dependent on your husband, and he shall rule over you.**

Learning while one is engrossed and entrapped in a physical body is more difficult and painful than learning from observation from the subconscious mind. In the seventh level of Mind one must discipline the conscious mind in order to receive the thought form through and from subconscious mind.

The engrossed consciousness is now entrapped and ensnared in sensory experience. Activity or physical effort is required to produce anything. A new idea, a new creation, a fruition in the physical life requires work, effort, exertion and often pain. Instead of functioning from Subconscious Universal Mind the individual, after entrapment in a physical body, is engrossed in the five senses. The soul in Universal Subconscious Mind-the husband-man, has the final say so concerning the point of birth and the time of death or permanent withdrawal of attention away from the physical life, and the conscious mind-woman.

17 And to Adam he said, Because you have listened to the voice of your wife, and have eaten of the tree of which I commanded you, saying, You shall not eat of it, cursed is the ground for your sake; in sorrow shall you eat the fruits of it all the days of your life;

The soul in Universal Subconscious Mind became entrapped in a physical body rather than continuing to learn from observation. Adam-the subconscious mind-soul allowed the conscious mind-woman to override the instruction I AM had given. This external stimulus lead to a desire that was not in accordance with the instruction of I AM.

Therefore, one needs to practice mental discipline to align conscious and subconscious mind in order to attune them to superconscious mind. Then one will know Self as I AM. Until then attachment to desires and external stimulus will keep one distracted from the lasting benefits that are the true purpose of life.

Now the subconscious mind-soul-man can no longer build permanent understanding from observation. Now the conscious mind must build the understanding through activity-effort combined with ideal and purpose.

18 Thorns also and thistles shall it bring forth to you; and you shall eat the herb of the field;

Thorns and thistles symbolize fears and doubts. The sensory entrapped life in a physical body gives rise to fears and doubts because the senses provide the illusion of separateness. In other words you see someone and the sense of sight gives you the impression that person is ten feet away.

The illusion of separateness is called Maya in India. The true nature of reality is connectedness and oneness. This illusion of separateness leads to fears and doubts about one's ability to create what is wanted or needed in the life and in the Self. Fear is a product of an undisciplined mind. Therefore, conquer fear and conquer the conscious mind with mental discipline.

> **19 In the sweat of your face shall you eat bread, until you return to the ground; out of it you were taken; for dust you are, and to dust shall you return.**

Face symbolizes identity. Bread symbolizes knowledge. Sweat symbolizes the physical or conscious life experience needed to know your real identity. Effort, action, or work is needed to have the opportunity to receive knowledge of the Self for anyone entrapped in a physical body.

Ground and dust symbolize Subconscious Mind substance. As long as you, the soul, inhabit a physical body, activity or effort will be required to gain greater Self awareness. At the end of a lifetime you will return to Universal Subconscious Mind-ground-dust to assimilate understanding and to prepare for the next incarnation.

> **20 So Adam called his wife's name Eve because she was the mother of all living.**

To call something is to name something. To name something is to identify something. Adam, the subconscious mind, has now more clearly identified the conscious mind-woman. Naming the woman Eve shows that the subconscious mind now knows the conscious mind is enticed by desires. This craving for sensory experience and desire for experience affects the subconscious mind. All aspects of the conscious mind are descendents or come from this desire for more and more sensory experience on the part of the conscious mind, the brain and five senses. It is this attachment to desire, this craving that produces the pain and misery of engrossment.

Therefore, be in the present moment and receive the eternal Truths of learning.

> **21 And the Lord God made for Adam and for his wife coats of skin, and clothed them.**

Coats of skin represent the physical body that the subconscious mind or soul became entrapped in. Since then the cycle of reincarnation has been in effect. Your physical body is a highly evolved animal body that is a coat or coating that the Real or Inner Self wears for a lifetime.

I AM continues to want to learn even though mistakes have been made. The Self can still become enlightened by using the physical experience correctly. Therefore, value and appreciate your physical body and the opportunity you have to use it to gain enlightenment. Discipline the physical body and conscious mind in order to follow the commands of I AM-Lord God instead of serpent-conscious ego.

> **22 Then the Lord God said, Behold, the man has become like one of us, to know good and evil; and now lest he put forth his hand, and take also of the tree of life, and eat, and live forever;**

The thinker-man-subconscious mind has attempted to move into the stage of growth known as adulthood of reasoning with little time or experience in adolescence. The thinker has gained the ability to reason, yet the thinker does not have the wisdom that comes from experience. This wisdom is absolutely necessary in order to use reasoning productively.

When children are forced to grow up too quickly because of violence, force, or war or lack of attention, the stage of adolescence is missed. Therefore, such children are emotionally immature. Because of eating of the tree of good and evil, humanity missed out on a stage of learning. This attempt to avoid or to understand adolescence of reasoning has been a major cause of all the wars that have been going on for thousands of years.

Therefore, look, perceive and identify the areas in which you have failed to mature your consciousness. Identify those areas in which you are stuck in old memories that produce emotional re-actions such as oversensitivity to certain people or circumstances. Life is the ability or the capability to perform one's functions and purpose which is different from re-actions or re-acting.

The tree of life symbolizes the ability to still the mind and to live and consciously breathe in the constant awareness of the true reality.

The tree of good and evil symbolizes the tendency of the mind to go to extremes until the Self learns these extremes are not necessary. This learning is the process of learning to reason. This process is the ability to develop the reasoning through the four stages of infancy, adolescence, adulthood, and wisdom. As the Self grows in awareness and understanding through the stages of reasoning, one eventually realizes that there is more to life than solving problems.

Whereas, previously one lived the life thinking the highest life was using the mind to solve problems, now it is realized that the mind itself is the problem. More accurately it is the undisciplined mind that is the problem. Then busy minded thinking stops being one's highest priority. As long as one has a busy mind, an undisciplined mind, the conscious ego-serpent will subtly control the Self. Therefore, such a one disciplines the mind, stills the mind, quiets the thoughts and learns to experience the true reality, enlightenment. The disciplined one learns to breathe the life force-tree of life through the medulla oblongata.

Such a one is no longer separate and therefore is not busy trying to solve problems. Such a one is consciously aware of the universal connectedness and oneness. Such a one then becomes a world teacher and a world server.

23 Therefore the Lord God sent him forth from the garden of Eden, to till the ground from whence he was taken.

Every child needs to learn responsibility. This ability to respond serves the child well through the maturing process. Because the maturing process had been artificially quickened by eating of the extreme food-knowledge of the tree of good and evil, the ones entrapped in a physical body need to apply physical effort in order to achieve permanent learning and maturity. This permanent learning, these understandings, are achieved through the threefold process of ideal, purpose and activity.

Activity is effort, action and movement.

Ideal is the mental image of what you want to be or become.

Purpose is personal benefit. Purpose provides the motivation to initiate activity in order to achieve the ideal of enlightenment.

The movement from the garden of Eden is the soul's subconscious mind's movement into the cycle of reincarnation-rebirth in order that after many lifetimes one could, through effort and learning, achieve enlightenment-the Christ consciousness. Individuals, entrapped souls, fulfill the command of I AM-Lord God to till the ground by activity and effort or work in the physical life. Work is effort without purpose. Activity is effort with purpose.

Ideal, purpose and activity are required to till the ground and cause it to produce. In order to add permanent understandings of Self and Creation to one's soul, one's subconscious mind, one must use the physical body and five senses to produce and receive the essence of the learning. This requires the will to direct the Self productively in the physical life.

The duty of the subconscious mind is to fulfill the desires of the conscious mind.

The duty of the conscious mind is to build permanent understandings of Self and creation. These understandings are then given to subconscious mind as permanent and lasting knowledge, enlightenment and soul memory.

This is the cycle that continues until one masters all lessons of life and creation that the physical world affords. **Then one's subconscious mind is filled full of understanding.** At that point all understandings are fully given to superconscious mind in fulfillment of the Divine and Perfect Plan of Creation. This plan, this seed idea, is held in superconscious mind.

> **24 So the Lord God drove out the man; and he placed at the east of the garden of Eden, Cherubim, and a flaming sword which turned every way, to guard the path to the tree of life.**

The Lord God-I AM moved the attention all the way out into the physical existence. No longer would man, the thinker, the soul, learn from observation. Now the soul became entrapped in a physical body. This cycle of re-incarnation has taken effect. Chakras or energy wheels are formed in the physical body in order to return energy into the higher levels of Mind. This gives anyone the possibility and opportunity to become enlightened. Until then most are confined to the lower three chakras.

The east is the third level of Mind, the deepest level of Subconscious Universal Mind. The cherubim and a flaming sword guard the path to the tree of life.

Eden is the Superconscious Mind. The garden of Eden is Subconscious Mind. The path is guarded making it much more difficult to go from Subconscious Mind to Superconscious Mind. A cherub is one of the order of angels. Angels are messengers from I AM and Superconscious Mind.

The flaming sword represents Karma, a word from India that means the physical manifestation of the Universal Law of Cause and Effect. The flaming sword that turns every way is an apt description of Karma. You can't get away from the Universal Laws and you can't get away from Karma.

Karma is created by intention.
Karma is relieved and fulfilled by understanding.

Karma is the Universal Lessons of life that keep coming at you until you get it. You have to learn the lesson that brings you into harmony and alignment with Universal Truths and Universal Laws before the Karma is fulfilled. When you learn the lesson of life you change for the better. You are less separate and more connected.

The tree of life is in Superconscious Mind. The medulla oblongata connects us to this life through life force. One needs to use the tree of the knowledge of good and evil to learn to reason. This occurs as one goes from one extreme to another until, through the disciplined mind, one gains equanimity. Then the still mind attunes to Superconscious Mind. One then gains enlightenment of Superconscious Mind. One has reached the wisdom stage of reasoning and one has achieved something beyond reasoning called the Intuitive Faculty.

This is discussed in more detail in the book of Revelation, interpreted and explained later in this book.

Summary of the Inner Meaning of Chapter 3 of the Book of Genesis
I AM, the Real Self, becomes engrossed in physical, sensory experience. The learning mode changes from observation to the activity called work.

Keys to Matthew

Chapter 4 of the Book of Matthew
Verses 1-17

Few word essence of Chapter 4, verses 1-17 of the Book of Matthew

The conscious ego in adolescence and adulthood

Brief and more expanded essence of Chapter 4, verses 1-17 of the Book of Matthew

Mental, emotional and physical discipline overcomes the conscious ego-Devil-Satan.

Chapter 4 of Matthew, verses 1-17

New Symbols and The Interpretation of Chapter 4 of Matthew, verses 1-17

1. Jesus - the knower

2. Holy Spirit - whole Breath

3. wilderness - untamed mind

4. the devil - conscious ego in adolescence

5. forty days and nights - stability in wielding the aggressive and receptive Principles of Creation

6. hungry - assimilation of knowledge gained in previous experience

7. Son of God - the one who chooses to create employing the aggressive quality

8. temple - stilling the Mind to be in the present moment

9. angels - thought forms from I AM

10. hand - purpose

11. mountains - challenge or obstacle

12. satan - conscious ego in adulthood

13. John - the quality of believing

Chapter 4 of Matthew
Verses 1-17

**1 Then Jesus was carried away by the Holy Spirit
into the wilderness to be tempted by the devil.**

Jesus symbolizes the knower. The knower is the one who stills the
mind through mental discipline. Through the still mind one is able and
capable of receiving the experience to the fullest. Thus, one is able to
receive the essence of the learning in every experience. Such a one is
then able to correlate the essence of the learning gained in the present
moment with the memories of learning in the past and the imagined
learning in the future.

It is through the full and correct use of memory, attention and imagination that one is able to bring about the full use of reasoning to know
the truth.

The Holy Spirit is the whole Mind and the use of the whole breath
to know the whole mind and all of consciousness.

The wilderness is a place where plants and animals are wild. The
wilderness is a place where humanity has not yet tamed. The area of
your mind and thoughts that you have yet to master is wild and untamed. This is the wilderness within you.

The devil is the conscious ego. The conscious ego attempts to control, manipulate and stimulate the part of Self called the conscious mind
that one has yet to discipline, master or to tame. The devil, who is the
ancient serpent-conscious ego, will tempt Jesus, the , just as the conscious mind-woman is tempted and deceived by the conscious ego in
the third chapter of Genesis.

As the conscious mind has matured to the disciplined, reasoning
knower so also has the ego grown in force, might and temptation or
stimulus. The conscious ego-serpent that becomes Satan, the adversary, will tempt you to become more sensory engrossed and physically
engrossed until you win the battle or war of your conscious mind. The
conscious ego-serpent becomes the dragon in the book of Revelation.
In the book of Revelation the dragon-conscious ego is tormented. This
means that your conscious ego will tempt you and beguile you until

you master the conscious ego. Then the dragon, the conscious ego, will be tormented for it can no longer control you by tempting you to go astray into sensory, physical engrossment.

2 So he fasted forty days and forty nights; but at last he was hungry.

Moses, the lawgiver, spent 40 days and 40 nights on a mountain in Exodus 24:18. And in Exodus 34:27-29, *"27 And the Lord said to Moses, Write these words; for by these words I have made a covenant with you and with all of Israel. 28 And he was there with the Lord forty days and forty nights; he neither ate bread nor drank water. And he wrote upon the tablets the words of the covenant, the ten commandments. 28 And it came to pass, when Moses came down from mount Sinai with the two tablets of testimony in his hand, when he came down from the mountain, Moses knew not that the skin of his face shone while the Lord talked with him. 30And when Aaron and all the children of Israel saw Moses' face, behold, the skin of Moses' face shone; and they were afraid to come near to him."*

Moses indicates the use of will and imagination to raise the Kundalini energy. The will and image making faculty are developed by the use of a disciplined mind.

The number 40 indicates stability gained by the disciplined mind. Four is the number of stability. Forty represents the power of stability that comes when one masters the essence of the lessons that physical life affords.

A fast is a time of not eating food. It is therefore a time of assimilation of the previous learning and knowledge-food.

Days or daylight symbolizes awareness. Night symbolizes lack of awareness.

When the previous learning and knowledge has been fully assimilated and integrated into one's being as permanent understandings then comes the need-hunger for greater learning and knowledge. One who fasts is steadfast in abstaining from food. One who mentally fasts is steadfast in abstaining from engrossment in the five senses of sight, sound, smell, taste and touch.

3 And the tempter drew near and said to him, if you are the Son of God, command these stones to become bread.

The conscious ego, the ancient serpent of Genesis, is here called the tempter-Devil. The serpent did tempt the woman to eat of the tree of the knowledge of good and evil in the third chapter of Genesis. The conscious ego tempted the inexperienced woman-conscious mind to eat of the tree that the Lord God had forbade. Now, the ego is at-tempting to place doubt in the mind of the knower-Jesus by trying to get him to perform a miracle. If Jesus refuses the conscious ego can say, "See, I told you there was no power beyond the physical. Therefore you should just lead a physical life."

Also, if Jesus tried to change the stones to bread and failed, then also the conscious ego would win. For this also would cast doubt on the belief that there is reality and power beyond the physical, sensory world.

The statement by the conscious ego-Devil, "If you are the Son of God," is a reference to Psalms 2:6-7. This verse from the book of Psalms says, *"I have appointed my king over Zion, my Holy Mountain, to declare my promise; the Lord has said to me, You are my son; this day I have begotten you."*

4 But he answered, saying, It is written that it is not by bread alone that man can live, but by every word which proceeds from the mouth of God.

In response to the conscious-ego-tempter-devil, the knower-Jesus quotes the truth of scripture.

Matthew, chapter 4, verse 4 is a quote from Deuteronomy 4:3. This is the scripture that the knower, Jesus, references. *"1 All the commandments which I command you this day you shall observe to do, that you may live and multiply, and go in and possess the land which the Lord swore to your fathers. 2 And you shall remember all the way which the Lord your God led you these forty years in the wilderness, that he might humble you, and prove you, to know what is in your heart, whether you would keep his commandments or not. 3 And he humbled you and suffered you to hunger and fed you with manna, which you did not know, neither did your fathers know; that he might make you to understand that man does not live by bread alone; but by everything that proceeds out of the mouth of the Lord does man live."*

It is not by bread-knowledge alone that the thinker-man can cause an expansion of consciousness. One must also learn to receive the truth and life force in every experience. This requires a still mind. A still mind is no thought and no thinking. Therefore, man the thinker, must learn to be a not thinker; at least one half of the time.

Genesis 1:3 states: *"And God said, Let there be Light; and there was Light."*

Therefore, it is the word of a creator that gives life, energy and motion to any creation.

Some people think they will become wise or authorities by reading a lot of books or by having a lot of experiences. Yet something more is needed to achieve the higher life. This something more is the ability to have a still mind with no thought and thereby, receive the cosmic life force into one's being.

The energy to sustain the body that we receive from food is its essence, life force. The 'word that proceeds from the mouth of God' is that life force that can be accessed directly rather than through the medium of food, through the medulla oblongata located at the back and base of the brain. The word of God is the truth of creation. The one who has achieved the still mind can align with this cosmic and Universal Truth and thereby directly receive the cosmic life force.

5 Then the adversary took him to the holy city, and he made him to stand on the pinnacle of the temple.

The conscious ego-Satan is called the adversary in verse five and the conscious ego-devil is called the tempter in verse 3. Therefore, your conscious ego is both your tempter and your adversary. The conscious ego will tempt you to engross yourself in sensory experiences, or if that is not available, the memory of sensory experiences. Anytime sensory experiences lead you astray from the True Purpose of Life, the conscious ego is your adversary because the conscious ego does not want you to know the True Purpose of Life that is lasting and eternal. The conscious ego motivates each person to move toward desires that have been stimulated through contact with the physical, sensory world.

The holy city is the whole Mind. The holy city is attained within the Self when one has aligned the conscious and subconscious minds through mental discipline. This discipline of the mind that Jesus achieved culminated after 40 days and 40 nights in the wilderness. The holy city is the New Jerusalem. The word Salem means peace. It is by the still mind that has attained a peaceful state that is able to receive and know the Holy and Whole Mind and the Whole Self.

The temple symbolizes one whose attention is on knowing the mind. To stand on the pinnacle of the temple shows one who has achieved the use of the whole Mind.

> **6 And he said to him, If you are the Son of God, throw yourself down; for it is written that he will command his angels concerning you, and they will bear you up on their hands so that even your foot may not strike a stone.**

The adversary-Satan quotes directly from Psalms 91:11-12. *"11 For he shall give his angels charge over you to keep you in all your ways. 12 They shall bear you up in their hands, lest you dash your foot against a stone."*

The devil-ego who is the tempter drew near Jesus in verse 3.

In verse 5, the adversary took Jesus to the holy city.

In verse 10, the adversary is identified by the knower-Jesus as Satan.

So either we have two different entities named the tempter-Devil and the adversary-Satan, or they are two different aspects of the same ego.

The book of Genesis 3:13 says, *"And the woman said, "the serpent beguiled me, and I did eat."*

The serpent is the first aspect of the conscious ego. The devil is the second aspect of the conscious ego. Satan is the third aspect of the conscious ego. The dragon of Revelation is the fourth aspect of the conscious ego.

1. **The serpent symbolizes the conscious ego in the stage of growth known as infancy.**
2. **The devil symbolizes the conscious ego in adolescence.**
3. **Satan is the conscious ego in adulthood.**
4. **The dragon is the conscious ego in old age.**

To beguile is to delude or to deceive by diverting the mind and attention. The conscious ego-serpent is the beguiler and will divert your attention from the true purpose of life.

The devil-tempter-conscious ego will attempt to distract you from the True Purpose of Life by becoming engrossed in food and other sensory experiences.

The adversary-Satan-conscious ego exposes itself for what it really is, an opponent and one who opposes your true purpose for which you are incarned in physical life. The adversary tries to make Jesus jump off the top of the temple. If angels save him, then Satan, the conscious ego, wins because you have chosen to use your spiritual or enlightened powers for purely self aggrandizement reasons. Self Aggrandizement is entrapping, engrossing, and feeds the ego. If Jesus, the knower, would say he is afraid, then also the conscious ego-Satan will win by employing fear. Fear is a product of an undisciplined mind that creates mental images of a future you don't want to create. In other words, fear gets you out of the present, the only true reality.

In the still mind one exists in the ever present, eternal now.

Therefore, the disciplined and still mind is the key to mastering the conscious ego.

Gautama the Buddha forbade his monks, his disciples, to demonstrate outward, supernormal abilities such as levitation and psychic abilities because he knew it was a distraction to their soul growth and spiritual development.

To command angels-messenger thought forms from I AM to carry you around is a misuse of the enlightenment one has gained. Enlightenment is to be used to further enlightenment and to aid others to enlightenment. This is the higher purpose-hand, will-stone and spiritual foundation-foot.

> **7 Jesus said to him, Again it is written that you shall not tempt the Lord your God.**

The knower-Jesus responds by quoting directly from the Old Testament book of Deuteronomy in the **Bible**, *"You will not tempt the Lord your God as you tempted him with temptations,"* (6:16).

Him refers to the adversary-Satan. However, the devil that speaks in verses one through four is not referred to as a him. Just as the serpent is not referred to as him.

The devil is referred to as the tempter rather than the male gender of him.

The serpent of Genesis 3 is called subtle and the beguiler.

Therefore, the devil still has many of the characteristics of the serpent while the adversary-Satan seems to take on a male form. This is because as one develops the discipline of the mind one develops an ego that goes beyond tempting and beguiling. Subtle, cunning, tempting and beguiling works for the conscious ego-serpent-devil when one is undisciplined with thoughts. Only when you have practiced concentration will you be able to recognize and know your own thoughts. When you are unconscious and unaware of most of your thoughts you will not know your own thoughts. Therefore, your thoughts may be yours or they may be the conscious ego's thoughts.

The conscious ego-devil will try to make you think that the ego's thoughts are your thoughts but they are not. The conscious ego-serpent is more subtle and cunning than all the wild beasts. Wild beasts symbolize habits. Animals possess a type of memory. Animals also have a limited kind of attention. Yet, animals lack imagination.

The conscious ego-serpent, however, has a type of limited memory-fantasy-imagination. Therefore, when the conscious-ego-devil is not successful at keeping your attention in the past, it will try to use a primitive type of imaging or day dreaming to try to distract you from the real purpose of life.

The conscious ego-serpent-devil has three methods of deceiving you. They are:

---

1. **Misuse of memory to keep your attention in the past,**
2. **Misuse of attention to keep you engrossed in sensory experiences, and**
3. **Misuse of imagination by trying to fantasize about the future that you will never create or to imagine a different past.**

All three forms of deception keep one from having all the mind and attention focused in the present moment. And the present moment is the only time that you can experience the true reality.

Jesus answers the adversary, Satan, by saying, *"You shall not tempt the Lord your God."*

The Lord-I AM is a god to the conscious ego-Satan. Lord-I AM is Jehovah-Yahweh of the Old Testament. Satan-the conscious ego attempts to oppose I AM. The conscious ego, that exists in your physical body, lives for sensory, physical experiences. The problem with this is that physical experiences alone will not give you enlightenment. The purpose of life is not physical. Temptation is a distraction to the real purpose of life. We are here to draw the essence of Universal Truth from every experience into the Self.

8 Again the adversary took him to a very high mountain, and he showed him all the kingdoms of the world and their glory.

Satan, the conscious ego, is your adversary. The adversary attempts to draw you and your attention away from the present moment. The adversary-Satan attempts to keep you from fulfilling the purpose of life in the present moment.

The conscious ego seeks physical, sensory engrossment or physical, sensory power-control.

A very high mountain symbolizes your challenge to achieve enlightenment, the Christhood. The glory of the kingdoms of the world are temporary, physical, sensory power and temporary, physical, sensory experience.

There is nothing permanent and lasting in what the conscious ego has to offer. The conscious ego, disguised as Mara, also offered all the kingdoms of the world to Siddhartha Gautama on the eve of his becoming the enlightened Buddha. Gautama also refused this conscious ego's offer as it was a distraction from the true purpose of life which is enlightenment.

9 And he said to him, All of these I will give to you, if you will fall down and worship me.

This statement, this temptation by Satan the conscious ego is in direct violation of the Lord God's-I AM's-commandments given in Deuteronomy that Jesus-the knower has been quoting. Specifically, Satan is contradicting Deuteronomy 16:22 which says, *"Neither shall you set up for yourselves any statue, which the Lord your God hates."*

The King James version of the **Bible** says the same verse this way, *"Neither shalt thou set thee up any image; which the Lord thy God hateth."*

An image or statue is a graven image. In the book of Revelation the second beast made an image-statue of the first beast. This will have much relevance later in this book as the inner meaning of Revelation is presented.

Therefore, the knower-Jesus cannot worship the conscious ego by giving all his attention to Satan because that will not fulfill the purpose of life. To become the Christ and Know the Real Self as I AM, one must give the whole attention to knowing I AM-Lord God. Also Deuteronomy 6:14-15 says, *"You shall not go after other gods, the gods of the people who are round about you."* Verse 15, *"For the Lord you God is a zealous God."*

The conscious ego will try to get you to give up the eternal for what is temporary.

In order to gain more temporary power or physical control one has to worship the conscious ego. To worship your conscious ego is to deny I AM and be distracted from your Real Self and Real Being. Nothing temporary is worth what is permanent and lasting. Enlightenment is eternal. Understandings of Self are permanent. Christ consciousness is lasting. Sensory experiences are temporary. Physical positions are temporary. Physical memories are temporary.

Siddhartha Gautama who became the Buddha had to overcome the same temptation by the conscious ego or Mara, as it is called in India.

When Siddhartha (first name) Gautama (last name) was born, the king, his father, brought all the wise men and astrologers to the court to predict and describe the child's future. All of them except one said the same thing: that the baby, Siddhartha, would either become the greatest king the world had ever seen and would rule the world, or he would become a fully enlightened being, a Buddha, and would raise the consciousness of the whole planet and all of humanity. The one that differed said Siddhartha would become the Buddha.

At the age of 28, Siddhartha Gautama left the palace and the kingdom, donned the clothes of a wandering monk, ascetic, and studied under a teacher who taught him all he knew. Then he studied under another spiritual teacher who taught him all he knew also. Then he tried extreme, bodily discipline to the point of death. Finding he was still not enlightened he ate food, regained his strength and then went to sit and meditate under a Bodhi tree.

He vowed he would remain in meditation under the tree until he was either enlightened or dead.

It was during this time of deep and committed meditation that the conscious ego-Devil-Satan-Mara appeared to Gautama just as it did to Jesus in the desert-wilderness. Both were tempted with all the sensory delights the temporary, physical world can offer. Both Jesus and Gautama chose the permanent and lasting over the temporary.

Both were offered the entire world as their kingdom. Both refused and instead chose the greater, eternal, true reality kingdom.

Jesus fasted for 40 days and 40 nights overcoming all attachment to physical sensory desires.

Gautama fasted and practiced Hatha Yoga disciplines for years until he grew weak and almost died.

In both cases the devil-Satan-Mara-conscious ego showed itself only after an incredible amount of mental, emotional, and physical discipline.

Therefore, the devil then found that guile, cunning and deceit no longer worked to control the disciplined one. Then Satan, the adversary, gave the ultimate physical promise of physical kingship over the entire planet. This also Jesus refused.

Mara promised the same things to Gautama. He also refused them because his goal, his ideal, was far beyond just physical satisfaction. Both Gautama's and Jesus's ideal was mastery over all 7 levels of Consciousness. To know Self as an awake, enlightened being they had to master the conscious mind, the subconscious mind, and the superconscious mind. The master of Mind knows Self as I AM beyond Mind, beyond time and beyond space.

10 Then Jesus said to him, Get away, Satan, for it is written, You shall worship the Lord your God, and him only shall you serve.

Deuteronomy 6:13 says, *"You shall reverence the Lord your God, and serve him, and swear by his name."* Verse 14 says, *"You shall not go after gods, the gods of the people who are round about you."* Jesus is also quoting Deuteronomy 5:8-9, the second commandment.

In verse 10 the adversary, of verses 5 and 8, is identified as Satan.

However, the devil of verse 1 is identified in verse 3 as the tempter.

So there are four aspects or stages of the conscious ego. These four stages of the conscious ego are:

1. Infancy - the serpent - subtle, cunning, beguiling,
2. Adolescence - the devil - tempting,
3. Adulthood - Satan - the adversary, and
4. Old age or Wisdom - the Dragon - fiery, enraged, angry.

Jesus' statement to *"get away, Satan"* indicates the ability to remove the distraction of the conscious ego. With what then do you replace the conscious ego-Satan? The conscious ego is replaced and overridden with I AM.

The conscious ego views and thinks everything is separate from itself. Therefore, it exists in a state of fear while trying to control everything. The conscious ego-Satan lives in a state of denial of the true reality of connectedness. Therefore, the conscious ego-Satan has no true power. In order to have true and real power one must align with the true nature of reality that is connectedness.

The conscious ego views the world through the five physical senses. The 5 senses of sight, taste, touch, smell, and sound give us a partial and imperfect perception of the world. The senses tell us we are separate from everything and everyone. This illusion of separation provided by the 5 senses is the basis upon which Newtonian physics is based.

Einsteinian physics, the theory of relativity and quantum mechanics, quantum physics, are grounded in the truth that there is reality beyond the reach of the 5 senses. This is the reality of the very small, the subatomic universe, and the very large, the solar system and galactic universe.

In verse 3 the devil tempts Jesus with a quote from Psalms 3. Jesus, the disciplined knower replies with a quote from Deuteronomy 8:3.

In verse 6 the adversary-Satan quotes Psalms 91:11-12, to which Jesus the knower replies with a quote from Deuteronomy 6:16.

In regard to the efforts of Satan in verse 9, Jesus, the knower of the disciplined mind, replies with a quote of Deuteronomy 6:5. While Satan's verse 9 is in direct violation or opposition to Deuteronomy 16:22.

Jesus quotes Deuteronomy because this book of the **Bible** contains the statutes and judgements that the Lord God gave to his people, the Israelites, through the enlightened Moses, his servant. The conscious ego as the devil-Satan quotes Psalms which was written by king David, an ancestor of Jesus. So Jesus has to choose between physical ancestry and the genetics of reasoning as symbolized by David or the spiritual ancestry and mental genetics of enlightenment as represented by Moses.

Lord God is I AM. Therefore, in his replies to the devil and Satan, Jesus, the disciplined knower, chose to be in alignment with and know I AM rather than succumb to the conscious ego.

11 Then the adversary left him alone; and behold, angels drew near and ministered to him.

Jesus, the disciplined knower, overcomes the conscious ego because he attained a still mind in the present moment and thus could know I AM. The conscious ego-devil-Satan is always in sensory experience. The knowing one remains true to I AM. Angels are messengers from I

AM. The one who achieves discipline of the mind in order to live in the present moment knows Self as I AM.

Receive everything you need in the present moment.

The meaning is, that you are the only one who can discipline your mind. You are the only one who can choose to be in the true reality, the ever present, eternal now. In the now, you defeat the adversary and the tempter. Thought is cause. Jesus, the knower, was then free to fulfill the soul's mission he had chosen.

12 Now when Jesus heard that John was delivered and imprisoned, he departed to Galilee.

John symbolizes the quality of believing. Believing-John comes before knowing-Jesus. Yet, the one with the disciplined and still mind, Jesus, the knower, conquers the conscious ego. Then does the quality of knowing gain prominence. To be imprisoned is to be restricted. The meaning of John-believing being imprisoned is that knowing is more expansive than believing.

The **Bible** says, *"Ye shall know the truth and the truth will set you free."* The knower, the one with a disciplined mind, is set free of the limitations and restrictions in consciousness. The one who exists in believing without knowing still exists in restrictions.

To know the Higher Truths, the Universal Truths of High Consciousness, one must have a disciplined mind that has achieved the still mind.

The wilderness, in which Jesus the knower spent 40 days and 40 nights, symbolizes the conscious mind that is not yet fully disciplined and directed.

Jesus' fast symbolizes the mental discipline of a still mind. Food symbolizes knowledge. To practice a fast is to not eat, to do away with food for an extended period of time. Jesus' fast symbolizes a disciplined mind that does away with mental knowledge of any kind, including thoughts. Jesus, the knower, exists in a thought free state during his fast. In order for you to conquer your conscious ego, you must exist in a thought free, disciplined state of mind. In the thought free, still mind the Self exists in the eternal now. In the eternal now you will know Self as I AM. In the eternal now, the conscious ego-devil-Satan has no power. Therefore, cultivate and master the still mind and the eternal now. Then you can consciously choose a thought with no conscious ego-devil interference.

13 And he left Nazareth, and came and settled in Capernaum, by the seaside, within the borders of Zebulun and of Napthali, 14 So that it might be fulfilled which was spoken by the prophet Isaiah, saying, 15 O land of Zebulun, O land of Napthali, the way to the sea, across the Jordan, Galilee of the Gentiles! 16 The people who dwelt in darkness saw a great light, and upon those who dwelt in the country and in the midst of the shadows of death, light shone. 17 From that time Jesus began to preach and to say, Repent, for the kingdom of heaven is coming near.

As soon as Jesus, the disciplined knower, achieved the still mind and mastered the conscious ego-devil-Satan, he began to fulfill his assignment in life. Jesus began to teach and lecture as a world teacher. The subject he chose was repentance. To repent is to feel pain or sorrow for mistakes of the past. To repent is to remember what brought pain and sorrow in the past, and therefore, change and do or be something different. To re-pent is to do penitence or be penitent for sins or offenses. The kingdom of heaven is the kingdom of the skies. Both sky and heaven symbolize superconscious mind. Therefore, change and stop living in the past. Instead, achieve the still mind in the ever-present eternal now and attune your consciousness to superconscious mind. This is what you must teach to many others in order to learn it in every aspect of your being.

Summary of the Inner Meaning of
Chapter 4, verses 1-17 of the Book of Matthew
Mental, emotional and physical discipline is the key to mastering the mind and conscious ego. In the still minded, present moment, the conscious ego has no control over you. Live according to Universal Truth and Universal Law.

The Secret Code
of Revelation

The Book of **The Revelation**
of
Saint John

The Book of the Whole Structure of the
Preparation to Receive the Plan of Creation

Few Word Essence
of Each Chapter of the Book of Revelation

1. Consciousness Revealed

2. The Root Chakra, The Spleen Chakra, The Solar Plexus
   Chakra, The Heart Chakra

3. The Throat Chakra, The Brow Chakra, The Crown Chakra

4. The Still Mind

5. The Full Commitment

6. The 7 Levels of Mind

7. The 144,000 Aspects of Self

8. The First and Highest Level of Mind

9. The Unconscious Part of the Brain

10. Aligning the Conscious and Subconscious Minds

11. Superconscious Awareness

12. The Birth of Enlightenment

13. The Brain, Memory, Imagination and Reasoning

14. The Choice of Entrapment or Enlightenment

15. Receptivity in the Conscious Mind

16. Kundalini and the Conscious Mind

17. Engrossment in Sensory Experience

18. Mastering the 5 Senses

19. Relieving Karma and Entrapment

20. The Second Death and the Book of Life

21. I AM and Superconscious Awareness

22. Full and Complete Consciousness

Book of Revelation
Chapter 1

Few Word Essence of Chapter 1
of the Book of Revelation

Consciousness Revealed

Brief and More Expanded Essence of Chapter 1
of the Book of Revelation

The Self realizes it is possible to attain enlightenment,
Christ Consciousness, this lifetime.

Symbols of the Book of Revelation
New symbols added chapter by chapter

Symbols & The Interpretation of Chapter 1 of Revelation

1. Jesus - the knower

2. the Christ - Enlightenment, Christ consciousness

3. John - the disciplined use of the quality of believing

4. the 7 churches of Asia - 7 chakras

5. spirit - breath and mind

6. kings - authority

7. Father - superconscious aspect

8. eye - perception

9. Patmos - emotional level of Mind

10. prophecy - imaging future goals

11. hair - conscious thoughts

12. fire - expansion

13. feet - spiritual foundation

14. water - conscious life experience

15. hand - purpose

16. two edged sword - cause and effect, Karma

17. dead - unconsciousness

18. Sheol, Hades, Hell - entrapment

19. angel - thought form from I Am or superconscious mind

20. voice - vibration

Revelation

Revelation, the last book of the **Bible**, reveals not only each person's potential, it also shows our destiny. Hidden within its passages is a hidden message. A message so important for the people of this planet that for the past 2000 years, millions of people have tried to understand its meaning. This book reveals the deeper meaning behind the symbology. As key after key is unlocked, the secret of secrets is revealed. Humanity's ultimate destiny is illuminated.

Chapter 1

1 The Revelation of Jesus the Christ, which God gave to him to show to his servants those things which must soon come to pass; he sent and signified it by his angel to his servant John; 2 Who bore record of the word of God and of the testimony of Jesus Christ and of all things that he saw. 3 Blessed is he who reads and they who listen to the words of this prophecy and keep those things which are written in it; for the time is at hand.

The word Revelation means reveal. The book of Revelation reveals in hidden, cryptic form, the destiny of each individual and all of humanity.

The word Christ is a Greek word meaning enlightened or anointed. Jesus was actually called messiah by his own people. The word messiah means anointed. The Aramaic word messiah was translated as the Greek word Christ or Christos.

The Aramaic name Joshua was changed in the translation to its Greek form, Jesus. The New Testament books of *Matthew, Mark, Luke* and *John* present an image, a story, of the one known as Jesus who became the

Christ. To become a Christ is to become enlightened. It is to become awake in full consciousness.

In the New Testament Jesus seems to always know what to do. He always has the answers to those questions posed to him whether by his students the disciples, or whether by the Pharisees, or the common people.

Jesus knew himself as a creator and as an enlightened being. The goal of all ancient temples of learning was to teach the individual to know the Self. This is why the words "man, know thyself" were inscribed above the entry ways to some of the ancient temples, colleges and schools of learning and high knowledge.

Therefore, when Jesus is referred to in the **Bible**, the quality being presented is knowing. Jesus symbolizes the knowing quality. Christ is a title. Christ was not Jesus' last name. Jesus the Christ was and is Jesus who became a Christ.

An angel is a messenger. As such, an angel symbolizes a message coming from I AM and superconscious mind to the conscious mind of this individual. The testimony of Jesus Christ is the truth that has been received and is now being shared.

John symbolizes the quality of believing. Believing always precedes knowing and John the Baptist preceded Jesus the Christ. In fact, John was known as the harbinger, for he prepared the way for Jesus' mission of teaching enlightenment. Anytime the name John is given in the **Bible**, the quality of believing is being presented.

A prophet is a goal setter, a prophecy is a goal. The book of Revelation presents the goal of enlightenment. It also presents the step by step process to become enlightened.

The time is at hand indicates that anyone who can understand the deeper meaning of Revelation has it within them to become enlightened this lifetime. A hand, whether in dream symbols or the **Bible**, symbolizes purpose. Therefore, verse 3 indicates the need to have both a goal and purpose for becoming enlightened. Purpose is personal benefit which provides motivation to pursue the goal of enlightenment.

Together, goal or ideal, purpose and activity-experience enable one to advance in consciousness and awareness.

**4 John to the seven churches which are in Asia:
Grace be to you and peace from him who is and who
was and who is to come; and from the seven Spirits
which are before his throne;**

The seven churches of Asia symbolize the seven chakras of the individual. Chakra is a Sanskrit word meaning *wheel*. The chakras are energy wheels or energy vortexes that return unused energy back into Mind for each person. Asia symbolizes the whole physical body. The seven chakras are located along the spinal column from the base of the spine to the crown of the head.

At present the vast majority of humanity is unaware of their own chakras. Those that progress rapidly in spiritual awareness and Self understanding become aware of the tremendous power of the chakras. The chakras are major keys to enlightenment. This is why they are presented in the very first chapter of the book of Revelation.

As the student progresses farther and farther in soul awareness, the chakras spin faster, and radiate greater LIGHT. This is why enlightened masters such as Jesus are often depicted as having a brilliant halo of spiritual energy around the head and an aura or energy field of LIGHT filled energy around the rest of the body.

I have perceived and become aware of all seven chakras of my energetic Self. Others have noticed and commented on these chakras also. This is not a theory but an actual fact that I and others have experienced and that more and more people are beginning to experience. This quickening is occurring as a movement in consciousness on planet Earth.

Mental discipline and the desire and effort to serve and aid the rest of humanity is what produces the quickening and enlightening of the chakras.

Because I have practiced mental discipline for over 30 years and have taught enlightenment and the Mind to millions of others during this time, I now offer this explanation of the book of Revelation directly from my experience.

I have experienced Revelation and have taught others to experience Revelation. I ask my students during the Revelation class I teach to identify the chapter of Revelation that most clearly presents their present state of consciousness. In other words I ask students which chapter of Revelation most aptly describes their current state of consciousness, awareness and understanding of Self and Mind. From this the student comes to realize it is possible to achieve all the enlightenment given in Revelation.

The throne referred to in verse 4 symbolizes superconscious mind and the authority that comes from using superconscious mind. The one who is, who was, and who is to come is I AM. I AM is you, the individual, beyond time, space, distance, and Mind. The past and the future are a function of time and space which are a function of Mind. I AM, which is your true individuality, is beyond time and space. Therefore, I AM, which is you the individual, existed in what seems to be the past, I AM exists in the present, the eternal now, and I AM will continue to exist in what seems to be the future.

Your goal in life is to know yourself as I AM.

Your ideal in life is to become en-LIGHT-ened and thus exist in Heaven. Heaven is not some far off place or in the future. Heaven exists in the here and now for those with eyes to see and ears to hear.

I AM exists in the present moment.

The seven spirits are the seven levels of Mind. Anytime the word spirit is used in the **Bible** it can also mean the Mind. *(See diagram 2)*

The word spirit comes from the Latin word spiritus, which means to breathe. The whole Mind (Conscious, Subconscious, and Superconscious) is a manifestation of the breath of God. The very same breath that moved upon the waters of Genesis 1:2, *"And the earth was without form, and void; and darkness was upon the face of the deep. And the spirit (mind, breath) of God moved upon the face of the water."*

> **5 And from Jesus Christ, who is the faithful witness, and the first to arise from the dead, and the prince of the kings of the earth. To him who loved us and washed us from our sins in his own blood.**

The knower, Jesus who has achieved enlightenment, is the first to arise and lift the consciousness out of the unconsciousness as symbolized by the phrase, "first born of the dead." The first born of the dead is without limitations. Such a one has achieved omnipresent consciousness.

Most people sleep walk through life. I have had students tell me that after they went through an initiation it was as though they had previously been walking around in a stupor. To be dead to the Higher and Universal Truth is to be unconscious and unaware.

The kings of the Earth are the five senses of sight, smell, taste, touch and hearing. The Prince of the Kings of the Earth is the one who has mastered the five senses and sensory engrossment. Such a one is a knower, an enlightened being, a Christ. Such a one has awakened from the death of unconsciousness.

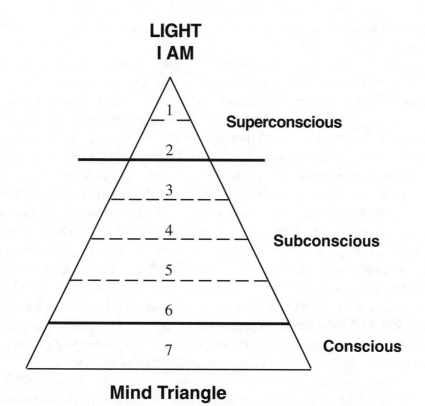

Mind Triangle

Diagram 2

The one who is gaining enlightenment is growing in the awareness of the connectedness of all beings and all creation. Love connects and the true nature of reality is connectedness. Therefore, an awakened, enlightened being lives a life of connectedness and love with the authority that comes from knowing the true nature of reality.

Water symbolizes the physical world that we experience with our conscious mind and the five senses. Thus, water symbolizes the conscious life experience.

Sins are mistakes. As recorded in the Gospels, after Jesus healed someone, he would often say, "Go your way and sin no more." In other words he commanded the person he healed to stop making the same mistakes. Sins are mistakes and since thought is cause, all mistakes begin in the mind with the thoughts of the individual. To sin no more is to correct your mistakes. To correct your mistakes is to **upgrade, update** and **improve** your thinking by practicing and developing a disciplined mind and by aligning with Universal Law and Universal Truth.

Blood symbolizes life force and truth. Truth enables us to know the essence of creation. Life force is the essence of things such as physical objects. Everything contains some life force. To know the essence is to know Universal Truth and the life force that comes from Superconscious Mind. To have Jesus Christ wash away our sins in his own blood is to identify with a greater and deeper truth, and therefore no longer make the same mistakes in thought, word or deed. The essence of truth as symbolized by blood only occurs in the present moment, not the past or the future. Now is the only time you can gain enlightenment. Only in the present moment can you learn and grow in awareness. Only in the present can you experience life and the life force from Superconscious Mind.

Thus, the symbolic meaning of Jesus the Christ washing away our sins in his own blood is that we come to live with full attention in the present moment. **The present moment is the only place and time where we can experience life.** In the present moment we can draw the essence of the learning in each experience, we can draw the permanent and universal learning in each experience into ourselves.

> **6 And has made us a spiritual kingdom to God and his Father, to him be glory and dominion for ever and ever. Amen.**

The **Bible** is a text book for knowing the whole Mind. The **Bible** is a book about you. It is a book that presents who you are, where you came from and where you are going. Therefore, each person in the **Bible** represents an aspect of yourself.

In order to make us a spiritual Kingdom to God and his Father we must come to know all of Mind. The Kingdom of God is Heaven. Heaven symbolizes Superconscious Mind. To gain enlightenment you must come to know Superconscious Mind.

> **To gain enlightenment one first practices discipline of the mind.**
> **1. Through the discipline of a concentration exercise one comes to know one's thoughts.**
> **2. From awareness of one's thoughts, the Self begins to choose one's thoughts.**
> **3. From choosing one's thoughts the Self begins to replace limiting and habitual thinking with more expansive and truth filled thinking.**
> **4. The conscious ego - which is the devil - re-acts to the mental discipline. Then the conscious ego begins to lose control of the physical brain and attempts to re-assert control.**
> **5. The one who maintains the commitment to know the Self experiences an inner struggle and either resists the temptation to become physically minded once again or else falls prey to this temptation.**
> **6. The one who resists the ego and brain limitations and maintains the commitment to know the whole Self experiences rapid progress in soul progression and a quickening of spiritual enlightenment.**
> **7. The Self, dwelling more on thoughts of Love, LIGHT, and Universal Truth comes to know Self as a world teacher, a being filled with the LIGHT of understanding.** *(See diagram 3)*

Verse 6 also says the following, *"To him be glory and dominion for ever and ever. Amen."*

The **Bible** is a story about you and teaches how you can have dominion over the many aspects of yourself. What is an aspect? An aspect is a quality of Self such as will, love, curiosity, power, truth, determination, openness, receptivity, aggressiveness, harmony, and discipline. There are many aspects. The more enlightened you become, the more aspects of yourself you know.

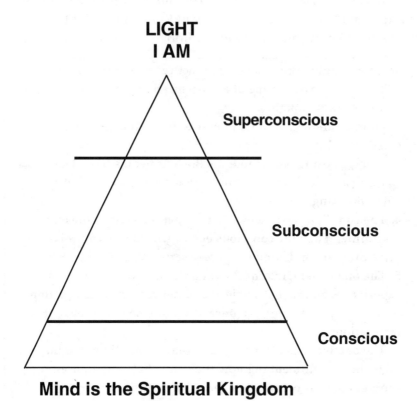

Mind is the Spiritual Kingdom

Diagram 3

The word glory comes from the Latin word gloria and the Greek Kleos, which mean fame, to celebrate, to hear. To give glory is to give praise, honor, admiration, or distinction. It is a state of greatness. Glory is also the radiation around the head or figure of a deity, saint, or angel.

Thus, glory is the one who has attained enlightenment, the Christhood, thus radiates light outward into the energy field or aura.

Domain comes from the Latin word dominus and means Lord. Domain indicates ownership and/or property. Dominion indicates a sovereign or supreme authority.

To have glory and dominion forever is to have gained understanding and authority in the use of the whole Mind and whole Self. One who has achieved this mastery of consciousness is worthy of honor and distinction. Such a one needs to be listened to for such a one is a teacher and brings the truth and LIGHT into the world.

Such a one, whether called a Christ, a messiah, a Buddha, a Zarathustra or a master teacher, is in a state of greatness that is permanent and lasting and filled with Light.

AMEN is a Hebrew word meaning, certainly or so be it, or let it be so.

7 Behold he will come with the clouds; and every eye shall see him, even the men who pierced him; and all the kindreds of the earth shall wail over him. Even so. Amen.

Clouds are in the sky and sky indicates heaven and Superconscious Mind. Clouds symbolize the Dome which is the separation between Subconscious and Superconscious minds. The word 'he' refers to Jesus who symbolizes the knowing quality. Jesus is the one who knows the Self and creation. Jesus knows the Universal Laws, Universal Truths, and Universal Principles.

Because the Knower knows all aspects of Self, so shall all aspects know, be aware of, and understand one who knows the Self.

Those who pierced Jesus symbolize the rebellious aspects of Self that are engrossed in physical, sensory, temporary experiences! When the knowing quality comes into the Self, any aspect that has yet to align with the true purpose of life will need to change from engrossment to enlightenment.

8 I am Aleph and Tau, the beginning and the ending says the Lord God, who is and who was and who is to come, the Almighty.

Aleph and Tau are the first and last letters of the Hebrew alphabet. Versions of the **Bible** that are derived from Greek use the words Alpha and Omega. Alpha and Omega are the first and last words of the Greek alphabet.

The **Bible** however was originally written in Aramaic - Hebrew. Therefore, the Aramaic is the more accurate translation. Because Alpha and Tau are the first and last letters of the Hebrew alphabet they indicate the beginning and ending. Alpha or Aleph and Tau or Omega are the end of the past and the beginning of the future. I AM is the beginning and ending. You began as I AM and you are here in this lifetime to gain awareness of Self as I AM, a creator in the present moment. I AM is neither past nor future. I AM exists in the eternal now, the present moment. **The only time you can know Self is in the present moment.**

Lord or Lord God symbolizes I AM. Lord symbolizes I AM and God is the Creator with both aggressive and receptive qualities.

Genesis 1:26-27 says "Then *God said, 'Let us make man in our image, after our likeness; and let them have dominion over the fish of the sea, and over the fowl of the air, and over the cattle, and over all the wild beasts of the earth, and over every creeping thing that creeps upon the earth. So God created man in his image, in the image of God he created him; male and female he created them.'"*

God created man the thinker in his likeness, which is to create individuals with like attributes to the Creator. What are those attributes? This question is answered in God's statement, *"Let us make man in our image."* To image something is to imagine or visualize something. Man, the thinker, whether male or female, has the ability to image.

The beginning of any and all caused creation is a visualized image. This is why "Thought is Cause" is a Universal Truth. It is universally true that all creation begins with a thought. A visualized image is a thought. ALL thoughts are images.

Therefore, the aggressive-receptive Creator gave us, the I AM's, the ability to create with choice. To choose is to visualize images that create or manifest in our lives. Before the sincere, conscious student can become enlightened, the image of enlightenment must be created in the Self.

Thus, the two tools or abilities that each of us, each I AM, uses to create with are:

1. **The ability to choose.**
2. **The ability to imagine.**

The ability to choose is in the present moment.
The ability to imagine is in the present moment.
To choose to imagine creates one's future.
I AM exists in the present as each person, each individual.
I AM existed in the past as each individual.
I AM will exist in the future as each individual.
Memory is drawing forth images of the past.
Attention is a still mind in the present.
Imagination is creating new images of the future.
In the present is the mind still. In the present can the individual know I AM. "Be still and know that I AM God." Psalm 46:10.

The I AM that is to come is the enlightened Self, which is any individual who has come to know Self. It is anyone who has become a Buddha, a Christ, an enlightened, awakened being.

The word might comes from a Saxon word meaning, able. To be almighty is to be able to do all, which is a definition of a creator and an enlightened being. Any individual I AM, any being who has gained enlightenment, is able to create. Such a one knows the Self.

> **9 I, John, your brother and companion in suffering and in the hope of Jesus Christ, was in the island which is called Patmos because of the word of God and because of the testimony of Jesus Christ.**

John, who symbolizes belief, is in suffering because he does not yet know Self as creator. He is not yet fully enlightened. Suffering occurs as a result of attachment to desires and identification with temporary, physical materiality. Knowing occurs as one realizes Self as an eternal being of LIGHT. Anyone who has developed the belief that he or she can become enlightened has a hope, an image of becoming a Christ.

An island symbolizes the emotional level of consciousness. The emotional level of consciousness is that level of Mind closest to the physical existence and the conscious mind. John, the believer, is on the island of Patmos because he wants to go deeper into Mind than just the emotional level. The believer wants to know all of Mind, including the Subconscious and Superconscious Minds.

The word of God, the Creator, is an image, a mental picture of the process of becoming a creator. The word of God is the Holy vibration of Creation that gives rise to all the multitude of forms in the physical world.

One who hears and receives the word of God is one who has accepted the ideal to become a knowing Christ, an enlightened being. Such a one is fulfilling the plan of creation held in Superconscious Mind.

The testimony of Jesus Christ is that we can all become Christs. Jesus said, *"Greater things that I do, you shall do also."* John 14:12.

10 The Spirit of prophecy came upon me on the Lord's day, and I heard behind me a great voice, as of a trumpet, saying,

The spirit of prophecy is the mind of one who imagines and visualizes the ideal of Christhood for Self and all beings. Spirit is mind. The word spirit comes from the Latin word spirare which means to breathe. A prophet is a goal creator. A goal setter decides what he or she wants the future to be and creates that future.

Since Lord symbolizes I AM, the Lord's day is the day or time of I AM. It is the time in your life when you decide to live your life for what is permanent and lasting instead of what is temporary. The Lord's day occurs when you reach your goal of awareness of Self as I AM. The Lord's day is the time set aside for communing with the Lord. The Lord is I AM. Physical life is temporary. Everything in the physical world is temporary. The Real Self, the Real You, which is I AM, is eternal and everlasting.

Ask yourself these questions. Are your motivations spiritual-mental or are they physical? Are your decisions based on physical gratification and sensory stimulation or are your decisions based upon the quickening of soul growth and spiritual development?

The day you decide that knowing Self, the Real Self, is the most important thing in the world, is the day you begin to know I AM. It is the beginning of the Lord's day.

The great voice behind John is the voice or instruction from I AM urging one on in the race to know the Self. It is the urge to enlightenment. This voice is the Holy vibration of creation. The one with a disciplined mind is able to receive this.

The reason the voice is behind John, the believing aspect of the Self, is because the awareness of I AM is not yet built in the conscious mind. Therefore, the perception of I AM is not yet apparent to one's conscious awareness.

The voice sounds like a trumpet because the voice is offering instruction concerning the seven chakras. The seven chakras when quickened become more than two dimensional wheels. Instead they evolve and grow into three dimensional vortexes that have a bell like a trumpet.

11 What you see, write in a book and send it to the seven churches, to Ephesus and to Smyrna and to Pergamos and to Thyatira and to Sardis and to Philadelphia and to Laodicea.

The mental image given in sending a book is to transfer information from one place to another. The information being sent and received is the knowledge of the chakras. The seven churches symbolize the seven chakras. The names of these seven chakras are the root chakra, the spleen chakra, the solar plexus chakra, the heart chakra, the throat chakra, the brow chakra, and the crown chakra.

1. Ephesus-the root chakra
2. Smyrna-the spleen chakra
3. Pergamos-the solar plexus chakra
4. Thyatira-the heart chakra
5. Sardis-the throat chakra
6. Philadelphia-the brow chakra
7. Laodicea-the crown chakra

12 And I turned to see the voice that spoke to me. And as I turned, I saw seven golden candlesticks,

The meaning of the seven golden candlesticks is revealed in the final verse of this chapter, verse 20.

13 And in the midst of the seven candlesticks one resembling the Son of Man, wearing a long vestment and girded round his breast with a golden girdle.

The one resembling a Son of Man is any individual who has activated and quickened the movement of the seven chakras. Such a one has awareness of the movement of energy along the spinal column. The seven chakras are located along the spine starting at the base with the root chakra and proceeding up the spine to above the crown of the head. This is why the crown chakra is so named.

The long vestment is clothing and clothing symbolizes one's outer expression, one's outer presentation. The reason such a one is girded about the breast is that the breast is the area of the heart chakra. The golden girdle indicates such a one has gained greater wisdom, value and understanding. The Son of Man has an open heart. This is why Jesus who became a Christ is depicted as being a divine example of Universal Love. As a disciplined one opens the chakras into conscious awareness of love and truth and teaches others, the heart chakra is opened. When this occurred with me it felt as if my heart had broken. After this my heart has remained open. Therefore, I am free to give and receive permanent understanding of myself and creation. The quality of the heart chakra is understanding, specifically permanent understanding of Self and creation. As the understandings are taught to others, greater and greater wisdom is developed in the Self. Hence the golden sash or girdle around the breast. **The heart chakra must be opened in order to fully comprehend the book of Revelation.**

14 His head and his hair were white as wool, as white as snow; and his eyes were as a flame of fire;

Hair symbolizes one's conscious thoughts. Head represents one's thinking ability as it relates to one's identity. The reference to the head and hair being as white as wool and snow indicates one who has learned to still the mind and thoughts. To still the mind is to enter into a state of no thought. White is a combination of all the colors of the rainbow.

A rainbow shows the separating of light into the different colors of the spectrum. This separation occurs because the rain droplets act as a prism. In a similar way, one's thoughts cause the LIGHT within the Self to be separated or broken down into the different colors of the spectrum. From this separation come the various colors in the aura or energy field of people. The predominant color in one person's aura or energy field may be blue while another person's energy field may be green or yellow or red.

In the enlightened one, the still mind is predominant. Therefore, the aura or energy field is white or LIGHT. When such a one decides to think a thought it is a productive thought in alignment with Universal Law and Universal Truth.

Verse 14 states that this one resembling the Son of Man had eyes that were as a flame of fire. Eyes symbolize perception. The one with mental perception can perceive what is beyond the five physical senses.

Fire symbolizes expansion. Thus, the one who has eyes like fire is the individual who is using the mind to expand the ability to perceive. Such a one is expanding consciousness into enlightenment.

> **15 And his feet were like the fine brass of Lebanon, as though they were burned in a furnace; and his voice was as the sound of many waters.**

Feet symbolize one's spiritual foundation. One's spiritual foundation is always built upon mental discipline. To have feet like the fine brass of Lebanon is, symbolically speaking, to have a very strong and firm spiritual foundation. The spiritual, mental, foundation of such a one is expanding for it is as if the feet are burned in a furnace. To burn requires fire.

The voice symbolizes one's ability to send forth the vibration of creation, the sacred sound of AUM.

Water symbolizes one's waking life experiences, one's conscious life experiences.

The voice had the sound of many waters, indicating one who is continually creating in the daily flow of conscious life experiences and is learning to be an enlightened creator.

> **16 And he had in his right hand seven stars; and out of his mouth came a sharp two-edged sword; and his countenance was like the sun shining in its strength.**

Stars symbolize conscious awareness or awareness in the conscious mind.

A hand represents purpose. The right hand symbolizes the productive, correct, or right use of one's purpose. It indicates one who is in the present moment. It is each person's duty to gain conscious awareness of the purpose of life and one's own, unique purpose in life. The one who has seven stars in his right hand is gaining awareness in all seven levels of mind.

Mouth symbolizes one's ability to digest the essence of the learning in life's experiences and then send it forth using that truth in one's life.

A weapon such as a sharp sword symbolizes a tool for change. A two-edged sword indicates karma. Karma is a word from India. Karma is the physical manifestation of the Universal Law of Cause and Effect, and is the tool for change being referred to.

Countenance is a French word meaning demeanor, way of acting or holding oneself and derives from the word contain. Countenance also means the whole form of the face, the features considered as a whole, the appearance or expression of the face. Face symbolizes one's identity. The sun shines forth to light the world. The sun symbolizes superconscious awareness. The one whose countenance was like the sun shining in its strength is a being whose identity is full of Self understanding and Self awareness. Such a one lives to aid others to enlightenment.

The sun gives light and light symbolizes awareness.

17 And when I saw him, I fell at his feet as dead.
And he laid his right hand upon me, saying, Fear not;
I am the first and the last;

John, the believer, fell at the feet of the One like a Son of Man as though dead indicating a total change in consciousness. Death symbolizes change.

Feet symbolize one's spiritual foundation. The feet of the One like a Son of Man are the spiritual foundation of one approaching spiritual mastery.

Man represents the thinker. The word man comes form the Sanskrit word Manu, which means thinker. Son indicates an aggressive motion forward in consciousness and in the life. Son of Man, therefore, symbolizes the one who is initiating action toward the goal of enlightenment. Such a one is directing the thoughts productively and in alignment with Universal Law and Universal Truth. Such a one moves and directs the thoughts to the ideal of enlightenment.

The One like a Son of Man laid his right hand on the believer, John. Right indicates righteous or correct. Gautama the Buddha called it Right Thinking. Hand symbolizes purpose. The One is I AM.

Therefore, the One like a Son of Man has a correct and productive purpose. John the believer is thus, gaining an awareness of a greater purpose for life. Such a person is coming to realize that there is a greater purpose to life and is beginning to fulfill that greater purpose. John, the believer, symbolizes anyone who is becoming aware of their purpose in life and realizes it will require mental discipline to fulfill that purpose.

This first chapter of the book of Revelation is the first realization and major push towards enlightenment. This chapter presents the recognition that it is possible for you to become enlightened this lifetime.

The first and the last is the I AM. I AM is your whole Self. I AM is the Real Self. I AM is an individualized unit of LIGHT. Each individual is I AM plus the permanent understandings of Self and creation earned since being created.

18 I am he who lives and was dead; and, behold, I am alive for evermore. Amen. And I have the keys of death and of Sheol.

Death symbolizes change. However, the word dead indicates unconsciousness. When we refer to someone as dead, it means they no longer exist as a conscious presence for us. Death, however, is a transition from one point of awareness, the physical life, to another point of awareness, the inner or soul life. The one who was dead and now lives and is alive for evermore is any individual who raises their consciousness out of gross materiality into higher realms of Mind and gains the Christ consciousness. Such a one has a continual, continuum of consciousness.

The physical world we perceive with the five senses of hearing, smell, taste, touch and sight is only one seventh of reality. There are seven levels of Mind. The physical world, and the conscious mind, make up only one level of the total Mind. *(See diagram 4)*

To overcome death, Sheol, and the netherworld, and live forever is the second coming of the Christ.

One who gains enlightenment never goes back to a state of unconsciousness or entrapment in physical existence. The one who is alive for evermore has the realization of alignment of all seven levels of Mind. The one who knows all of Mind and the whole Self possesses the keys to change. Such a one is able to continually evolve the Self.

Some of the exercises to practice to learn about the keys to death and Sheol are concentration, meditation, breathwork-life force exercises, Kundalini energy, visualization-imaging, service, teaching, learning about and living within the Universal Laws.

The seven levels of Mind are seven dimensions or realms of existence.

The first level, Christ consciousness, is for those who have attained the full use of Mind. It is enlightenment.

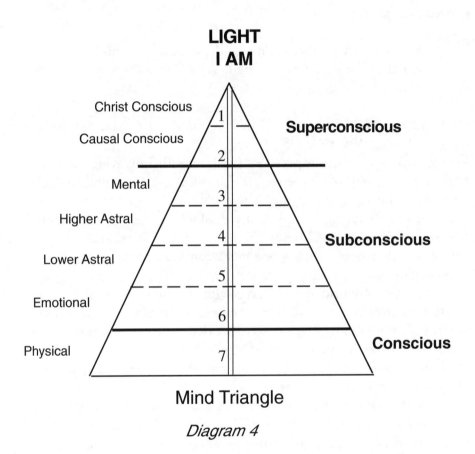

LIGHT
I AM

Christ Conscious

Causal Conscious

Superconscious

Mental

Higher Astral

Subconscious

Lower Astral

Emotional

Physical

Conscious

1
2
3
4
5
6
7

Mind Triangle

Diagram 4

The second level of Mind is called the causal level because from this point on through the levels of Mind, you become responsible for caus- ing your learning, soul growth and spiritual development.

The third level of Mind is the mental level. It is the point from which our thoughts begin to manifest in our physical life.

The fourth level is the higher astral. It is the final level before thought begins to take on form.

Between the fourth and fifth levels of Mind is located the Akashic Records. The Akashic Records, also called the Hall of Records, is an imprint or recording of everything that has ever been said, thought and done.

The fifth level of Mind is the beginning of physical form.

The sixth level is the emotional level. It is from this level that thoughts are emoted, or moved out to become manifested as a part of one's outward life.

The seventh level of Mind is the physical universe. This level and Division of Mind is used by the conscious mind.

19 Write, therefore, the things which you have seen and the things which are and the things which shall be hereafter,

To write something down is to make a record of an event. This record is then more permanent and lasting than otherwise would be the case.

1. The things which you have seen, are of the past and therefore relate to memory.

2. The things which are, pertain to the present and therefore relate to attention in the moment, the now.

3. The things which shall be hereafter are of the future and there- fore relate to imagination.

These three factors of memory, attention and imagination together make up reasoning.

Thus, the message is, to use memory, attention, and imagination to build one's reasoning and thus produce permanent understandings of Self and Creation. This relates to the duty of the conscious mind, which is to produce permanent understandings of Self and Creation that are then given to one's subconscious mind or soul.

When the subconscious mind of the individual is filled full of un- derstandings then all lessons of the physical life are complete. The subconscious mind then gives all these understandings of Self and Creation to the superconscious mind and the Self then exists with superconscious awareness. The Plan of Creation held in superconscious mind has been fulfilled. The Self is enlightened which is to be full of the LIGHT of awareness and understanding.

> **20 The mystery of the seven stars which you saw in**
> **my right hand, and the seven golden candlesticks.**
> **The seven stars are the angels of the seven churches**
> **and the seven candlesticks are the seven churches.**

The seven stars are the angels of the seven churches. Stars symbolize awareness in the conscious mind. Angels are messengers from superconscious mind and I AM. The seven churches are the seven chakras. Therefore, the awareness in the conscious mind must be built and enhanced through mental discipline in order to receive from superconscious mind and to know one's chakras.

In order to gain and achieve enlightenment one must know, perceive, enliven and be aware of all seven major chakras. These seven as given are the root chakra, the spleen chakra, the solar plexus chakra, the heart chakra, the throat chakra, the brow chakra, and the crown chakra.

The seven candlesticks are the seven churches. Therefore, both the candlestick and the churches symbolize the seven chakras. Candlesticks are designed to hold candles. Candle flames bring awareness. When the chakras are lit up they also bring awareness.

One can also enliven the chakras by bringing greater awareness into one's everyday experience. This is accomplished by learning how to learn about the whole Self. To learn about the whole Self at an accelerated rate requires a disciplined and still mind. It requires a willingness to be a student, to be humble in order to receive and to be taught the Eternal Principles of Life.

This chapter is a preview of the enlightenment that is to come for one who is determined to know the Real Self, and to become an enlightened being, which is to receive the Christ Consciousness.

Summary of the Inner Meaning of Chapter 1 of the Book of Revelation
The Self gains awareness of the seven chakras. The physical life is temporary and is therefore to be used to find and know the eternal.

Chapter 2 of Revelation

Few Word Essence of Chapter 2
of the Book of Revelation

The three lower chakras and the middle chakra

Brief and More Expanded Essence of Chapter 2
of the Book of Revelation

The Self realizes, the four lower chakras exist within
the Self and they need to be opened to all life.

Chapter 2

New Symbols & The Interpretation of Chapter 2 of Revelation

1. the church of Ephesus - the root chakra

2. Nicolaitanes - pretending to discipline the mind

3. the Tree of Life - continual awareness

4. ears - the ability to listen with the mind

5. the church in Smyrna - the spleen chakra

6. Satan - the adversary, the resisting conscious ego

7. the devil - the tempting, cunning, subtle conscious ego

8. prison - mental restriction

9. the crown of life - caused continual awareness and creation

10. the second death - entrapment in the physical body

11. the church in Pergamos - the solar plexus chakra

12. Balaam - perception and listening to the inner Self

13. Balak - an aspect uncommitted to the Real Self

14. the hidden manna - life force, cosmic energy

15. white stone - will power

16. the church of Thyatira - the heart chakra

17. Jezebel - the seduction of the senses

18. idols - worshipping the physical life

19. rod of iron - Universal Laws

20. the morning star - new awareness in the conscious mind

Chapter 2

1 To the angel of the church of Ephesus write: These things says the Omnipotent One who holds the seven stars in his right hand, who walks in the midst of the seven golden candlesticks.

The church in Ephesus symbolizes the root chakra.

An angel is a messenger from the I AM or High Self. This message conveys one of the keys to enlightenment and Christ consciousness.

The root chakra is located at the base of the spine. The quality of the root chakra is physical creation.

The root chakra recycles used mental energy back into the subconscious mind. The quality of the energy of the root chakra relates to physically creating.

The Omnipotent One is I AM. I AM is the one who holds the seven stars, which is the awareness of the seven levels of Mind. Mind is the vehicle to know the Self. The seven levels of Mind are the seven universes or dimensions that the individual may learn to enter with conscious awareness for the purpose of knowing the whole Self.

Seven stars in the right hand indicate, one who is using the seven levels of Mind productively and with awareness.

The seven golden candlesticks are the seven churches and symbolize the seven chakras.

The One who walks in the midst of the seven, golden candlesticks is the one who has conscious awareness and conscious use of the seven chakras. In order to know I AM, which is to gain enlightenment, one must master the seven levels of Mind and the seven chakras.

2 I know your works and your labor and your patience and how you cannot endure those who are ungodly; you have tried those who say they are apostles and are not, and you have found them liars;

The works, labor, and patience are the unceasing efforts of anyone who devotes the whole life to enlightenment and to helping others achieve the same.

As such a one progresses in soul awareness there is the constant upgrading and updating of one's thoughts and attitudes. This is done for the purpose of bringing them into alignment with the Universal Laws and Universal Truths. The one who practices concentration exercises soon comes to know the thoughts of Self. Then the process of weeding out the unproductive thoughts, attitudes and emotions as well as actions, begins in earnest. The ungodly are those that refuse to create a greater consciousness for the Self.

Disciples are students who practice mental discipline.

Apostles are teachers who teach mental discipline and the understanding of the whole Mind. A true teacher, an apostle, is one who practices and teaches mental discipline.

The Self and all aspects of Self must come to know that enlightenment is not achieved by only talking about the **Bible** or metaphysics or the Mind. Nor is enlightenment achieved by work, activity, or experience alone. These ideas are incomplete. Enlightenment and gaining the Christ Consciousness is achieved by mental discipline. This mental discipline must then be applied in all experiences in the life in order to draw forth the essence of the learning from all experiences. Then mental discipline and the higher truths must be taught to others. This is a true apostle.

3 And you have patience; and have borne burdens for my name's sake, and have not wearied.

To have patience is to be willing to apply mental discipline such as concentration, meditation, and life force in the life, minute to minute, day after day, until the awareness of the Christ within is achieved.

A burden is a load one carries. The burden that the disciple, that is the mentally disciplined one, carries is due to the fact that changes in the Self occur more often and more rapidly. When one is approaching a time of change or a need to change there is resistance. For the old thoughts, the old habits, the old mental images are strong because they have been practiced. Therefore, diligence, vigilance, and constant practice of the new, more expansive thoughts and actions are required.

Such a one has not wearied because of Self created purpose. Purpose is a strong motivating factor. Purpose comes from within and is

Self created. Purpose is personal benefit.

The average sensory, engrossed person relies on environmental stimulus for desire and motivation. Whereas, the purpose filled individual creates his or her own desires and is therefore not at the whim and mercy of the environment to create or to fulfill the desires.

To use the root chakra correctly, one must be able and willing to create purpose for the Self.

4 Nevertheless I have something against you, because you have left your first love.

Your first love is your inner mind, your soul, your subconscious mind. The marriage made in heaven is the commitment made in the conscious mind to align with one's soul or subconscious mind. The conscious and subconscious minds must be aligned in order to attune both to superconscious mind and thereby fulfill the purpose of life.

A lot of people create in the physical. However, in order to fulfill the purpose of life and become enlightened, that is not enough. Creating wealth, riches, or accumulating property will of themselves not give anyone enlightenment. The creative power associated with the root chakra must be used to create not only physically. The root chakra must be also used to create a greater enlightenment within the Self. Most people miss the permanent or soul learning in the experiences of life. To draw the essence of the learning in each experience, one must discipline the mind. To be re-united with your first love, you must see or perceive the learning in every experience and draw it into yourself. Then the universal learning must be practiced everyday and taught to others. This is how one makes learning Universal Laws and Truths a permanent part of the whole Self.

Concentration, meditation, breathwork, truth and love must be incorporated into one's being to forge the marriage made in heaven.

5 Remember therefore from whence you have fallen and repent and do the first works; or else I will come to you very soon, and I will remove your candlestick from its place unless you repent.

Each person, each soul inhabiting a physical body, is entrapped in that body.

Each I AM has fallen or moved from Superconscious Mind to the Universal Subconscious Mind and finally to entrapment in the physical body and conscious mind. Ever since the time of entrapment the individuals of humanity have been on the cycle of re-incarnation and karma. Incarning souls can no longer build permanent understandings of Self through observation. Instead, humanity must now gain understandings through activity, experience and reasoning.

Genesis, the first book of the **Bible** says, *"By the sweat of your face shall you eat bread until you return to the ground; out of it you were taken; for dust you are, and to dust shall you return."*

'By the sweat of your face shall you eat bread' means that effort, work, activity, and experience will now be necessary to produce permanent and lasting knowledge of Self and Creation. This has been so since the first time we became entrapped in a physical body. This has been so since that time when the conscious ego, as symbolized by the snake or serpent, tempted us to become engrossed in physical experiences.

To repent is to feel sorrow, pain or regret for something done or left undone by one Self. To repent is to experience such sorrow for sin that one amends the life. To repent is to be penitent. To repent and do the first works is to change the way you have been doing things. It is to change your perspective. It is to remember to learn in every experience. It is to remember to receive the essence of the learning in every experience. It is to observe your experiences while in the activity of daily life.

Remember, the learning is always about you. The seven candlesticks are the seven churches and the seven churches symbolizes the seven chakras.

The phrase "I will remove your candlestick from its place" means the root chakra will cease spinning and cease returning used mental energy back into Mind. When this happens the individual dies, which is to permanently withdraw the attention from the physical body. At the point of death, the soul withdraws its attention from the physical body and returns to the Universal Subconscious Mind. In such a case the individual has no more opportunity to experience physical existence this lifetime. To keep the root chakra functioning at full capacity, one must be willing to change and grow in awareness and consciousness, constantly and consistently. This capability requires that the conscious ego surrender to I AM.

**6 But this you have in your favor, you hate the works
of the Nicolaitanes, which I also hate.**

Nicolaitanes were those in the early Christian church that attempted to bring elements of other teachings, such as the pagans, into the church. Yet the teaching of the Christian church is of one God. This means you should not get distracted in your quest to know the one Self, which is I AM. They often did not believe everything that Jesus taught. See John 3:1-16.

The worship of many gods is the worship of the many aspects of the Self. The worship of the Lord is the effort and desire to know I AM. To hate the work of the Nicolaitanes is to refuse to be distracted from the goal of knowing the whole Self as I AM.

The process of soul growth is one of consistently upgrading the thoughts from habitual and undisciplined to the use of will power with discipline.

The process also includes the will power and mental discipline needed to still the mind and still the thoughts. As one progresses in soul awareness and enlightenment, one thinks less and less thoughts and therefore has less and less distractions. Having less and less distractions is how one overcomes the practices of the Nicolaitanes.

Even though the enlightened one thinks less and less thoughts, the thoughts are more powerful. The thoughts are more powerful and productive because they are focused and directed with will power and discipline. **The disciplined, enlightened being either consciously chooses to think a thought or consciously chooses to still the mind, which is to have no thought.**

When the mind is stilled the Higher Truths and realization of the High Self as I AM can occur.

**7 He who has ears, let him hear what the Spirit says
to the churches: To him who overcomes, I will give to
eat of the tree of life, which is in the midst of the
paradise of my God.**

Ears symbolize the ability to receive the Truth into the Self. The meaning of one who has ears is the one who can still the conscious mind thoughts and thus be capable of receiving the higher truths from the subconscious and superconscious minds. Hearing is a receptive function. Hearing is the ability to receive sound waves into the ear and

ear drum. The sound is then transmitted to the brain when it is interpreted.

The one who has ears symbolizes the one who is willing to receive
the higher truth.

The mind or spirit must be directed by the individual to come to
use the chakras consciously, wisely, and with understanding. The one
who overcomes physical engrossment and physical entrapment will
receive knowledge and awareness of how to build permanent understanding of Self and Creation. Such a one will gain the higher consciousness and awareness of the eternal, everlasting Real Self. Such a
one will know how to cause growthful change in consciousness and
will master the motion of creation.

Physically the Tree of Life is the medulla oblongata which is located
at the base of the brain. The medulla oblongata is the point in which
the life force or cosmic energy flows into the physical body.
(See diagram 5)

The "paradise of my God," physically is the interaction between
the pituitary gland, the pineal gland, and the medulla oblongata. Mentally the meaning is that the one who overcomes physical entrapment
will master the motion of life and will experience the superconscious
mind and awareness. The body and mind must be disciplined in order
that the still mind may receive the higher consciousness which is life.
The Tree of the Knowledge of Good and Evil is described in Genesis
2:9.

**8 And to the angel of the church in Smyrna write:
These things says the first and the last, which was
dead and is alive:**

The church in Smyrna symbolizes the spleen chakra.

The quality of the spleen chakra is power. To manifest one's true
power one must discipline the mind. A disciplined mind then has the
capability of developing a still mind. A still mind can then make a
choice to imagine, to move and to create, using the aggressive principle. Thus, a still mind can access the power of the spleen chakra.

The root chakra aids or enables one to create in physical life. The
spleen chakra adds power to this creation. This power enables one to
create on a large and expansive scale.

Although chakras are not physical and are therefore not a physical

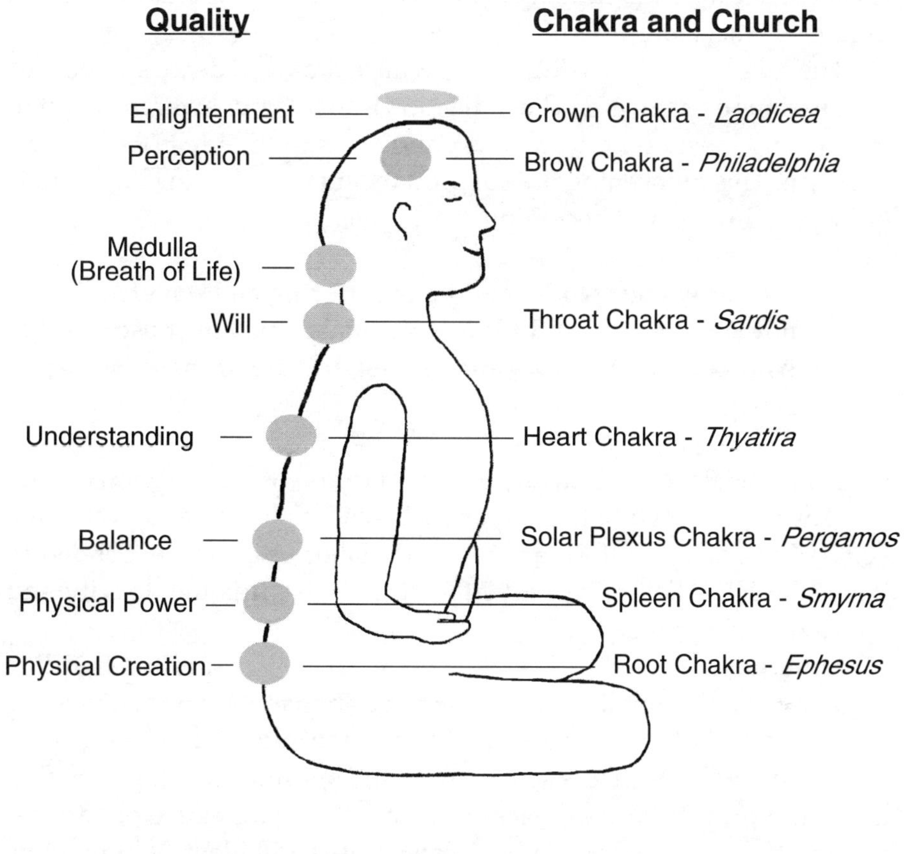

Quality

Chakra and Church

Enlightenment ——————— Crown Chakra - *Laodicea*

Perception ——————— Brow Chakra - *Philadelphia*

Medulla
(Breath of Life) ——

Will —————— Throat Chakra - *Sardis*

Understanding ——— Heart Chakra - *Thyatira*

Balance ——— Solar Plexus Chakra - *Pergamos*

Physical Power ——— Spleen Chakra - *Smyrna*

Physical Creation——— Root Chakra - *Ephesus*

Diagram 5

organ, they are nonetheless associated with that area of the body. Thus, the spleen chakra is located in the area of the spleen which is above the area of the root chakra.

The first and the last is I AM. You were created as an individualized unit of LIGHT known as I AM. Now, through many millennia of experiencing, you have grown in awareness and understanding. As I AM evolves, the individual becomes enlightened, yet remains I AM, a unique, connected individual.

The reason I AM was dead was because the word dead, symbolizes unconscious or unaware. The indication is to lift your awareness out of the unconsciousness of fears and darkness into the LIGHT of understanding. This quickening of soul growth and spiritual development is one of waking up and becoming more alive.

> **9 I know your works and your suffering and poverty,**
> **but you are rich, and I know the blasphemy of those**
> **who say they are Jews and are not, but are of the**
> **synagogue of Satan.**

I AM, the Real Self is aware of the condition of the conscious mind.

'Your works' symbolize anyone who earnestly strives to know the Self. Works are the effort, action, work, labor or energy expended to know the High Self and quicken soul growth. It is the activity and effort to discipline the mind.

Suffering is caused by the attachment to desires says the Buddha. Once one chooses to direct the life and attention toward understanding the purpose of life, one's attachments become apparent. The one who would be the Christ places soul growth and spiritual development first as the top priority. New choices often cause one to release old attachments. The one who is growing in awareness will identify limitations in consciousness, which are often associated with attachments. Then an effort will be made to transform, upgrade and improve the thoughts and consciousness.

The poverty referred to in verse 9 indicates the attachment to physical objects and possessions as a focus of security. However, the One, which is I AM, says anyone who is disciplining the mind and quickening soul growth is rich. Such a one is able to harmonize with and draw upon the abundance of the whole Mind, Conscious, Subconscious, and Superconscious. This is why enlightened beings are never poor. Jesus, who became the Christ, did not even have a place to lay his head, yet he was not poor. He had riches beyond compare. His teachings continue to enrich the world 2000 years later. True riches are lasting. Physical, illusory, riches are temporary.

Jews symbolize those who believe in the coming of Christ consciousness in a future time while Satan symbolizes the conscious ego. The control over the conscious ego, the battle for the Real Self is fought in the present moment, not the future or the past.

The synagogue of Satan is anyone who lets the conscious ego control their life in such a way that they are motivated to achieve physical things only. The choice is to practice becoming enlightened or practice being engrossed in the physical senses. The conscious ego dwells in the solar plexus. However from the solar plexus the conscious ego can control many aspects of Self related to physical power and the spleen chakra. The synagogue of Satan, in the pit of the stomach, relates and often controls the action of the spleen chakra.

> **10 Fear none of those things which you shall suffer; behold, the devil will cast some of you into prison, that you be tried; and you will be oppressed for ten days. Be faithful even to death, and I will give you a crown of life.**

Do not fear becoming aware of your unconscious attachment to the past or to past memories or to physical objects. It is lack of awareness or unconsciousness that one should see and become aware of to transcend. Fear is a warning that one should change and move out of physical thinking to mental thinking. **Fear is a product of an undisciplined mind.**

The one who practices mental thinking understands that thought is cause and thereby accepts responsibility for the life. You create your life by the choices you make. One's choices are based upon one's thoughts.

The devil, one's own conscious ego, is a physical reflection of I AM in the conscious mind. As such, the conscious ego tries to rule the conscious mind of each individual on planet Earth. However, the conscious ego is only temporary and is gone or destroyed along with the conscious mind when the physical body dies. The conscious ego is a reflection and like all reflections it is temporary. The devil or conscious ego will cast some aspects of Self into prison because prison represents one's own limitations in consciousness. When one has refused to exercise free will and refuses to be responsible by responding to the inner urge, then such a one lives in a Self created prison. This is a prison of one's own thoughts, attitudes, and limitations.

To be tried and oppressed for ten days is to judge yourself to determine the degree you have changed and grown in consciousness. The number 10 symbolizes the completion of one cycle and the beginning of the next higher cycle with understanding and power. This means that you will be trapped in your own limited thinking until you expand your consciousness.

To be faithful even unto death, metaphorically speaking, is to be committed to the quickening of your soul growth and the understanding of the whole Mind until you change. Keep changing and growing in awareness and understanding until enlightenment is achieved. Enlightenment is the crown of life. It is the mastery of the crown chakra and the motion of the mind. The Crown of Life is the ability to still the mind and know Christ consciousness in the present moment.

> **11 He who has ears, let him hear what the Spirit says**
> **to the churches: He who overcomes death shall not**
> **be hurt by the second death.**

To have ears as referenced in the **Bible** means to be able and capable of receiving the Higher Truth. This Higher Truth is the Universal Truths, the Universal Laws, and the Universal Principles. The one who is able and willing to receive the Higher Truth shall understand and receive the full use of the chakras. Therefore, it is of utmost importance for the one who desires to know the Self to learn to still the mind. A restless or busy mind can never receive the High Knowledge any more than a busy mind can hear what another person says.

Only a disciplined, still, mind can be receptive. Only a quiet, still mind can receive the Higher Truth. In meditation one needs to still the thinking in the outer, conscious mind in order to receive, first from the subconscious, and then from the superconscious mind.

The second death is entrapment in a physical body and engrossment in sensory experience. You are not your physical body. You are an I AM engrossed and entrapped in the vehicle known as the physical body. Any person who overcomes limitations in consciousness will overcome the entrapment in a physical body. Such a one will be able to enter and leave the physical body at will with full conscious awareness. This is how Jesus, the Christ, was able to disappear near Jerusalem after the crucifixion and reappear almost immediately in Galilee.

The one who overcomes the second death knows he or she is not a physical body. Such a one has a continuum of consciousness and conscious awareness beyond the body in the Superconscious and Subconscious. For the enlightened one this is true whether in a physical body or not, whether before death or after the death of the physical body. The spleen chakra contains a powerful key to overcome the unconsciousness of death.

12 And to the angel of the church in Pergamos write: These things says he who has the sharp two-edged sword:

The church in Pergamos symbolizes the solar plexus chakra.

The quality of the solar plexus chakra is balance. The quality of balance relates to the balance between the inner Self and the outer Self, the mental and the physical, the conscious mind and the subconscious mind.

The sharp two-edged sword symbolizes karma. Karma is the physical manifestation of the Universal Law of Cause and Effect. A sword symbolizes a tool for change. The One or I AM has the two-edged sword because the efforts to know the Self provide the opportunity for continuous change, which is growth in consciousness as well as the relief of karma.

Karma is indebtedness as an individual.
Karma is created by intention.
Karma is relieved by understanding.

The one who has the sharp two-edged sword is anyone who has been taught and learned to cause continual change and growth in consciousness. Such a one causes the consciousness to expand, increasing one's awareness. Then one can make better and more productive decisions that add to one's understanding thereby relieving one's karma. Karma can be perceived in the experiences one draws to the Self. It is your duty to harmonize with all the Universal Laws and Truths and to align your conscious and subconscious minds with superconscious mind.

> **13 I know your works and where you dwell, even where Satan's seat is; and you upheld my name, and you did not deny my faith, even in those days when that witness of mine appeared, that faithful one of mine who was slain among you, where Satan dwells.**

Your works are the effort you give forth to advance your consciousness and the learning you receive from your efforts be they mental, emotional or physical.

The area of the solar plexus is where the conscious ego resides. For the solar plexus is the seat of the conscious and subconscious minds, and Satan is the conscious ego.

The conscious ego motivates you to achieve physical goals. Satan, the conscious ego, feeds on desires. As such it is temporary. The conscious ego does not know the subconscious mind or superconscious mind. The conscious ego does not know what is permanent and lasting. Therefore, to get control of your conscious ego you will need to understand the solar plexus chakra. When you experience fear, such as stage fright or fear of public speaking, you will notice the uneasy or queasy feeling in the pit of your stomach. This is the ego re-acting. The conscious ego resides in the solar plexus. This means in order for you to get control of your conscious ego, Satan, you must understand, harmonize with and align with the energies of the solar plexus chakra. *(See diagram 6)*

The conscious ego is mastered by the disciplined, conscious mind that has achieved a still mind. Only in a still mind can you choose to think a thought-aggressive or choose to receive a thought-receptive. The name being upheld is I AM. The faith referred to is the belief that you can know your Real Self as I AM, your true individuality.

The faithful witness that St. John the Divine refers to is the still mind in the present moment that produces Christ consciousness. Such a consciousness was achieved by Jesus of Nazareth who gained the Christ consciousness. Jesus, who became the Christ, was crucified as given in the gospels of Matthew, Mark, Luke and John. He was the faithful one who was slain. An accurate witness must have been present and given full attention to an event or experience. The faithful witness keeps the

**Person who is entrapped in a physical body,
engrossed in the five senses and ruled by the conscious ego.**

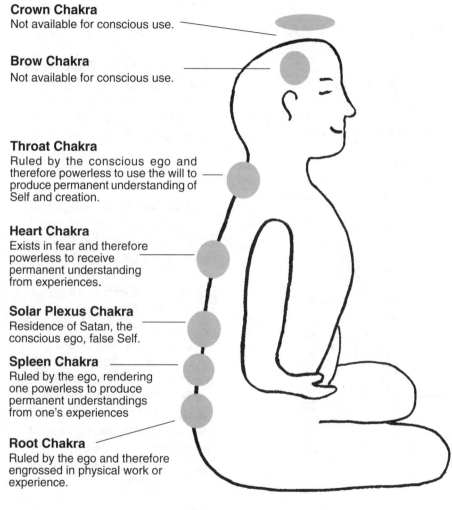

Crown Chakra
Not available for conscious use.

Brow Chakra
Not available for conscious use.

Throat Chakra
Ruled by the conscious ego and
therefore powerless to use the will to
produce permanent understanding of
Self and creation.

Heart Chakra
Exists in fear and therefore
powerless to receive
permanent understanding
from experiences.

Solar Plexus Chakra
Residence of Satan, the
conscious ego, false Self.

Spleen Chakra
Ruled by the ego, rendering
one powerless to produce
permanent understandings
from one's experiences

Root Chakra
Ruled by the ego and therefore
engrossed in physical work or
experience.

Diagram 6

In the ego based, undisciplined one Satan, the conscious ego, rules from the solar
plexus chakra as given in Revelation 2:13. From the solar plexus, Satan, the conscious ego, also rules the spleen chakra as given in Revelation 2:9 and the root
chakra as given in Revelation 2:5.

HEBREW ALPHABET

א	1
ב	2
ג	3
ד	4
ה	5
ו	6
ז	7
ח	8
ט	9
י	10
כ — ך	20*
ל	30
מ — ם	40*
נ — ן	50*
ס	60
ע	70
פ — ף	80*
צ — ץ	90*
ק	100
ר	200
ש	300
ת	400

Each letter of the **Bible** has a numerical correspondence. In ancient days the letters of the alphabet were also the numbers used. Thus, Aleph, the first letter of the Hebrew alphabet equals the number 1.

Words therefore, being made up of letters, have numerical equivalents. The numerical equivalent for Satan is 360. Now, 360 degrees is the number in a circle. Therefore Satan, the conscious ego, will keep you running around in circles all your life chasing your tail of endless physical desires. The other option is to realize that all physical life is temporary, and therefore, seek out and learn the permanent and lasting. The permanent gets you out of the circle and into the cycle.

Diagram 7

attention in the present, the here and now. This is the key to fully using the solar plexus energies. Otherwise one lives in egoic re-actions to past memories stimulated by present experiences. *(See diagram 7)*

Jesus symbolizes the knowing quality in each of us. As we build a greater knowledge of the Self and move forward in consciousness, we face obstacles that are actually restrictions and limitations in attitudes and consciousness. This limited thinking and restrictions in mind must change in order for expansion to occur. To be slain is to change.

This great change of the ego must and needs to occur in the balance of inner and outer, conscious and subconscious mind. The student of Mind who desires to know the Self must choose the permanent and lasting over the temporary, thereby climbing higher and higher cycles of growth until the Christ consciousness is achieved.

> **14 But I have a few things against you because you have there those who hold the teaching of Balaam, who taught Balak to cast a stumbling block before the children of Israel, to eat things sacrificed to idols and to commit adultery.**

Throughout the Old Testament of the **Bible**, the Israelites are instructed by I AM, symbolized by the Lord, not to worship false idols and false gods.

Balaam was a prophet and an interpreter of dreams in the Old Testament book of Numbers. Balak was a King of Moab, who was afraid of being destroyed by the Israelites. Therefore, he sent for Balaam who lived in Mesopotamia to come to him and curse the Israelites. Balaam came to Balak in Moab, but instead of cursing the Israelites he blessed them because this is what the Lord told him to do.

Balaam symbolizes one who listens to the inner Self and practices that truth in the life. Balaam is the one who meditates every day and receives from the superconscious mind, yet has not reached Christhood. Balaam represents the parts of Self that listen to the night dreams and apply them in the life.

Balak symbolizes one whose attention is on the temporary, physical world and disregards the value of the permanent and lasting. As such Balak is allied with the conscious ego. To eat things sacrificed to idols presents an image of trying to gain your value out of physical experience alone while refusing to gain the learning of the higher truths and higher knowledge. Adultery symbolizes the refusal to maintain one's commitment to fulfill the soul urge and to build permanent understandings of Self and Creation.

Such a one as described in this verse has aspects of Self that are not fully committed to knowing the Self. There is also the indication of aspects that are engrossed in the five senses and sensory experience.

The Israelites, metaphorically speaking, are the teacher aspects of Self. As you teach you learn. To make the higher consciousness permanent, the disciplined student must become a teacher.

15 And also you have those among you who hold to the teaching of the Nicolaitanes.

The Nicolaitanes were also present in verse 6 of this chapter. They symbolize those aspects of Self that act as if their attention and efforts are toward knowing I AM and what is permanent and lasting. When in truth they tend to be physically engrossed and worship physical, sensory experience.

Verse 6, which refers to the church in Ephesus, the root chakra, gives credit for hating the works of the Nicolaitanes. While verse 16 says while referring to the solar plexus chakra, *"You have those among you who hold to the teaching of the Nicolaitanes."*

Such a one has learned how to create in the physical world-root chakra but still has aspects of Self that are controlled by the conscious ego. A student of the Mind at this level of development is devoting much of the physical life-root chakra to soul growth and spiritual development, yet still is not fully disciplined with the conscious mind. Therefore, one at this level of development has not fully aligned conscious and subconscious mind. Therefore, the conscious ego-devil-Satan of verse 10 still has some power over one's thoughts and consciousness. A person at this level of awareness also has aspects of Self that appear to be spiritual yet are still engrossed in sensory experience.

16 Repent; or else I will come to you very soon and will fight against them with the sword of my mouth.

To repent is to turn from sin. To repent is to regret what you have done and therefore turn from your mistakes. The sword of I AM's mouth is the ability to cause change in the way one assimilates the learning in each experience. This change is the ability to more fully receive and rapidly process the essence of learning in each experience.

To repent is to experience pain or sorrow for past conduct and to change in order that the pain will not be produced again. To repent is to be penitent again.

The mouth is used for eating food. Food symbolizes knowledge. The mouth is also used for communication. In order to change and relieve one's karma, one must talk and listen to others. One must share this inner Self with others, and one must receive the learning in the experience.

When your experiences produce pain then change your thoughts so that your decisions, actions and emotions will change. Then there will be growth in consciousness.

A sword is a tool for change. However, when there is alignment of all aspects of Self with the soul's purpose, there is no need for fighting. Therefore, learn to align the inner and the outer minds by building a disciplined and still mind.

17 He who has ears, let him hear what the Spirit says to the churches: To him who overcomes, I will give to eat of the hidden manna, and I will give him a white stone, and on the stone a new name written, which no man knows except he who receives it.

Ears symbolize the ability to listen. The spirit is the whole mind.

The hidden manna is life force, which is cosmic energy as it enters the physical body.

The manna is referred to in Exodus 16:4, *"The Israelites were fed manna from God while wandering in the desert for 40 years after they left Egypt."*

The one who overcomes physical thinking and aligns with the subconscious mind and superconscious mind will gain the ability to consciously draw upon this cosmic life force to cause a further quickening of one's soul evolution. The one who has the hidden manna is able to fill the body with LIGHT and gain the higher consciousness.

A stone symbolizes the will. A white stone symbolizes will power. A correct choice to discipline the mind produces will. Repeated choices to apply the disciplined mind in the life produce will power.

The word 'man' symbolizes the thinker. The new name is the identification of Self with the subconscious and superconscious minds. It is a new identity that goes beyond physical thinking. The new name is for the one who has gained awareness of Self as more than a physical being.

Will is required to access the inner levels of Mind and to know the Self. The one known as Jesus of Nazareth gained a new identity and became known as the Christ. Only a Christ can fully know a Christ. Only a Buddha, an awakened one, can know a Christ, an awakened one. In Genesis 2:19, Adam called or named every living creature. To name something is to identify it. To receive a new name is to receive and achieve a new identity as a Son of God.

> **18 And to the angel of the church in Thyatira write:
> These things says the Son of God, who has eyes like
> a flame of fire, and whose feet are like fine brass
> from Lebanon;**

The church in Thyatira symbolizes the heart chakra.

The quality of the heart chakra is understanding. Compassion comes from understanding. Love is necessary for understanding. Love makes it easier to receive the learning in order that one may understand Self and Creation.

The Son of God is the one who disciplines the mind and thereby chooses the thoughts that produce more understanding of Self and Creation. Such a one is learning to live in the Light.

Eyes symbolize perception. Fire symbolizes expansion of consciousness. Feet symbolize one's spiritual foundation. Brass fee symbolize a disciplined, mind, foundation. Feet of brass indicate a very strong, durable and lasting spiritual foundation. The one who is building the disciplined mind has increased perception, is expanding consciousness, and is building a strong foundation for knowing the whole Self.

> **19 I know your works and your love and faith and
> service, and also your patience; and your last works
> are to be more abundant than the first.**

Works symbolize one's actions or activity directed to knowing the Self.

Love is a product of opening the Self up to learning and connectedness.

Faith comes from hearing or receiving the higher Truth and acting upon it. Service is one's efforts to aid others in their learning and soul growth. Service is the effort to teach and share the Universal Truth and High Knowledge one has received.

Such a one's most recent activity, effort and accomplishment are greater than anything this entrapped soul has achieved before. This lifetime you have disciplined your mind and have been willing to re-place limited thinking with higher truth. Such a one is teaching the disciplined mind to others. Such a one is using the disciplined mind to achieve a still mind.

Patience is endurance. Any individual desiring enlightenment needs endurance. Patience and endurance are related to will power, a series of repeated choices towards a goal or ideal. Your last works are more abundant and prosperous because a disciplined mind can more effi-ciently and productively know the Self and quicken soul progression. Soul progression is the process of building permanent understandings of Self and Creation.

> **20 Notwithstanding I have a few things against you because you allowed that woman of yours Jezebel, who calls herself a prophetess, to teach and to seduce my servants to commit fornication and to eat things sacri-ficed to idols.**

The word 'woman' in the **Bible** symbolizes the conscious mind. The word 'man' symbolizes the subconscious mind.

The woman 'Jezebel' symbolizes the conscious mind that is en-grossed in sensory experience. Jezebel also relates to ego gratification. To be engrossed in sensory experience is to forget who you are as a soul in Universal Subconscious Mind, as a spirit in Superconscious Mind and as an I AM existing in and beyond Mind and vibratory creation. To be engrossed in sensory experience is to think you are your physical body with its attendant brain and sense organs. To be engrossed is to live one's life for temporary, sensory experience. It is to forget the true purpose of life which is to build permanent and everlasting understand-ings of Self and Creation. This is accomplished by disciplining the mind so you direct the mind instead of the conscious mind, brain, and con-scious ego directing you.

A prophet is one who creates a goal that aligns with subconscious mind. A prophetess is one who sets a goal for the conscious mind. Jezebel calls herself a prophet, yet is not a true prophet, which indicates her goals will not produce soul growth. Jezebel produces only physical goals.

Fornication symbolizes one's creative energy being used only for short term, temporary, physical results rather than eternal, permanent, understanding of the true reality.

Idol worship indicates one's attention is misdirected towards making physical existence and the physical world your god. To eat things sacrificed to idols is to go through experiences, yet never assimilating and processing the essence of the learning in the experience in order to produce permanent understandings of Creation and Self.

21 And I gave her time to repent, but she did not repent from her fornication.

Time is the opportunity needed to have the experiences to learn and grow in consciousness.

To repent is to experience pain as the result of one's actions and thoughts and then to do penance. To do penance is to change one's thoughts in order to relieve the pain by learning the life lesson. Since Jezebel did not repent from her fornication, the indication is that the individual has stubbornly refused to discipline the mind, to still the mind, and to create a higher purpose for the life. The solution is to examine your life to discover any areas of your thoughts and life that are unproductive. Look for areas of your life including thoughts and emotions that are not producing lasting fulfillment. Eliminate these areas. Replace them with time better spent in fulfilling your mission in life.

22 Behold I will cast her into a sick bed and those who commit adultery with her in great tribulation, unless they repent of their deeds.

A sick bed is the place one lays the body when one is immobilized due to disease and pain. Dis-ease and pain are created when one has limiting thoughts and attitudes such as fear, hate, doubt, guilt, or jealousy.

Marriage symbolizes commitment to the soul, one's subconscious mind. To forget that commitment to the inner Self causes one to be more and more engrossed in sensory stimulation. This causes one to miss the purpose of life. The one who repents of such deeds re-estab-lishes the commitment to align conscious and subconscious minds. Such a one becomes more and more committed and determined to know the Self. Such a one disciplines the mind until the still mind is mastered. In the still mind one lives in the present, the eternal now. The eternal now is the true reality.

> **23 And I will smite her children with death; and all the churches shall know that I am he who searches the minds and hearts; and I will give to everyone of you according to your works.**

The children of Jezebel are any aspects of Self that allow themselves to be engrossed in sensory stimulation and refuse to discipline the mind.

The result of engrossment is that the environment forces you to change or else you exist in pain.

The result of a disciplined mind is you cause consistent change that is the expansion of consciousness.

All the churches are the seven chakras. I AM searches the whole mind to know the level of understanding and enlightenment of each individual. Each person creates his or her life situations, circumstances, experiences and awareness of reality based on understanding or lack of understanding of Self and Creation. You draw to you the experiences you need for soul growth and illumination.

> **24 But I say to you, the rest of you in Thyatira, those who do not have this doctrine, and those who have not known, as they say, the depths of Satan, that I will not put upon you another burden.**

Thyatira symbolizes the heart chakra. The quality of the heart chakra is understanding.

The word understanding or the plural, understandings, is used to indicate permanent soul memory and integration of the consciousness and use of all of Creation plus the knowledge of Self as I AM.

Satan symbolizes the conscious ego. The purpose of the conscious ego is to motivate the Self to gain the physical experiences needed for soul learning. Most people, being engrossed in physical experiences, miss the real essence of the learning, the learning of Self in the experi-ences.

If you permanently change and grow in awareness through your experiences, you are learning. If you go through experiences and remain essentially the same, you are not learning as a soul.

Those who have not allowed the conscious ego to motivate them deeper into physical, sensory engrossment will find their life's burden getting lighter. Satan, the conscious ego, has a subtle, cunning, beguiling way of making you believe that your self serving, unproductive thoughts are valuable and good for you. This is false. This is the depths of Satan.

25 But hold fast to that which you already have till I come.

Keep disciplining the mind. Continue to apply the disciplined, concentrated mind in the life. Gautama the Buddha said, as quoted in the Dhammapada 3:42-43, *"More than those who hate you, more than all your enemies, an undisciplined mind does greater harm. More than your mother, more than your father, more than all your family, a well disciplined mind does greater good."*

Only a disciplined mind can develop a still mind.
Only a still mind can then choose a thought.
Continue to practice the still mind that then chooses higher and more elevated thoughts until you become enlightened. To be enlightened is to be a Christ, a son of God.

The one who continually practices the still and disciplined mind will experience the second coming of the Christ. The second coming of Christ occurs when the Christ consciousness is fully received via the still mind into one's whole being and consciousness.

26 And he who overcomes and keeps my works until the end, to him I will give authority over the nations;

The end occurs when you overcome physical time by expanding your consciousness beyond the sensory physical existence and become enlightened. This requires a disciplined and still mind. What is it that one needs to overcome? One needs to overcome the limitations of the brain, the conscious ego and the conscious mind, which are the first beast, the second beast, and Satan. The first and second beast are referred to later in the book of Revelation. The works of the Son of Man and of I AM is the process of building permanent understandings of

Self and creation. To accomplish this, one must discipline the mind, create with others, and teach others how to discipline the mind and know the Self.

People symbolize aspects of Self. A nation is made up of people with something in common. Authority over the nations indicates one who knows all aspects of Self and thus knows Self as an I AM and as a Christ.

To have authority is to know and create. To have authority is to consciously author your life. It is to understand your creation and to author it.

27 And he shall shepherd them with a rod of iron; like the vessels of the potter, they shall be shattered, even as I was disciplined by my Father.

Jesus the knower is the good shepherd. His flock is anyone or any aspect of Self that is willing to give the effort to know Self and Creation.

A rod of iron symbolizes one's ability to wield and harmonize with the Universal Laws.

Vessels indicate receptivity. Vessels symbolize the one who is willing to receive the greater and higher truth into the Self.

At some point in the disciplined student's study of Mind and Self one's world view will be shattered. You will never be able to pick up the pieces and put it together because you have outgrown the vessel. Like a chicken breaking out of an eggshell, the time for a new life more abundant has arrived.

The statement "Even as I was disciplined by my Father" represents one who practices mental discipline and applies it in the life until one's conscious and subconscious minds attune to superconscious Mind. Father indicates the aggressive principle of creation operating in Superconscious Mind.

Jesus, who gained Christ Consciousness, said, *"I and my Father are One."* He also said that his Father was in Heaven. Heaven symbolizes Superconscious Mind. The one who practices and masters the still mind then has a consciousness that is capable of receiving Superconscious Mind into the waking, day to day life on Earth. This is called bringing Heaven down to Earth. This is the new Jerusalem which will be presented and explained in later chapters of this book and Revelation.

Then the Divine Plan of Creation held in Superconscious Mind will take over and aide one in the life to accomplish one's dharma, one's duty of enlightening the planet. Discipline is the foundation for enlightenment.

28 And I will give him the morning star.

The morning star is the dawning of new awareness of greater consciousness in the Self.

I received this morning star, this greater consciousness shortly after my heart broke. I have never been the same since. My mind is more disciplined and still than ever before.

Once you have the morning star you have insight into life that you never had before. Now I learn the lessons of life quicker, often the first time.

The morning star gives earlier and quicker awareness just as the morning star in the sky gives light before the sun, of Superconscious Mind.

29 He who has ears, let him hear what the Spirit says to the churches.

Learn to discipline your mind in order to listen with the whole mind. Receive the Higher Truth concerning the energy transformers of life energy, the chakras, in order to know the whole mind and the whole Self as I AM.

Summary of the Inner Meaning of Chapter 2 of the Book of Revelation
The keys to the successful utilization and harmonization with the root chakra, the spleen chakra, the solar plexus chakra and the heart chakra. This brings greater awareness, understanding, wisdom and enlightenment to the Self.

Chapter 3 of Revelation

Few Word Essence of Chapter 3
of the Book of Revelation

The higher chakras
The throat, brow, and the crown chakras

Brief and More Expanded Essence of Chapter 3
of the Book of Revelation

The Self realizes the three higher chakras exist within the Self,
and they need to be opened to all life.

Chapter 3

New Symbols & The Interpretation of Chapter 3 of Revelation

1. church in Sardis - throat chakra
2. spirits - breath, mind
3. name - recognition of identity
4. dead - unconscious
5. thief - aspect that steals valuable learning opportunities from Self
6. hour - time and the present moment
7. white - the disciplined, still mind
8. robes - outer presentation
9. ears - ability to still the mind and receive
10. church in Philadelphia - brow chakra
11. key of David - reasoning
12. open door - doorway to the inner mind
13. satan - conscious ego
14. worship - where the attention is directed
15. the world - conscious mind
16. crown - authority to be the conscious author of your life
17. man - the thinker-subconscious aspect
18. temple - the still mind
19. New Jerusalem - superconscious awareness
20. church in Laodicea - crown chakra
21. money - value
22. poor - without value
23. sight - perception
24. blind - without perception
25. clothes - one's outer expression
26. naked - without an enlightened expression
27. wanderer - one who does not know where he or she is going

Chapter 3

**1 And to the angel of the church in Sardis write:
These things says he who has the seven Spirits of
God and the seven stars: I know your works; you
have a name that you are alive, and yet you are
dead.**

The church in Sardis represents or symbolizes the throat chakra.

The quality of the throat chakra is will.

Will is a series of conscious choices acted upon toward an imaged goal or ideal. Will power is developed as one moves toward the goal or ideal until completion.

He who has the seven spirits of God and the seven stars is I AM, for I AM manifests through all seven levels of Mind. The seven spirits are the seven levels of Mind. The one who exercises the will to discipline the mind comes to know the whole Mind and the whole Self as I AM.

Chapter 2, verse 19 of Genesis states, "*And out of the ground the Lord God formed every beast of the field and every fowl of the air; and brought them to Adam to see what he would call them; and whatever Adam called every living creature, that was its name.*"

The first death was our movement away from Light into the levels of Mind. The second death is entrapment in a physical body.

To call or name something is to identify it. To have a name that you are alive is to have identified the areas of your life and your consciousness that is able to produce learning, growth, and forward motion.

However, verse 1 of Revelation 3 says, "*you have a name that you are alive yet you are dead.*" To be dead is to be unconscious. The meaning is that outwardly it looks like or appears that you know a lot, are doing a lot and have a lot of motion, but inwardly you are not growing rapidly in consciousness and are somewhat unconscious.

Most people only use a small portion of their mind. In order to wake up one must discipline the mind. From the discipline one can learn to still the mind. In the stillness of the mind one is awake and no longer dead. All this requires will and will is a function of the throat chakra. This is why verse two begins with the word awake.

**2 Awake, and hold fast to the things which
remain but are ready to die; for I have not found
your works perfect before my God.**

To become awake is to move through the initiations that produce a higher consciousness. When a person goes through a great initiation such a one never views life the same again. Such a one is more awake to life and is initiated into a greater state of awareness.

Each movement forward in consciousness produces greater understanding, wakefulness and Self awareness. Will is always required to achieve greater Self understanding and Self awareness.

Those things that remain but are ready to die are the permanent understandings you have built. Use these permanent understandings so that you can cause the conscious mind to change. To die is to experience transformation in consciousness through a new beginning. The individual subconscious mind or soul is the storehouse of all one's permanent understandings of Self and Creation. The subconscious mind or soul stores these understandings as permanent memory. When the soul or subconscious mind of the individual is filled full of understandings, one's work on the physical Earth is done. One no longer needs to re-incarn. All understandings are given to superconscious mind in fulfillment of the Divine and Perfect Plan of Creation held in superconscious mind. Then one exists as a fully enlightened superconscious, I AM, being.

Work symbolizes the effort you have given to knowing the Self. This includes mental discipline such as concentration, meditation, life force, breathwork exercises, visualization, imaging and stilling the mind.

Continue your mental discipline to develop the still mind. For one's works to be perfect before God one must have gained mastery of the Mind. The Mind is the vehicle to know Self. The Mind is the vehicle Self uses and must use to come to know the Self.

Therefore, perfect or master your ability to wield the mind. Strive to apply mental discipline of the mind more and more each day. Use your permanent understandings to build new complete understandings. Apply the will to choose to be in the present moment in each experience, each moment. For the present is the only time you can learn. The present is the only time you can be awake.

> **3 Remember, therefore, just as you have received and heard, so hold fast and repent. And if, therefore, you do not awake, I will come against you as a thief, and you shall not know at what hour I will come upon you.**

One who disciplines the mind gains the ability to receive and hear to a much greater degree. This is because of two reasons:
1. A disciplined mind leads to a still mind.
2. A still mind can receive and can be receptive.
Only the one with a still mind can choose a thought or choose to be receptive.

To hear one must receive the words of the one speaking. Hearing is a receptive act. Receiving is a receptive act. To choose to receive and to choose to be receptive is an act of will. The will is best exercised from the vantage point of a still mind.

To hold fast requires will power. To repent is to change unproductive ways of thinking and acting to productive thoughts and actions. This also requires repeated, conscious and awake choices of the will.

The one who awakens to a greater consciousness is aware of the thoughts and is aware of the environment. A thief will try to steal when one is unaware. To awaken requires a disciplined and still mind in order to know the true reality.

The word Buddha means awake. The one who is to use and master the will chakra, the throat chakra, must awaken in consciousness. Most people do not realize they are unconscious. Put another way, most people do not realize there is a much greater awareness, realization and consciousness that they could be using and applying in the life.

To awake is to use every minute to the fullest for soul growth and spiritual development while constantly being in the present moment. To refuse to awaken is to remain enmeshed mostly in the physical brain and some in the conscious mind.

An hour is a physical measurement of time. An hour, therefore, measures physical time. Physical time is somewhat of an illusion in the sense that the past is over, the future has not yet occurred. Therefore, the only Real Time is the Present, the Eternal Now. Now is the time to accomplish, achieve, and fulfill. Now is the time to become enlightened. Now is the time for the still mind that observes.

> **4 But you have a few members at Sardis who have not defiled their names; and they shall walk with me in white, for they are worthy.**

Members represent those aspects of the Self that relate to the will. Since this instruction concerns the throat chakra, the members are aspects of the individual that indicate one who exercises the will consciously.

Those members that are not defiled symbolize any individual who is using the will and will power to know the Self and is striving to improve the use of the will every day.

There is a reference to names as in verse one. The correct name or identification of the throat chakra is the will. Therefore, learn to make many conscious choices every day. Make choices that quicken one's awareness and understanding of Self. Choices to discipline the mind, choices to meditate, choices to concentrate, choices to still the mind, choices to go beyond one's limitations and choices to be aware of one's surroundings.

The color white symbolizes the stilling of the mind. For in stilling the mind, thoughts cease and mind forms cease to be created. Only those with a still mind are worthy to know the Self. Only the one with a still mind, with no thought, is capable of discovering who is behind the thoughts. The conscious use of the chakras is for the purpose of knowing the Self.

When light is split into the colors of a rainbow by a glass prism or by water droplets, the aspects, colors or parts of light, are seen. Without the filter of the prism or rain drops, light remains in its pure, unadulterated state. This natural state of white light is indicated by the use of white in the **Bible**. It symbolizes one who can maintain a still mind. In the still mind one identifies the Real Self.

The one with a still mind is worthy and able to walk and be with I AM, the ONE.

> **5 He who overcomes, the same shall be clothed in white robes; and I will not blot**

**his name out of the book of life, but I will
confess his name before my Father and
before his angels.**

What is to be overcome? The limitation of the entrapped physical existence that is the second death.

Since the time of entrapment, over 10,000 years ago, souls have
been moving out of Universal, Subconscious Mind to exist in a physical
body for a lifetime. Then at death they return to Universal, Subconscious Mind. This is the cycle of re-incarnation or rebirth. This is the
process that has been used by the people on planet Earth for many thousands of years.

When all the lessons of physical existence have been gained and
received into the whole Self as permanent memory, permanent understandings, then the Real Self, the soul, no longer needs to reincarn into
a physical body. Such a one shall be clothed in white robes, meaning
the mind has been disciplined. The will has been applied until one
knows the Self as a Christ, an enlightened being.

The Book of Life is the record in Superconscious Mind of one's
progress in fulfilling the Divine Plan of Creation. Such a one must have
learned how to attune to the Aggressive and Receptive Principles of
Creation held in Superconscious Mind.

A name indicates one's identity. Such a one as this has a
superconscious identity that is aligned and attuned to Superconscious
Mind. This indicates the achievement of the still mind and therefore a
rapidly expanding consciousness.

The word Father indicates superconscious mind. Jesus referred
to, "My Father in Heaven," indicating he had attuned his own consciousness to Superconscious Mind.

Angels are thought forms from superconscious mind. One
whose mind is stilled and disciplined can receive messages, insight,
awareness and realization from superconscious mind.

**6 He who has ears, let him hear what the
spirit says to the churches.**

Ears symbolize the ability to listen, to receive and to practice
receptivity. The spirit is the mind and breath. The one who can still the
mind in meditation or any other time has the capability to receive from
all of Mind. The one who masters breath raises the Kundalini and causes

the chakras to quicken and be filled with LIGHT. Such a one can receive the full knowledge and awareness of the chakras, their functions, and their use for enlightenment of the whole being.

Both consciously creating a thought and consciously receiving a thought begin in a still mind. A busy mind is not capable of this.

> **7 And to the angel of the church in Phila-**
> **delphia write: These things says he who is**
> **the holy one, he who is true, he who has**
> **the key of David, he who opens and no**
> **man shuts, and shuts, and no man opens;**

The church in Philadelphia symbolizes the brow chakra.

The brow chakra is also known as the third eye and the eye of perception.

The quality of the brow chakra is perception.

The individual who develops a disciplined and still mind can know the whole Self and whole Mind. Such a one is Holy for the disciplined one unites all five senses into the perceiving consciousness.

The one who masters the brow chakra aligns with Universal Truth and Universal Law and therefore is true.

David symbolizes reasoning. David was one of the great kings of the Old Testament. He became great by being a good reasoner. The key of David is the ability to use the brow chakra, the perceptive ability, to reason and to understand the Universal Truth, "As above, so below."

The reasoner opens the doorway to the mind. Only the one with a disciplined mind can know the Real and Whole Self. Only the still mind can master perception. The still mind is in the present. Only in the present, the eternal now, can the Real Self be known.

The one with the disciplined mind may choose the thoughts consciously with conscious will. Man indicates the thinker, yet until the mind is disciplined and perception developed, most so called free will or free choice is really just stimulus-response, action-reaction in the brain, not the mind of the individual.

When one develops the still mind, the choice is available to either choose to think a thought aggressively or to receive a thought receptively or to maintain a thought free state in the still mind. The still mind can experience the bliss of I AM.

**8 I know your works and behold, I have set
before you an open door which no man can
lock, for you have but little strength and yet
you have obeyed my word and have not
denied my name.**

The works referred to are efforts and activity to concentrate, discipline the mind and combine the senses to form the 6th sense called perception. The open door is the still mind combined with the brow chakra. The one who has developed a disciplined and still mind can open the doorways to the subconscious and superconscious minds by the action of the will and imaging. Such a one has access to the whole Mind.

The one who has a still mind can then make conscious choices concerning thought and action. The person without a disciplined and still mind allows the thoughts to control the Self. Memory thoughts arise seemingly of their own accord. Such random or will-less thoughts are of the brain, not of the Mind. They are habitual and compulsive, even if the person thinks they are chosen.

The little strength one has built refers to the will and will power. There has been progress and there is still much more to do. This is just the third chapter of Revelation. There are 19 more chapters of evolving and evolution yet to come.

To obey the word of the Holy One, the I AM, is to still the mind, receive and perceive the learning in the present moment and learn to be a creator.

To not deny the name of I AM is to perceive and admit you are I AM, an immortal being.

**9 Behold, I turn over those of the synagogue
of Satan, who say that they are Jews and are
not, but do lie; behold, I will make them to
come and worship before your feet, and to
know that I have loved you.**

Satan symbolizes the conscious ego. The conscious ego functions with the conscious mind and brain to provide motivation to achieve physical goals. The conscious ego is concerned with physical and sensory motivation.

The synagogue of Satan represents anyone who worships physical achievement and physical gratification to the exclusion of, and with higher priority than the discipline of the mind and the understanding of the whole Self.

The word worship comes from the Anglo Saxon words worth and ship. The word worship indicates worth and honor. What you worship is where you place your worth. Where you worship is what you honor. One worships where one's attention dwells.

Many of the early Christians were Jews who had converted to the new faith or held on to both faiths, new and old. The Jews believed in the coming of the messiah, the Christ. The second coming of Christ symbolizes the coming of the Christhood, the Christ consciousness in each individual. The second coming is the full enlightenment.

The first coming of Christ was in a man that lived over 2000 years ago in the middle East of Asia.

The second coming of Christ is in anyone, in the present moment, who stills the mind and receives the universal life lessons of LIGHT.

When enough LIGHT is received one becomes full of Light. This is known as enlightenment, Christ consciousness or Buddha consciousness.

Those aspects that worship or give their value and worth to temporary, physical goals, gratification and physical thinking will come to realize the error of their ways of thinking. The value of the disciplined mind of one committed to knowing the whole Self will be realized as one progresses. Feet symbolize one's spiritual or mental foundation. Your spiritual foundation is mental discipline.

The I AM gives Love, Light, and Truth to Self at all times. However, only the disciplined and still mind is prepared to receive the Divine Love.

Mental discipline produces a still mind which can cause the receptivity needed to receive the Higher Love.

> **10 Because you have kept the word of my
> patience, I also will keep you from the hour
> of temptation which shall come upon all the
> world to try those who dwell upon earth.**

The brow chakra, the eye of perception, is patient because a disciplined and still mind is required to perceive. The still mind receives the present experience fully and thus has patience. A patient person bears pain or trials without complaint. So does the one building enlightenment.

Temptation comes from the conscious ego, the 5 senses and the brain. The word temptation comes from the Latin temptare and the Sanskrit tan, meaning to stretch. Temptation is the act of the brain, senses and conscious ego attempting to stretch out, into the physical existence. Temptation is the action of getting caught up in physical experiences while forgetting who you really are and what your true purpose is in life.

Temptation has to do with experiences that only produce temporary results, stimulation, or effects. It is more important to be the master of your own soul and mind than king of the physical world. This is the answer Jesus gave to Satan and the Devil in the fourth chapter of the book of *Matthew* in the New Testament. In each case, Jesus was offered something temporary, such as food or physical power. And each time Jesus instead chose what was permanent and lasting. Matthew 4:1-4, *"1 Then Jesus was carried away by the Holy Spirit into the wilderness to be tempted by the devil.. 2 So he fasted forty days and forty nights: but at last he was hungry. 3 And the tempter drew near and said to him, 'If you are the Son of God, command these stones to become bread'. 4 But he answered, saying, 'It is written that it is not by bread alone that man can live, but by every word which proceeds from the mouth of God.'"*

The one who is driven by the inner Self will choose what is permanent and lasting. The one with the undisciplined conscious mind will become engrossed in temporary, sensory experience and memories of those experiences.

11 Behold, I come quickly. Hold that fast which you have, so that no man take your crown.

The crown symbolizes the crown chakra. The crown also symbolizes your authority to still the mind and know the whole Self, which is enlightenment. The one who has authority is the author. The author is the beginning, former, or first mover of anything. The author is the originator or creator of anything.

The crown of life is the ability to create or initiate a greater life within the Self.

The word man comes from the Sanskrit word "manu," which means thinker. Yet, the one who is enlightened and has the crown of authority or creatorship, has developed a still mind. Such a one exists in a state of no thought and occasionally, consciously chooses to think a thought.

To let a man take your crown is to allow random thoughts to arise, unwillingly and without choice. Those thoughts disturb and distract the disciplined and still mind.

The one who would master the Brow chakra must develop and gain the disciplined and still mind. To hold fast is to be able to direct your attention where you want it, for as long as you want it. This requires mental discipline. Once the disciplined and still mind is developed, the awareness of I AM, the One, comes much more rapidly and quickly, for such a one is overcoming physical, horizontal time.

> **12 He who overcomes I will make a pillar in the temple of my God, and he shall not go out again; and I will write upon him the name of my God and the name of the New Jerusalem which comes down out of heaven from my God; and I will write upon him my new name.**

What is to be overcome is the engrossment and entrapment in physical existence. To overcome entrapment in the physical body you must realize that you are not the physical body. Next, learn that the purpose of life is not just temporary experiences. Rather, the physical body and physical experiences are to be used to draw into the Self the permanent and lasting lessons of life.

We are here on the Earth plane or level of existence to learn to harmonize with the Universal Laws and Truths. In this process we align conscious and subconscious minds and attune them to superconscious mind.

To be a 'pillar in the temple of my God' is to attune the mind to Superconsciousness. The temple symbolizes superconscious mind. The pillar is the spinal column and chakra system. The spinal column becomes a pillar in the temple of my God when the Kundalini, creative energy is raised upward from the base of the spine, thereby enlightening all seven major chakras from the root chakra to the crown chakra. This opens the Middle Pillar to the Tree of Life.

Sometimes individuals will have brief and brilliant flashes of superconscious awareness and cosmic consciousness. No matter how wonderful these experiences are, they are not able to repeat them. Nor are they able to cause this high consciousness to be a permanent part of Self. The phrase 'he shall not go out again' is indicative of one who has entered Superconscious Mind and is able to maintain that High Consciousness of Superconscious Understanding permanently at all times. Achieving Superconsciousness permanently enables the spiritual being to never need to incarn again.

The name of my God shall be written on him permanently because such a one is rapidly becoming a creator and has learned the secrets of creation. God equals Creator. My God is the Creator. I, being made in the image and likeness of the plural God as given in Genesis 1:26, 27, am learning to be a creator. Until finally I or you may proclaim as did Jesus the Christ, *"I and the Father are One!"*

To name something is to identify it. The name for the New Jerusalem is Superconscious awareness and enlightenment while still in the physical body. It is the full enlightenment.

The New Jerusalem comes down out of Heaven. Heaven symbolizes and is Superconscious Mind. The new name or new identification for such a one is no longer Homo Sapiens, or human or reasoner. The new name for such a one is enlightened Christ or awakened Buddha.

Instead of the identity being only the conscious mind and brain personality, the identity of such a one is the Superconscious, awakened, enlightened being. *(See diagram 8)*

13 He who has ears, let him hear what the Spirit says to the churches.

Verse thirteen repeats what was said in Verse 6 of this chapter as well as Verses 17 and 29 of Chapter 2. When a thought or phrase is repeated over and over in the **Bible** it will indicate something of great importance.

Therefore, it is very important to understand what ears mean. Ears, in the **Bible**, symbolize the ability to listen. What does one need to listen to and hear? One needs to listen to what the subconscious and superconscious minds, symbolized by the Spirit, have to offer the conscious mind.

The Spirit mind is offering instruction concerning the brow chakra, the eye of perception. This is some of the highest and greatest knowledge one can receive.

ENLIGHTENMENT

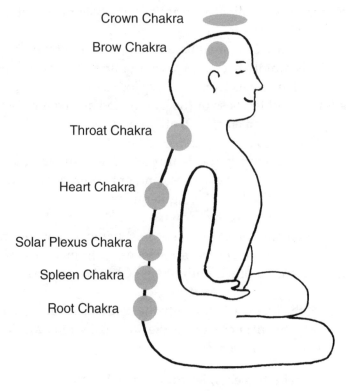

Crown Chakra

Brow Chakra

Throat Chakra

Heart Chakra

Solar Plexus Chakra

Spleen Chakra

Root Chakra

Diagram 8

All 7 chakras working in harmony under the conscious direction of I AM, the disciplined one with a still mind.

The Kundalini energy is released from its dormant state at the base of the spine and the Kundalini rises up the spine vivifying and lighting up each chakra in turn until the crown chakra is achieved. The one becomes full of Light. "I and the Father are One," as Jesus, who achieved Christhood, proclaimed.

The one with a disciplined conscious mind gains the ability to still the thoughts of the brain and conscious mind thus aligning the conscious mind with the subconscious mind or soul. Then the still mind is used to function with Universal Law and Universal Truth in order to attune conscious and subconscious minds to superconscious mind. This produces enlightenment, the Christ consciousness.

14 And to the angel of the church in Laodicea write: These things says the Amen, the faithful and true witness, the beginning of the creation of God;

The church in Laodicea symbolizes the crown chakra.

Amen comes from the Hebrew word meaning verily, certainly or let it be. Verily means true or truth. This is why the Amen is described as the faithful and true witness. 'Let it be' is to be in the present moment fully. A witness is one who is present and observes what is occurring in the present moment. The Amen is the witness of the beginning of creation. The Amen is the act of being in the present moment, which requires a still mind.

The crown chakra's quality is enlightenment. The crown chakra returns used mental energy from the conscious mind to the first level, the highest level of Superconscious Mind. The first level of Mind is the beginning of all creation. The one who is gaining rapid enlightenment quickens the conscious awareness and use of the crown chakra.

In order to understand, draw upon, and harmonize the crown chakra, one must be the witness, which is to have the still mind in the eternal present, the now. Only the still mind can witness and observe.

In the average human being the crown chakra turns down. In the enlightened being the crown chakra turns up and outward like a fountain of golden LIGHT energy that spreads out to all the world.

All enlightened beings have the disciplined mind, which leads to the still and present mind, which enables them to be the silent witness. They are silent witnesses to the present. Yet, when there is a need to act and create, they respond.

AMEN can also be interpreted as Let It Be. Let It Be is an accurate statement of the crown chakra. The crown chakra's energies function in a state of being. One who is attuned to the crown chakra is in a state of be-ing in the ever present, eternal now. I AM is in the eternal now.

15 I know your works: that you are neither cold nor hot: it is better to be either cold or hot.

Your works are the efforts and activity you have given to build permanent understandings of Self and Creation.

Hot and cold symbolize the Aggressive and Receptive Principles of Creation. The receptive and aggressive principles are referred to as Yin and Yang in Chinese Holy books and literature. Cold is receptive. Hot is aggressive. It is better to be either aggressive or receptive than neither. Why? Because these are the two qualities that produce soul growth and spiritual development. When one is passive or forceful there is no soul growth. Both are lukewarm as Revelation says.

To be aggressive is to initiate action on one's creation. To be aggressive is to move toward the learning.

To be receptive is to still the mind and receive the present moment, the present situation and circumstance. Then one is able to draw to the Self the learning needed.

> **16 So then because you are lukewarm, and
> neither cold nor hot, I will spew you out of
> my mouth.**

Being lukewarm symbolizes the refusal to either still one's mind and receive or to make a choice, a decision to learn that is acted upon.

A decision is not a decision until action is initiated on that imaged decision. Then one is aggressive.

To still the mind and be present is also a choice, a decision.

An undisciplined mind is a busy brain. An undisciplined mind is never still and therefore, is unable to create a condition of receptivity. Without a state of receptivity one is unable to receive the universal learning available in each experience. The undisciplined mind is also ineffectual in being able to develop sustained effort toward the ideal of enlightenment. The undisciplined one too often becomes distracted.

Food is received through the mouth of a person. Food symbolizes knowledge. To be spewed out of the mouth of the crown chakra is to miss the opportunity to receive and assimilate enlightenment into the whole Self, one's whole being.

> **17 You say, I am rich and my wealth has
> increased and I need nothing; and you do
> not know that you are miserable and a wan-
> derer and poor and blind and naked.**

This verse is a statement of one's lack of awareness of one's state of unconsciousness. Physical riches and wealth are temporary.

The crown chakra and Superconscious Mind give and receive the eternal, lasting, permanent benefits.

There are 22 chapters in the book of Revelation. Each chapter is a part of life's journey. This journey is quickened by the one who takes up the study of Mind, Self, and mental discipline. To begin this quickening one must realize a need to know the truth about Self and life. When you find your life wanting and are willing to do something about it, then does the journey to enlightenment begin. As each chapter progresses we will uncover the obstacles to learning the universal life lessons and the way to go beyond these obstacles to achieve enlightenment. Once you have earnestly begun this journey of enlightenment and Christhood the areas of understanding that have yet to be built in the Self become apparent. This is the meaning of being poor and naked.

Those who achieve chapter 3 of Revelation within the Self are just beginning to know where they are going and how to get there. They are beginning to learn and know the keys and steps to enlightenment.

18 I advise you to buy of me gold refined in the fire, that you may become rich; and white raiment, that you may be clothed, so that the shame of your nakedness may not be seen; and anoint your eyes with salve, that you may see.

Gold symbolizes value. Fire symbolizes expansion. Gold refined by fire indicates permanent and lasting value that produces a permanent expansion of consciousness. To become rich as a soul and spiritual being is to learn how to build permanent understandings of Self at an ever increasing rate.

Raiment comes from the word arrayment, or array. Clothing symbolizes one's outer expression. To be arrayed in white clothing symbolizes the ability to express and share one's full understandings of Self and Creation outwardly with others.

Naked means one is not aware of and not sharing one's permanent understandings with Self and others. As one disciplines the mind through concentration and meditation exercises, the conscious mind becomes receptive to the subconscious mind. Then, as one teaches many students, the soul understandings and wisdom come pouring forth from one's subconscious mind and is given to the students. Then the shame of one's nakedness is no longer seen.

Eyes symbolize perception. To anoint your eyes with salve means to improve one's mental perception in order to develop the reasoning and intuitive faculties. In this manner one comes to learn to be able to draw into the Self the learning in every experience, thus, adding to one's enlightenment.

**19 I rebuke and chastise all those whom I
love; be zealous, therefore, and repent,**

To rebuke is to reprove or to reprimand. The work with and conscious use of the crown chakra entails a willingness on the student's part to identify all of one's limitations in consciousness. It involves placing one's soul growth and spiritual development above all else. The love of understanding becomes so great that one will give whatever effort is needed to know the Self, to know Truth and to gain enlightenment. The conscious mind must become humble or lower to receive the Superconscious Mind which is the higher.

To be zealous is to be passionate in the pursuit of enlightenment. The command is to be passionate and eager in the commitment to change. Change is to be used to replace limited thinking and consciousness with more expansive and truth filled thoughts, attitudes and consciousness.

The more enlightened one is, the more easily one embraces change that adds to one's permanent learning and soul growth. This aligns with Universal Law and Truth.

**20 Behold, I stand at the door and knock; if
any man hear my voice and open the door, I
will come in to him and will sup with him,
and he with me.**

The beginning of each person's creation was or is as I AM. I AM is the 'I' that stands at the door and knocks. The door is the opening to the inner levels of Consciousness. The door is the opening to Subconscious and Superconscious Minds and beyond.

Man symbolizes the thinker. Any thinker that stills the mind will be able to hear the voice of I AM. Hearing the voice of I AM is heeding one's inner purpose and opening the doorway to the inner levels of Mind.

When this occurs, I AM, one's true identity, will move through Superconscious Mind, Subconscious Mind and into the conscious mind and brain. The higher knowledge and wisdom will be received by such a one. This is indicated by the statement, "I will come to him and sup with him." To sup with someone is to eat food together. Food symbolizes knowledge.

The still mind must be developed for the conscious mind to be able to receive the higher consciousness. The still mind is necessary for the ultimate receptivity. The inner Self, the High Self is always attempting to get the attention of the conscious mind. The High Self, the Real Self always continues to give to the lower mind that is willing to receive.

> **21 To him who overcomes I will grant to sit**
> **with me on my throne, even as I also over-**
> **came and have sat down with my Father on**
> **his throne.**

The one who overcomes has learned the lessons of creation that the physical world holds. The individual has overcome the entrapment in the physical body and the engrossment in the five senses. Such a one has gained conscious use and awareness of the inner levels of Mind and gained enlightenment.

The throne is one's ability to direct one's mind with undivided attention using all levels of Consciousness. The Father in Heaven is Superconscious Mind. Father is the aggressive principle and mother is the receptive principle of Superconscious Mind.

Jesus who became the Christ said, *"I and my Father are one."* To be one with the Father in Heaven is to sit down with the Father at his throne. The one who overcomes physical entrapment will gain the Christ consciousness, the enlightenment of the whole Self.

> **22 He who has ears, let him hear what the**
> **Spirit says to the churches.**

Ears symbolize listening. In order to listen one has to receive. In order to receive one must have a still mind. One with a still, conscious mind is able to receive from the subconscious and superconscious minds. Spirit is the breath used to know the Mind and Self.

Listen to what is being said about the crown chakra.

I have gained the ability to still my mind. Therefore, I listen. Therefore, I can also choose to think a conscious thought. Therefore, I am either hot or cold.

To be cold is the still mind that receives.

To be hot is to consciously choose to move the Mind or to give.

Being receptive is a choice.

Being aggressive is a choice.

Both choices come from a still mind.

Summary of the Inner Meaning of Chapter 3 of the Book of Revelation
The keys to the successful attunement and receptivity to the throat chakra, the brow chakra and the crown chakra.

Chapter 4 of Revelation

Few Word Essence of Chapter 4 of the Book of Revelation

The still mind

Brief and More Expanded Essence Chapter 4 of the Book of Revelation

The disciplined one has achieved the still mind and is thus able to begin to receive Superconscious awareness.

Chapter 4

New Symbols & The Interpretation of Chapter 4 of Revelation

1. voice from heaven - being receptive to Superconscious Mind

2. throne in heaven - directing the attention into Superconscious Mind

3. one - I AM

4. rainbow - LIGHT experienced as separateness through seven levels of Mind

5. stone or rock - will

6. elders - major aspects of Self

7. white robes - the still mind taught to others

8. lightening - flashes of higher awareness

9. seven lamps of fire - the 7 chakras

10. sea of glass - still consciousness with no thought

11. animal - compulsion

12. six - service

13. wings - the ability to produce motion in the life

14. Holy - whole and complete

15. Lord God - I AM

16. day - awareness, the aggressive quality

17. night - stillness, the receptive quality

18. eyes - perception

19. thunder - vibration of movement through the levels of Mind

20. twenty four - stability in the use of the aggressive and receptive principles through service

Chapter 4

**1 After these things I looked and behold, a door
was open in heaven; and the first voice which I
heard was like a trumpet talking with me, which
said, Come up here and I will show you things
which must come to pass.**

One who has gained some conscious use of all seven chakras has
opened a doorway to Superconscious Mind. This doorway begins to
give one access to insights and awareness of what one needs to accomplish in order to gain enlightenment. Chapter four is a vision of what is
to come in the future. You be the judge as to whether it has already
come to pass within you or not.

Hearing a voice indicates one has gained the ability to listen to the
inner Self, the Real Self in Superconscious Mind. The sound is like a
trumpet. This indicates one is becoming receptive to the vibration of
thought coming from the inner levels of Mind.

The instruction to 'come up here,' means one is to raise the consciousness to the Superconscious Mind. Most people are still enmeshed
in the brain. A few have learned to use the conscious mind. Fewer still
the subconscious mind. A very few receive superconsciousness into
their conscious awareness.

What are the things which must come to pass? All the steps to enlightenment must come to pass.

**2 And immediately I was in the spirit; and be-
hold, a throne was set in heaven, and one sat on
the throne.**

In the spirit is in the Mind. The Mind has seven levels, planes, or
dimensions. The Mind has three divisions. A throne set in heaven is
the division of Mind referred to as Superconscious Mind. The throne
indicates one is able to still the individual mind and direct the thoughts

or receive thought images from superconscious mind.

The one that sat on the throne is I AM. I AM is singular. I AM is one. I AM is above and beyond Mind, and therefore beyond the illusion of separation, and therefore beyond physical time and space.

The still mind is able to attune to the superconscious mind. The attention and awareness is capable of receiving superconscious awareness. This verse offers a picture of a person who receives a glimpse of the Self as I AM in Superconscious Mind.

3 And he who sat resembled a stone of jasper and sardonyx, and round about the throne was a rainbow resembling emeralds.

A stone symbolizes the will. Jesus said to Peter, *"You are rock and on this rock I will build my church."* The name Peter or the Latin Petros means rock. Rock or stone symbolizes will. Will is the foundation of all soul growth and spiritual development. Will is the ability to make conscious choices that move one to the ideal of enlightenment. Jasper and sardonyx are stones of value indicating the value of the use of the will and will power.

The rainbow represents one's ability to separate and identify one's learning in every experience. A rainbow is a separation of LIGHT into different wavelengths. The seven colors represent one's ability to learn to use and gain awareness of all seven levels of Mind and all seven chakras. The predominate color of each chakra before enlightenment is:

red	root chakra
orange	spleen chakra
yellow	solar plexus chakra
green	heart chakra
blue	throat chakra
purple	brow chakra
violet or indigo	crown chakra

After enlightenment the chakras reverse themselves offering a cascading radiance of white light.

Superconscious perception reveals the permanent understandings needed to be enlightened. Emeralds indicate the tremendous value of this perception and awareness.

**4 Round about the throne were four and twenty
seats; and upon the seats I saw four and twenty
elders sitting, clothed in white robes; and they had
on their heads crowns of gold.**

The 24 elders are the 24 major aspects of Self. They are represented
in the **Bible** as the 12 tribes of Israel and the 12 disciples of Jesus. The
12 tribes symbolize the 12 outer, subconscious aspects of Self. The 12
disciples symbolize the 12 inner, conscious aspects.

The 24 are aspects or qualities or parts of the ONE, which is I AM.
There are 12 major, inner aspects and 12 major, outer aspects.

White robes symbolize one whose outer expression is in alignment
with knowing all of Mind and the whole Self. The image offered here is
of one who has developed the still mind and is offering this to the world.

Crowns of gold symbolize one who understands the value of directing all aspects of Self and has the authority to do so. One who has
authority is one who authors the life. This occurs from a still mind that
can then choose thought images or can receive.

**5 And out of the throne proceeded lightnings and
thunderings and noises; and there were seven
lamps of fire burning before the throne, which are
the seven Spirits of God.**

Light is awareness. Lightning symbolizes flashes of awareness.
Thunderings indicate a powerful movement of vibration. These flashes
of awareness and movement of vibration occur because one has begun
to receive superconscious awareness into the Self.

The seven lamps of fire are the seven chakras that work in conjunction with the seven levels of Mind. The seven spirits of God is the
breathwork needed to master the chakras.

Fire symbolizes expansion. One who accesses, enlivens and uses
the chakras consciously raises the awareness of the Self.

The throne symbolizes directing one's attention to Superconscious
Mind. One must achieve a disciplined and still mind for the attention
to be mastered. This process must be well underway before
superconscious mind can be received into one's conscious awareness.

**6 And before the throne was a sea of glass resem-
bling crystal; and in the midst of the throne, and**

round about it and in front of it were four animals,
full of eyes before and behind.

The sea of glass is the still mind. Waves on water indicate a busy mind that is full of thoughts. A sheet of glass is smooth. A sea of glass is smooth. A disciplined mind that produces a still mind has a consciousness that is smooth. A busy mind is chaotic and turbulent like large waves on water. In order to enter into superconsciousness one must achieve a still mind. The still mind is required to achieve communion with I AM, LIGHT, and Creator.

Water symbolizes conscious life experience. Conscious life experience is your day to day waking experience and your thoughts throughout those waking experiences.

The throne symbolizes one's attention being in superconscious. Crystal is usually clear as is glass. The reason windows are made of glass is so we can see or perceive through them and to receive light into a room. Sight symbolizes perception. Therefore, the mental image being portrayed symbolically is the still mind that is beginning to perceive and receive superconscious awareness. There is much more to gain, perceive and understand before the full superconsciousness or Christ consciousness is perceived. The rest of these steps are presented and explained in chapters five through 22 of the Book of Revelation.

The four animals symbolize the four levels of Subconscious Mind. Eyes symbolize perception. The four animals being full of eyes before and behind indicates omniperception and the ability to master memory and imagination. Prometheus in Greek mythology symbolizes imagination. Epimetheus, his brother, symbolizes the use of memory. To use the mind correctly we must master not only the use of memory but also attention and imagination.

7 And the first animal was like a lion and the second
animal was like a calf and the third animal had a face of
a man and the fourth animal was like a flying eagle.

Each of the four animals symbolize a level of Subconscious Mind. The calf symbolizes the 6th level of Mind. The animal with the face of a man symbolizes the fifth level of Mind. The fifth level of Mind is the place or level of Mind when manifesting thoughts begin to take on physical form. Face in a dream symbolizes identity. Man symbolizes the thinker. The fifth level of Mind is the location that developing thought forms can begin to be identified by the perceiver.

The lion symbolizes the fourth level of Mind.

The animal that was like a flying eagle symbolizes the third level of Subconscious Mind. The third level is the deepest or highest level of the division of Mind known as Subconscious Mind. As one develops a disciplined mind, the capacity is developed to receive and use each of the qualities of energies of these levels of Mind.

Animals symbolize habits and compulsions. The four levels of Subconscious Mind perform their functions through the structure provided by Universal Law. They function whether you believe in them or not. To learn to harmonize and align with the Universal Laws and levels of Mind is a science not an act of faith.

**8 And the four animals had each of them six wings;
and they were full of eyes within; and they had no
rest day and night saying, Holy, holy, holy, the Lord
God Almighty who was and is and is to come.**

Each of the animals had six wings each. Six is the number of service. The meaning is that all who would come to know and master the Subconscious Mind must live a life of service. And the highest service is teaching. And the highest teaching is of the Mind and Self. I have been teaching the Mind and Self for over a quarter of a century and have come to know the truth of this.

Eyes symbolize perception. To be full of eyes within is to develop one's inner perception with the disciplined and still mind. Teaching others how to know the mind brings one out of the physical brain to the mental mind. Teaching Self awareness enables one to receive Self awareness on a higher and higher level. The one who has developed and earned the disciplined and still mind is able to perceive and have the higher perception continually, day and night. Holy means whole and complete. Lord God Almighty is I AM. I AM was created as an individualized unit of LIGHT.

I AM exists now. Those who are not yet enlightened will come to know I AM.

**9 And when those animals give glory and honor
and thanks to him who sits on the throne, who
lives for ever and ever,**

The four levels of the Subconscious Mind are subservient to and aid in the fulfillment of the Divine Plan of Creation held in Superconscious Mind.

The Subconscious Mind owes its existence to Superconscious Mind. Therefore, anyone who fulfills the Divine Plan and attains to Superconsciousness will find their subconscious mind is their faithful servant. One's subconscious mind or soul will work diligently to aid the productive conscious mind to learn and grow by fulfilling the true and deep desires or needs of the Self to know.

> **10 The four and twenty elders fall down before**
> **him who sits on the throne, and worship him who**
> **lives for ever and ever, and cast their crowns**
> **before the throne, saying,**

All the major aspects of the Self, as symbolized by the 24 elders, can be brought into alignment with I AM as symbolized by the one who lives forever and ever. Crown symbolizes authority.

They cast their crown before the throne of the I AM and Superconscious Mind because the lower authority recognizes and aligns with the higher authority. When this occurs in one's life no longer are the conscious and subconscious minds the author of one's life. Now superconsciousness is the author of one's life.

The authority is the one who authors.

The author is the one who consciously creates.

When one creates from superconscious mind, one rapidly fulfills the plan for enlightenment and Christhood.

> **11 Thou art worthy, O our Holy Lord and God, to**
> **receive glory and honor and power, for thou hast**
> **created all things, and by thee they are, and by thy**
> **will they are and were created.**

I AM is the Real Self. You are I AM whether you recognize it or not. Very few people in the history of the planet have known Self as I AM. Now more and more are waking up to this awareness of the Real Self. Mind is the vehicle I AM uses to create. Mind is the vehicle I AM uses to learn to be a creator. For we were made in the image and likeness of the Creator with similar and like attributes and qualities.

Each individual is constantly creating the life based upon one's thoughts and consciousness whether they are aware of this or not. Therefore, upgrade and improve your thoughts by use of the disciplined mind. Then the false reality one perceives through the filtering brain will be transformed into the perception and understanding of the connectedness of all reality. This is brought about through the still mind.

Summary of the Inner Meaning of Chapter 4 of the Book of Revelation
The awareness of all seven levels of Mind. The awareness of the Conscious Mind, the Subconscious Mind and the Superconscious Mind.

Chapter 5 of Revelation

Few Word Essence of Chapter 5 of the Book of Revelation

The full commitment

Brief and More Expanded Essence of Chapter 5 of the Book of Revelation

The Self realizes there are seven levels of Mind and is determined to achieve all seven.

Chapter 5

New Symbols & The Interpretation of Chapter 5 of Revelation

1. right - correct, productive
2. hand - purpose
3. book - storehouse of knowledge or information
4. seven seals - keys to the seven levels of Mind
5. wept - movement of energy through the emotional level of Mind
6. Judah - productive use of ego through the developing reasoning
7. David - reasoning
8. the Lamb - one committed to attaining Christhood
9. harp - harmony in mind
10. cup - receptivity
11. incense - expansion in Mind that carries thoughts to superconscious mind
12. songs - harmony in Mind
13. blood - truth and life force
14. people - aspects of Self
15. nation - many aspects of Self with a common ideal
16. priests - aspects committed to gaining Christ consciousness
17. kings - authority within Self to direct aspects
18. 10,000 X 10,000 = 100 million = complete understanding
19. four - stability
20. sea - conscious life experience
22. zero - the power that derives from understanding
23. one - the aggressive quality, the ability to initiate action on a decision
24. two - the receptive quality

Chapter 5

1 And I saw on the right hand of him who sat on the throne a book, written within and on the back and sealed with seven seals.

The one who sits on the throne is I AM. I AM is above and beyond Mind. The throne is the point or place from which one's mind is directed. The attention moves outward from I AM through all seven levels of Mind and reaches the physical or seventh level of Mind. In the seventh level of Mind; in the physical body of people, I AM is reflected as the conscious ego.

Right indicates righteous or correct. Hand symbolizes purpose. The right hand denotes one who has a correct, productive and right purpose. A correct purpose while in a physical body is one that brings about the fulfillment of the Perfect Plan of Creation held in superconscious mind. The book symbolizes the degree that each individual has fulfilled that Plan of Creation held in Superconscious Mind.

The book in the right hand of him who sat on the throne is sealed with seven seals symbolizing the seven levels of Mind. The one who would know the Self must come to know all of Mind, for Mind is the vehicle to know the Self. The book is written within and on the back indicating who and what you are to become. It is up to you and your effort to reveal the Christhood, the full understanding of Self that is your eternal birthright.

2 Then I saw a mighty angel proclaiming with a loud voice, Who is worthy to open the book and to loose the seals thereof?

A mighty angel is a thought form from I AM and Superconscious Mind. The loud voice indicates one's ability to listen and hear the inner Self, the inner voice that is guiding one to make the full commitment to know the Self. Few people have a disciplined mind. Therefore, they lack a still mind, which is necessary to hear the voice of the inner or High Self. The one who is worthy to open the book and loose the seals thereof is one who has disciplined the mind through concentration and meditation and has developed a full commitment to know Self, all of Mind, and Creation. This is when the disciplined student of the Mind becomes worthy to open the seals to the seven levels of Mind. Such a one is giving service of the highest kind, for such a one is a teacher and is, therefore, worthy to receive. For as you give so shall you receive. As you sow so shall you reap. Therefore, the one who truly and earnestly desires to know all of Mind and Self will first be disciplined, which is to be a disciple. Then, one will become a teacher which is to be an apostle.

From this continued effort to grow in consciousness and become a world server, one attains the Christhood, the Christ consciousness.

3 And no man in heaven above, nor on earth, neither under the earth was able to open the book, neither to look on it.

Man represents the thinker. The word man comes from the Sanskrit word 'manu' which means thinker. No 'man' was able to open the book because thinking will not give you Superconscious awareness. Thinking will not move one's attention and consciousness into Superconscious Mind.

Thinking keeps one engrossed in the conscious mind and brain. Thinking produces self created mental pictures and images.

To know Superconscious Mind one must still the thoughts and still the mind. Then and only then is the Self capable of receiving Superconscious Mind.

Heaven symbolizes Superconscious Mind. 'On Earth' symbolizes Subconscious Mind. 'Under the Earth' symbolizes Conscious Mind. To look on something is to receive the reflected light image into the Self. A thinking mind is aggressive. A still mind can choose to be receptive.

4 And I wept exceedingly because no man was found worthy to open the book, neither to look on it.

No man-thinker is worthy to open the book of the Mind because thinking does not reveal the Subconscious and Superconscious Minds.

Only an individual, still mind that then chooses to be receptive can reveal the secrets of the whole and Universal Mind, the dimensions of consciousness.

To look on something is to receive the reflected light image. To receive the reflected light image is a receptive act.

A person weeps or cries when the emotions have been pent up and blocked. The emotional or sixth level of mind is the level closest to the physical, the seventh level of Mind. Thought forms move through the emotional level of Mind before they manifest as a part of one's outward, physical life. To weep exceedingly comes from a long held need or desire to know the Self and the purpose of life that is not being fulfilled.

> **5 And one of the elders said to me, Weep not; behold the Lion of the tribe of Judah, the Scion of David, has prevailed and he will open the book and the seven seals thereof.**

The elders symbolize the major aspects of Self. The Lion of the tribe of Judah, the Scion of David, is the one who has developed a disciplined and still mind and thus has control of both the conscious ego and reasoning.

Judah and its Greek derivative form Judas indicate the productive use of the ego to motivate one to know Self.

David symbolizes the ability to develop one's reasoning ability. David in the **Bible** was/is of the tribe of Judah. Reasoning proceeds from a still mind that has its foundation and is grounded in the present moment. The one who prevails to open the book of the whole Mind and whole Self must have developed a still mind. A still mind is the key to both reasoning and mastering the conscious ego. David was a mighty king of Israel in the Old Testament of the **Bible**. He became a mighty king because he was disciplined, committed to serving I AM and could therefore reason well.

> **6 And I beheld, and lo, in the midst of the elders, stood a Lamb as it had been slain, having seven horns and seven eyes, which are the seven Spirits of God sent forth into all the earth.**

The 24 elders are the major aspects of the conscious and subconscious minds. The Lamb in their midst is the one committed to following and fulfilling the Divine Plan of Creation held in Superconscious Mind.

Jesus who became the Christ is the good shepherd. Anyone who follows, practices and teaches the mental discipline Jesus taught, with commitment, is a Lamb of God. Jesus the Christ said, *"I AM the good shepherd; a good shepherd risks his life for the sake of his sheep."* John 10:11. *"I AM the good shepherd, and I know my own, and my own know me. Just as my Father knows me, I also know my Father; and I lay down my life for the sake of the sheep."* John 10:14-15.

The Lamb is of the flock of Jesus. Jesus symbolizes the knower who is committed to gaining Superconscious Mind and Christ consciousness. The Lamb is following the commitment of the knower, Jesus.

To die is to change. To be slain is to change without control. To gain control one must develop a strong will and imaging capability. Then the still mind and will power can be applied to mastering the seven chakras symbolized by the seven horns. The seven eyes are the ability to perceive in all seven levels of Mind.

The seven spirits are the controlled use of prana-life force through the breath which gives the mentally disciplined one control of the seven horns-chakras.

**7 And he came and took the book from the right
hand of him who sat upon the throne.**

The Lamb came and took the book, indicating that the one who is committed to quickening soul growth and spiritual development aligns the consciousness with I AM. The One who sat on the throne is I AM. To accomplish this alignment one must discipline the mind and be committed to knowing and being I AM. Such a one must have the attention in the present moment, for I AM exists in the ever present, eternal now. The book, symbolizing the Divine Plan of Creation, is known by one who has right purpose motivating the Self to have the attention in the present moment.

I AM is not I was or I will be. I AM is of the now, the present. Only a still mind can know the ever present now. The undisciplined mind goes to the imagined future or memories of the past.

"I was" is of the past.

"I will be" is of the future.
Only "I AM" is of the ever present, eternal now.

> **8 And as he took the book, the four animals and the**
> **four and twenty elders fell down before the Lamb,**
> **and everyone of them had a harp and a cup of gold**
> **full of incense, and these were the prayers of the**
> **saints.**

All 24 major aspects of Self recognize the importance and elevation of the one who is disciplined and committed to becoming and being a Christ, an enlightened being. This is because the dedication and discipline to become a master of Self and Mind brings about an alignment of all aspects of Self and of the conscious and subconscious minds.

Music indicates harmony. Harps are musical harmony and symbolize the harmony produced in the Self when one dedicates the life to becoming enlightened.

Gold symbolizes value, Self value and the value of one's efforts to know the Self. A cup indicates receptivity and a receptive state of mind. Incense symbolizes using one's attention to the fullest to know superconscious mind. A cup of gold filled with incense connotes one who values the still mind and can therefore choose receptivity while maintaining an attunement to superconscious mind.

Prayers are the thought images of gratitude and request one gives to the Creator.

Harmony in mind is the alignment of conscious and subconscious minds. Attunement to superconscious mind, symbolized by incense that rises to heaven, is, in effect, the greatest prayer.

The saints are those aspects fully in alignment with being a whole, functioning Self. Saints are those aspects that are a part of Self as permanent memory or permanent understanding.

> **9 And they sang new praise saying, Thou art worthy to**
> **take the book and to open the seals thereof; for thou**
> **wast slain and hast redeemed us to God by thy blood out**
> **of every tribe and tongue and people and nation;**

The change that has occurred within the Self is in alignment with the Divine and Perfect Plan in Superconscious Mind. This is why there is singing. Singing indicates harmony within all levels of Mind. Worthy or worth comes from the continual willingness to receive into the Self new awareness and greater understanding which is then given to others.

Blood symbolizes truth. It is by aligning one's consciousness with Universal Truth that one comes to use change productively. Then the consciousness is transformed into a creator. Such a creator creates greater enlightenment in the present moment, continually. The tribes and people are all the myriad aspects of the Self. It is by stilling the mind to receive truth that one becomes worthy and able to open the seven seals to the inner levels of Mind.

10 And hast made them for our God kings and priests; and they shall reign on the earth.

People symbolize aspects of Self. Aspects of Self are thoughts, attitudes, and ways of being.

A king symbolizes those parts of your own consciousness that direct aspects of Self. A priest symbolizes an aspect of Self that is totally committed to knowing Self as a creator. The message is that such a one as this has aligned conscious and subconscious minds through service. Such a one is fully committed to understanding Self and Creation and is a director of many aspects of the Self.

To reign on earth is to align conscious and subconscious mind and thereby direct the fulfillment of one's soul purpose in this lifetime.

11 And I looked, and I heard as it were the voice of many angels round about the throne and the animals and the elders; and their number was ten thousand times ten thousand, and thousands of thousands,

To look is to receive the reflected light image and thereby perceive. To look effectively one must direct the sight with the will. Then one must hold the attention where it has been directed. The voice of many angels around the throne indicates one whose thoughts are directed to enlightenment. When still, the mind of such a one receives superconscious awareness.

Numbers have meaning.

Ten thousand indicates one who is using the aggressive principle with much power and understanding.

Zero indicates power from understanding as in the number 10. The number 100 indicates 10 times more power and understanding than 10. The number 1000 indicates 10 times more power and understanding than 100.

Ten thousand times 10,000 indicates a complete or full understanding of an area of one's life. In this case the area is commitment and mental discipline as indicated by the Lamb, the four animals, and the 24 elders.

**12 Saying with a loud voice, Worthy is the Lamb that
was slain to receive power and riches and wisdom
and might and honor and glory and blessing.**

One is worthy because one has received worth. To be receptive and receive one has to develop a still mind. A loud voice indicates one receives the truth from the inner levels of Mind.

Power comes from understanding. Riches are permanent understanding of Self and Creation. Wisdom is the ability to teach others who then teach others what one has learned concerning Universal Truths and Universal Laws. To have might is to be able to achieve and receive. Honor is esteem paid to worth. Glory is fame and praise.

The Lamb, the one committed to know the whole Self, is capable and able to receive all that is permanent, lasting and real that the Mind and Creation have to offer. The following chapters describe the changes and challenges as one progresses with that capability. Such a one encounters obstacles to Self knowledge yet is able to overcome.

**13 And every creature which is in heaven and on the
earth and under the earth and all that are in the sea
and all that are in them, I heard saying , To him who
sits on the throne and to the Lamb be blessing and
honor and glory and dominion for ever and ever.**

Every level of Mind and every aspect of Self has its fulfillment in the one who is committed to knowing the whole Self with a disciplined mind. Such a one is capable of learning to receive the enlightenment. Such a one can progress rapidly to Christhood.

To have dominion is to have sovereign or supreme authority. To have authority is to author your own enlightenment. To author your life and enlightenment is to create a greater consciousness in and through each experience, in each moment, of each day. What is authored or created in the Self is to be permanent, lasting and eternal and of LIGHT, Love and Truth.

> **14 And the four animals said, Amen. And the four and twenty elders fell down and worshipped him who lives for ever and ever.**

The four animals are the four levels of Subconscious Mind. Conscious and subconscious mind follow the directions of the mentally disciplined creator. The one committed to knowing Self brings all aspects into alignment with the common ideal of enlightenment. The one with enlightenment has continual consciousness. Like the Buddha, such a one is awake. Awake to the higher consciousness and the higher life. Immortality is eternal, connected consciousness. To live forever and ever is immortality.

Summary of the Inner Meaning of Chapter 5 of the Book of Revelation
The one who has made the full commitment to the whole Self to achieve Christ Consciousness will master all 7 chakras and all 7 levels of Mind.

Chapter 6 of Revelation

Few Word Essence of Chapter 6
of the Book of Revelation

The 7 Levels of Mind

Brief and More Expanded Essence of Chapter 6
of the Book of Revelation

The disciplined one receives six levels of consciousness
through the power of the still mind.

Chapter 6

New Symbols & The Interpretation of Chapter 6 of Revelation

1. the seals - opening the doorways to the inner levels of Mind

2. the 4 animals - the 4 levels of Subconscious Mind

3. bow - directing one's mind with an ideal

4. conquering - mastering consciousness

5. pair of balances - Aggressive and Receptive factors of Creation

6. wheat, barley - knowledge

7. oil - understanding

8. wine - wisdom

9. see - perception

10. earthquake - massive movement or shift in consciousness

11. sun - superconscious awareness

12. hair - conscious thoughts

13. moon - subconscious awareness

14. tree - subconscious experience, understanding

15. mountain - obstacle, challenge

16. island - emotional level of Mind

17. caves - unconsciousness

Chapter 6

**1 I saw when the Lamb opened one of the seven
seals, and I heard one of the four animals saying in a
voice as of thunder, Come and see.**

The one with commitment and discipline, the Lamb, can open the
seal to the sixth level of Mind, the emotional level.

This animal that is speaking symbolizes the quality of the energy in
the sixth level, the emotional level of Mind. To come forward is to use
the will, the aggressive principle. To see is to receive the reflected light
image which is to use the receptive principle.

Anyone who would gain access to, enter into or receive the higher
planes of existence must learn to use, practice and apply both the Aggressive and Receptive Principals of Creation. In this way one gains
greater and greater alignment with superconscious mind.

**2 And I looked and beheld a white horse, and he
who sat on him had a bow, and a crown was given to
him; and he went forth conquering, and to conquer.**

A horse symbolizes will. A white horse indicates the productive
use of will to discipline the brain, body and conscious mind in such a
way as to be able to enter into the inner levels of consciousness.

A bow symbolizes a covenant, which is a commitment. To have a
covenant is to agree to come, to convene. It is a mutual consent or
agreement between two or more persons.

A bow propels arrows. To aim a bow and arrow one must direct the
attention to a point. This point of attention is a goal or ideal. *"And God
said to Noah, this is the Sign of the covenant which I make between me and you
and every living creature that is with you, for perpetual generations. I set my
bow in the clouds, and it shall be for a sign of a covenant between me and the
earth. And it shall come to pass, when I bring clouds to the earth that the bow
shall be seen in the clouds."* Genesis 9:12-14.

This covenant, symbolized by the bow, is the one who has a singular ideal of Christ consciousness. The rainbow reveals how our seem-

The caduceus symbolically
portrays the movement of the
energy of the Kundalini as the ida
and pingala move like a serpent
upward around the shushumna.
This is the opening of the seals.

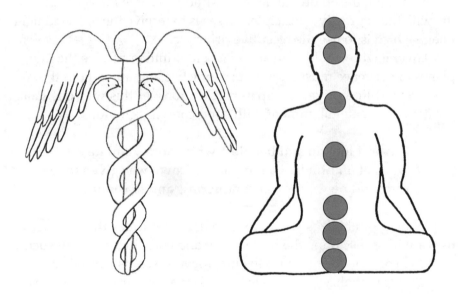

Diagram 9

ingly separate existence or many colors of Light, is in reality, only the one true Light of existence that is all connected in oneness without separation.

A crown indicates sovereign, regal power and authority. The one who sits on the horse, therefore, has will, commitment and authority. A white horse indicates the aggressive use of the will. The color white reflects light indicating the aggressive quality. To author a book, one must write a book. To write a book, one must use the imaging ability.

This first seal opens the doorway from the conscious mind, the seventh level of Mind, to the 6th level of Mind, the emotional level. The emotional level is the level of Mind closest to the physical world and conscious mind.

To open the first seal and move one's consciousness into the sixth level of Mind, one must have a highly developed will, imaging capability and commitment to know the whole Self.

Such a one may conquer, which is to master and harmonize with the sixth level of Mind. Then the Self may function with awareness in two levels of Mind at once, the sixth level and seventh level. *(See diagram 9)*

**3 And when he opened the second seal, I heard the
second animal say, Come and see.**

Opening the second seal indicates one's ability to move the attention into and receive the fifth level of consciousness. This requires a still and disciplined mind on the part of the one who thus attains.

The second animal represents the vibration and quality of the energy exchange in the fifth level of Mind. This quality is contraction. The words 'come and see' indicate the use of both the Aggressive and Receptive Principles of Creation. To come is to choose to move forward. To choose to move forward to engage the aggressive quality requires an act of will. To see is to choose to receive the light that is being reflected. To receive is the use of the receptive quality.

The eyes receive light that is reflected off an object. This is called the reflected light image. All the five senses are sense receptors. All five senses of sight, smell, hearing, taste and touch are receptive. Most learning occurs through the senses. Therefore, most learning is receptive and receiving. The aggressive quality and the will move us to a position or place of being able to then receive the learning.

To enter, receive and know the inner levels of Mind, one must master the aggressive and receptive principles of Creation.

As the individual gains mastery or receives fully a higher level of Mind it is as if the two levels become one. Then one can function in more than one level of Mind at the same time with awareness. *(See diagram 10)*

> **4 And there went out another horse, and it was red, and to him who sat on it was given power to take away peace from the earth, that people should kill one another; and there was given to him a great sword.**

The second horse indicates one who has earned and gained the capability to move into the next inner level, the fifth level of Mind. The fifth level of Mind is one of the four levels of Subconscious Mind. The one who is prepared to open the second seal, the second doorway to the mind, fully receives the 6th level, the emotional level of Mind. Therefore, thoughts, ideas, memories, attitudes or images that have not been understood or reasoned with become a point of emotional re-action in the brain and conscious mind of the individual.

The degree to which one is undisciplined in the conscious mind is the degree that thought forms moving out from subconscious mind react in and on the conscious mind and brain. Emotional re-actions rob the earth, one's consciousness, of peace.

The reason that the one who sat on this horse has the power to take away peace from the earth is because change is inevitable. The one who disciplines the mind learns to cause growthful, enlightening change at an accelerated rate. People that are engrossed in sensory experience often view change as undesirable or disruptive. People that pursue enlightenment diligently come to accept change as a way of life and learn to cause regular, consistent change in their consciousness.

The conscious use of the fifth level of Mind gives one the ability to direct and create more effectively in one's outer life by adjusting what is forming in the fifth level of Mind before it fully manifests in one's outward, physical life.

Death symbolizes change. A sword symbolizes a tool for change.

The one who receives awareness into the Self or the fifth level of Mind, gains the power to change and therefore transform the consciousness at an accelerated rate. To transform is to reform into a higher state of being. The red horse signifies one who uses the will to master the

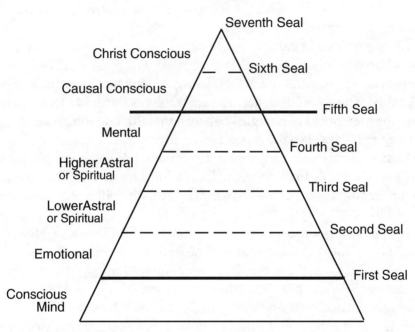

Diagram 10

emotions and the emotional or sixth level of Mind and thereby prepare to align with the 5th level of Mind.

> **5 And when he had opened the third seal, I heard the third animal say, Come and see. And behold, I saw a black horse; and he who sat on him had a pair of balances in his hand.**

The third seal symbolizes the reception of the fourth level of Mind into one's waking consciousness.

Will is required to gain access to each of the inner levels of mind. Thus, a horse, symbolizing will, is presented with each level of Mind. The black horse indicates one who is using the will to master the receptive quality. The color black absorbs and receives the light. In order to master the movement of energies between the fifth and fourth levels of mind one must develop the receptive quality.

The pair of balances are the balance of mental thought and physical form. For it is at the junction of the fourth and fifth levels of Mind that thoughts begin to take on the form that eventually will manifest in our outward lives.

This balance point between the fourth and fifth levels of Mind is the location of the Akashic Records. The Akashic Records are a recording, a record of everything that has ever been said, thought and done. The Akashic Records are the giant or great library of the Mind. The Records can be accessed and are available to one who gains entry into the fifth level of Mind. The Akashic Records are also referred to as the Great Hall of Learning or the Universal Library.

Black is the opposite of white indicating an opposite reflection of the sixth level of Mind, the white horse, to the fourth level of Mind. This is because of the shift from energetic thought in the fourth level of Mind to a thought with form in the sixth level of Mind.

> **6 And I heard a voice in the midst of the four animals say, A measure of wheat for a penny, and three measures of barley for a penny; and see that you do not damage the oil and the wine.**

The midst of the four animals is the location of the Akashic Records, also called the Hall of Knowledge. The midst or middle of the four levels of Subconscious Mind is between the fourth and fifth levels of Mind and is the location of the Akashic Records. The voice being referred to is one's own inner Self or soul. Both wheat and barley are food and as such symbolize knowledge. This kind of knowledge is not information received into the brain. This is the knowledge that adds to one's mind and whole being.

Money symbolizes value. Knowledge and the true value that adds to the whole Self are available to the one who disciplines the mind and gains awareness of the fifth level of Mind. One symbolizes the aggressive movement of thought or action. Three symbolizes the caused creation of a new structure or learning. As thought moves from the fourth to the fifth level of Mind, it changes from the aggressive action symbolized by the number one to the creation of the number three.

The color of the fourth horse is green. Green is the opposite color of red. Red is the color of the horse for the movement into the fifth level of Mind. Green is the color of the horse for the movement into third level of Mind. Red and green are opposite colors showing the movement from energetic movement to thought form structure.

Oil and wine symbolize the permanent understandings of Self and Creation gained by the individual. Wine symbolizes the wisdom that has been achieved by such a one as is ready to enter into the fourth level of Mind.

The four stages of growth are infancy, adolescence, adulthood and wisdom. By causing one's learning to progress through these four stages one gains wisdom and completion. It is in completing the wisdom symbolized by wine that we may build the permanent understanding symbolized by oil.

7 And when he had opened the fourth seal, I heard the fourth animal saying, Come and see.

The opening of the fourth seal symbolizes the movement of one's attention into the third level of Mind. The third level of Mind is the deepest level of the Subconscious Mind. The opening of the fourth seal symbolizes the openness within the consciousness of the individual to receive the third level of Mind.

8 And I looked and beheld a green horse; and the name of him who sat on him was Death, and Sheol

> **followed after him. And power was given him over
> the fourth part of the earth, to kill with sword and
> with famine and with death and with the wild beasts
> of the earth.**

Green is the color of healing. The third level of Mind is the point of cause and, therefore, the point of the development of true healing. When a strong, repeated desire is created in one's conscious mind, it then moves to the third level of Mind and begins its outward manifestation through the third, fourth, fifth and sixth levels of Mind. Then the thought form or desire moves into the seventh level of Mind to become an outward part of one's physical life.

Name signifies the ability to identify. Death symbolizes change that can transform one's consciousness.

The green horse represents the will of one who causes change and transformation from the point of cause. Such a one causes growthful change in the Self.

Sheol symbolizes entrapment and engrossment in physical life. Sheol has also been referred to as Hell, Hades and the Netherworld. Hell or Sheol is experienced when you refuse to use life experiences to the fullest for soul advancement and greater enlightenment.

The one who sat on the green horse was named Death. This indicates the one who accesses the third level of Mind has the power to cause growthful change. For death is change. The third level of Mind is one of the four levels of Subconscious Mind or 1/4 of the Subconscious Mind. The four levels of Mind are the northern quarter, the western quarter, the southern quarter and the eastern quarter. The four riders are sometimes referred to as the four horsemen of the apocalypse.

One who has mastered the third level of Mind has the power to cause change. To kill with the sword symbolizes the ability to master change. Green is the color of growth and healing. Growth and healing are the most productive ways to change.

Food symbolizes knowledge. Famine symbolizes one who realizes the life is not producing fulfillment and high knowledge of Self. Therefore, such a one changes the life and the Self to receive more knowledge and awareness in the life.

Wild beasts of the earth symbolize habits, compulsions and brain pathways. One who masters thought as cause has achieved the ability to override and update old patterns of brain thinking with the higher use of the mind and consciousness.

Such a one is gaining the still mind.

**9 And when he had opened the fifth seal, I saw
under the altar the souls of those who had been slain
for the sake of the word of God and for the testimony
of the Lamb which they had;**

Opening the fifth seal symbolizes one whose consciousness has moved into the second level of Mind. The second level of Mind is located in Superconscious Mind. The altar symbolizes one's attention in Superconscious Mind. The altar is where you worship. People worship the heavenly Father. Heaven is Superconscious Mind. The Superconscious Mind holds the blueprint for enlightenment, that is the Christ consciousness.

The souls of those who had been slain for the sake of the word of God represent those aspects of Self that have been changed and transformed so as to be in full alignment with becoming a Christ. The word of God is the Plan of Creation held in Superconscious Mind.

The testimony of the Lamb is the commitment to become a Christ. Such a one disciplines the mind.

**10 And they cried with a loud voice saying, How
long, O Lord, holy and true, dost thou not judge and
avenge our blood on those who dwell on the earth?**

Asking a question with a loud voice symbolizes one's desire to listen and receive truth from Superconscious Mind. Lord symbolizes I AM. The ideal is to come to know I AM. Then one can rightfully say as Jesus the Christ did, *"I and the Father are One."* Blood symbolizes truth and life force. Life force is a powerful key to knowing and receiving greater awareness and understanding of truth.

The one who would become the Christ strives constantly for the quickening of soul growth and spiritual development. The meaning of this verse comes in evaluating one's progress to enlightenment.

The desire and effort to live in harmony with Universal Truth plus the desire to be Holy, whole and complete, enables one to receive Superconscious Mind. To be Holy is to know the whole Self and the whole Mind.

11 And a white robe was given to every one of them; and it was said to them that they should rest yet for a little while, until the time should be fulfilled when their fellow servants and their brethren should be killed also as they had been.

A white robe symbolizes understanding of Self and Creation. A person receiving a white robe represents an aspect of Self that is understood and fully applied in the life for enlightenment and to aid others to enlightenment. To rest is to prepare for one's next step. In rest one can anticipate one's next step and gain the energy needed for it.

Time is fulfilled when one gains a still mind. Death symbolizes change. Until the mind is stilled, physical time still controls the Self. Physical thoughts enable physical time to control one.

A still mind enables one to know Superconscious Time.

12 And I looked when he had opened the sixth seal, and behold, there was a great earthquake; and the sun became black as sackcloth of hair, and the moon became as blood;

The opening of the sixth seal represents the movement of one's consciousness from the second level of Mind to the first level of Mind. The first level of Mind is the highest level of Mind and is in Superconscious Mind.

The great earthquakes denote the shift in one's whole consciousness as the first level of Mind is received consciously into one's whole being. The make up of one's whole mind is shifting.

The sun symbolizes superconscious awareness.

The moon symbolizes subconscious awareness.

The sun becoming black is an indication that one's conscious mind has become receptive to Superconscious Mind. Only a still mind can be receptive.

The moon became as blood shows that one who has achieved this stage of evolution is able to align the conscious and subconscious minds of Self. Thereby the truth and life force flows into one's being.

Hair symbolizes conscious thoughts. The sun became black as sackcloth of hair indicating that one who would know the whole Self must develop a still mind that is receptive to Superconscious Mind. The

Superconscious Mind provides life force to the other two divisions of Mind.

There are three knots located along the spinal column in relation to the chakras.

The first knot is located at the root chakra.

The second knot is located at the heart chakra.

The third knot is located at the brow chakra.

I pierced all of these in a period of five days. This was after more than 20 years of preparation.

These knots are located at the junction of the ida, pingala and shushumna energies.

These knots are referred to as the first, fourth, and sixth seals of Revelation. Chapter 6, verse 2 refers to the one who sat on the white horse went forth conquering. The release of the Kundalini from the root chakra is the beginning of the conquest of the mind and chakras. This indicates the piercing of the first knot, the root chakra.

The opening of the 4th seal, which is the piercing of the knot at the heart center, is explained in the eighth verse. The one who sat on the green horse was named Death. Death symbolizes change. There is a tremendous change between one who operates from the solar plexus or lower chakras and the one who functions from the higher chakras.

The third knot is located in the conjunction of the ida, pingala and shushumna in the area of the brow chakra. The brow chakra is really a functioning together of the medulla oblongata located at the base of the brain and the third eye-pituitary. The medulla oblongata is sometimes referred to as the mouth of God. The sun referred to in verse 12 is the sun center, the single eye located between the eyebrows. The moon is the medulla oblongata.

The sun becomes black indicating the piercing of this knot leads one to become fully receptive.

The moon became as red as blood means that life force is now capable of moving freely into the body and consciousness through the medulla oblongata.

13 And the stars of heaven fell to the earth, even as a fig tree casts its green figs when it is shaken by a mighty wind.

Heaven symbolizes Superconscious Mind. Stars symbolize conscious awareness. Stars of heaven falling to earth symbolize one who has developed a disciplined and still conscious mind and can thus receive superconscious awareness.

Figs being food symbolize knowledge of one's whole being. Normally fruit falls off a tree when it is ripe. However, a strong wind will blow fruit off a tree prematurely. This indicates that the one driven to know Self may begin to have awareness of the inner levels of Mind prematurely. This is a sign of what is to come. It is a sign that such a one is to develop these awarenesses into permanent and lasting illumination.

Wind symbolizes one's thoughts in motion. This mighty wind indicates such a one needs even more discipline of the mind in order that the mind may be stilled in a thought free state.

**14 And the heavens separated, as a scroll when it is
rolled separately; and every mountain and island
shifted from its resting place.**

The symbolic message of the heavens separating, is the ability of the one with a still mind to separate and identify each level of Superconscious Mind. Also indicated is the Plan of Creation located in Superconscious Mind. Awareness of this Divine Plan is present for the one with a still mind.

Every mountain and island represents the levels of Subconscious Mind. Shifting from their resting place portrays an image of the levels of Subconscious Mind moving into greater alignment.

The separation between the levels and divisions of Mind is becoming less and less. The limitations in consciousness no longer need to exist. What was prior to this initiation, obstacles, as symbolized by mountains, is now seen to be empty. The movement in Mind is bring ing about a greater alignment of conscious and subconscious minds and attunement to Superconscious Mind.

**15 And the kings of the earth and the great men and
the commanders of thousands and the rich and the
mighty men and every bondman and every freeman
hid themselves in caves and in clefts of the mountain,**

Those aspects that have yet to break free of entrapment attempt to avoid the change, this major shift in consciousness that is coming. Caves and clefts of the mountain symbolize the unconscious part of the brain. The brain cannot make you enlightened. The mind is the vehicle the Self needs to discipline and master in order for enlightenment to come about.

All these men symbolize physical aspects, which are physical ways of thinking and being. Physical things cannot give one enlightenment. Physical experience can be received in order that understanding may be incorporated into the Self.

Hiding is avoidance. Avoidance never produces soul growth and spiritual development.

16 And said to the mountains and rocks, Fall on us, and hide us from the face of him who sits on the throne and from the wrath of the Lamb;

One who asks the mountains to 'fall on us,' is one who has accepted obstacles to enlightenment as limitations that cannot be overcome. Such a one has accepted obstacles to greater awareness as a false security. These aspects of Self must be , for all is LIGHT. Hiding is avoidance. Obstacles are to be overcome or expanded beyond. Accept no limitations.

Why would anyone or any aspect want to hide from Superconscious Mind? The answer is, a practice of living in fear. Fear is of the darkness. Truth and enlightenment are of the LIGHT.

The face of him who sits on the throne is one's own true identity in Superconscious Mind. It is the Real Self, I AM. The wrath of the Lamb is emotional re-actions one has in areas of Self that are not fully committed to knowing the Self. Your emotional re-actions are indicative of your own resistance to change, growth and expansion of consciousness.

17 For the great day of his wrath is come, and who shall be able to stand?

The great day of wrath is the time when the great shift in consciousness will move through the emotional level of Mind and into the conscious mind of the individual.

Wrath is anger.

Anger is an emotion.

Emotions are of the sixth level of Mind.

The sixth level of Mind is the emotional level.

Advancements in one's consciousness must move through the levels of Subconscious Mind. The last level before the physical is the sixth level, the emotional level of Mind. The emotional level binds the conscious mind to the subconscious mind.

The highest, greatest transformations of consciousness move all the way through from the Superconscious Mind to the conscious mind of the individual.

Those aspects that live according to the Aggressive and Receptive Principles of Creation shall stand. To stand is to still the mind and achieve the changelessness of Superconscious Mind.

Summary of the Inner Meaning of Chapter 6 of the Book of Revelation
Six levels of Mind have been opened to one's consciousness and conscious awareness. The Self has conscious awareness of Superconscious Mind.

Chapter 7 of Revelation

Few Word Essence of Chapter 7
of the Book of Revelation

The 144,000 aspects of Self

Brief and More Expanded Essence of Chapter 7
of the Book of Revelation

The disciplined one with the still mind becomes aware
of the 144,000 aspects of the Self.

Chapter 7

New Symbols & The Interpretation of Chapter 7 of Revelation

1. four corners of the Earth - north, west, south, east - the four
   levels of subconscious mind

2. brow - brow chakra, pituitary gland

3. 144,000 - aspects of Self

4. hands - purpose

5. face - identity

6. temple - mastery of time through the still mind

7. hunger - need for knowledge

8. thirst - need for experience that fulfills the soul

9. living water - prana, awake conscious, life force, cosmic energy

10. tears - emotional attachment to memories

Chapter 7

**1 And after these things, I saw four angels standing
on the four corners of the earth, holding the four
winds of the earth, that the wind should not blow on
the earth nor on the sea nor on any tree.**

Verse one is a picture, a description, a mental image of a still mind.

Angels symbolize thought forms from I AM and Superconscious
Mind. The four corners of the earth are the four levels of Subconscious
Mind.

The winds represent thought in motion. When the mind is stilled
there is no thought. Therefore, symbolically there is no wind.

Trees symbolize subconscious experience. The sea, being water,
symbolizes the conscious life experience. Thus, the image is one of
both the conscious and subconscious mind of the individual being
stilled. This means no thought and the mind is stilled.

**2 And I saw another angel, and he ascended from the
direction of the rising sun, having the seal of the
living God; and he cried with a loud voice to the four
angels to whom it was given to hurt the earth and the
sea, saying,**

East is the direction of the rising sun. The direction of east symbolizes the third level of Mind. The third level of Mind is the highest or
deepest level of Subconscious Mind.

To ascend as the angel did from the third level of Mind is to enter
Superconscious Mind.

The living God is I AM. The seal of the living God is your own
individuality. It is your ability to use your brow chakra. The brow
chakra, also called the third eye, or eye of perception, is the interpreter
of energies.

Reasoning is a function of the third eye, the pituitary gland, while the intuitive faculty is a function of the brow chakra.

To receive, experience and know the seven levels of Mind, you must develop a still mind. A busy mind only knows part of the seventh level, the physical, sensory part.

> **3 Do not hurt the earth, neither the sea nor the trees,
> until we have sealed the servants of our God upon
> their brows.**

Each individual needs time, opportunity, experience and instruction in the use of Mind.

The servants of our God are the Universal Laws of Mind. The Universal Laws are our servants in that they work for anyone that harmonizes with them. To have the servants of our God sealed on one's brow chakra is to learn, apply and live true reasoning. True reasoning means you are the cause of your life. You cause your life to be as it is because **thought is cause.**

To practice conscious rationalization is to say someone else is to blame. **Conscious rationalization is of the brain. Reasoning is of the mind.**

When the earnest student takes up the study of the Mind and Self, there is usually a grace period as the student learns.

> **4 And I heard the number of those who were sealed;
> and it was a hundred and forty and four thousand, of
> all the tribes of the children of Israel.**

As the student disciplines the mind, reasoning improves.

One hundred forty-four thousand is the number of aspects of the Self. The zeros indicate the power that comes from understanding. Three zeros indicate complete understanding. Each person must unlock the seals to all aspects of Self which is to fully understand and to know Self. The numbers 144 when added together total nine. Nine is the number of completion.

> **5 Of the tribe of Judah were sealed twelve thousand;
> of the tribe of Reuben, twelve thousand; of the tribe
> of Gad, twelve thousand;**

6 Of the tribe of Asher, twelve thousand; of the tribe of Naphtali, twelve thousand; of the tribe of Manasseh, twelve thousand; 7 Of the tribe of Simeon, twelve thousand; of the tribe of Levi, twelve thousand; of the tribe of Issachar, twelve thousand; 8 Of the tribe of Zebulun, twelve thousand; of the tribe of Joseph, twelve thousand; of the tribe of Benjamin, twelve thousand.

The numbers 144 when added together total nine. The numbers in 12,000 when added together total three. Three is the number of creation and occurs when one practices using both the aggressive and receptive qualities. The aggressive quality is symbolized by the number one. The receptive quality is symbolized by the number two.

Each of the 12 tribes of Israel symbolize one of the 12 major aspects of the Mind learning to use physical existence. The 12 disciples of Jesus symbolize the one who is striving to gain mastery of the inner and outer Mind and to know the Real Self. I have detailed these aspects in my book, The Universal Language of Mind: the Book of Matthew Interpreted.

The 12 aspects are represented in the 12 sun signs of the Zodiac, 12 inches to a foot and 12 hours in a day. The numbers 1 through 12 also represent the 12 major aspects of Self.

9 After these things, I beheld, and lo, a great multitude which no man could number, of every nation and people and kindred and tongue stood before the throne and in the presence of the Lamb, clothed with white robes and with palms in their hands,

The great multitude is made up of people. People symbolize aspects of Self, and the whole **Bible** is a book about the individual. The **Bible** instructs us concerning how to use the mind to come to know the Self. The **Bible** is a textbook of the mind. The Book of Revelation is a textbook for the movement in consciousness from reasoning to enlightenment.

The throne symbolizes directing all aspects according to Superconscious Mind. The Lamb symbolizes one's full commitment to know the Self and gain the Christ consciousness. White symbolizes one's ability to give fully of one's learning, knowledge, wisdom and understanding. Clothing symbolizes one's outer expression. White robes symbolize one who gives fully of knowledge, wisdom and understanding to others. The highest giving is teaching. The highest teaching is of the Self and Mind.

Hands symbolize purpose. Palm leaves symbolize subconscious experience, thus indicating one who is consciously building permanent understandings of Self and creation that are then stored in subconscious mind.

> **10 And cried with a loud voice, saying, Salvation to our God, who sits upon the throne, and to the Lamb.**

When many aspects of the Self cry together with a loud voice, it is because of a singular ideal and purpose within one's being.

An ideal is what you want to become. One who achieves those abilities given in Revelation has an ideal of enlightenment for Self. I AM sits upon the throne of attention in Superconscious Mind. The Lamb symbolizes one who is fully committed to realize and know Self as I AM.

> **11 And all the angels stood round about the throne and about the elders and the four animals, and fell before his throne on their faces, and worshipped God,**

The angels, who are thought forms from Superconscious Mind, worship and recognize the greatness of one who comes to know Self as I AM. The throne symbolizes one's attention in Superconscious Mind. The elders symbolize the major aspects of Self. Faces represent one's identity and the growing awareness of Self. God is the Creator. We are made in the image and likeness of the Creator as given in Genesis.

To worship is to give honor and to recognize worth. The greatest honor is given to the Creator when one disciplines one's mind. For mind is the vehicle to know the Self.

The greater the discipline of the mind, the more one is capable of knowing the Self behind the thoughts. The Self behind the thoughts is learning to be a creator.

The more one grows in awareness and understanding of Self, the more one learns to create greater awareness and understanding, the more one knows Self as a son or daughter of the Creator. Then one can know, not just believe, as Jesus did when he said, *"I and my Father are One."*

12 Saying, Amen! Blessing and glory and wisdom and thanksgiving and honor and power and might to our God for ever and ever. Amen.

Amen means so be it, verily, certainly. To bless is to invoke divine favor on. To give glory is to celebrate and to hear. To advance one's consciousness rapidly, one must be certain of one's commitment to know the Divine, the LIGHT within the Self. One must learn to listen to the inner Self, the soul, in order to know I AM.

One must learn to give in order to receive the higher consciousness. Gratitude and thanksgiving open one up to receive greater understanding. Honor is esteem paid to worth. One must learn to know one's true value and worth as an individual to be enlightened.

To have power is to be able. To know Self as a creative being one must be able to use the will to act and to move forward in one's consciousness. One must also be able to receive in the deepest levels of meditation. To have might is to be able to cause enlightenment.

Forever is the ever present, eternal now achieved through the still mind.

Through the still mind is the Real Self known.

13 And one of the elders answered, saying to me, Who are these who are arrayed in white robes? And from whence did they come?

One of the major aspects of Self, symbolized by the elders, desires to be aware of what is causing permanent understandings of Self and creation to be built. What is the process and key to quickening one's soul evolution? Who are those aspects of Self that are disciplined and have full understanding?

The question, 'From where did they come?' indicates a desire to know where one has come from, how one came to know the mind and Self so that, therefore, one can know how to build the full enlightenment in the Self and offer this to others.

**14 And I said to him, My lord, you know. And he
said to me, These are those who came out of great
tribulation, and have washed their robes and made
them white in the blood of the Lamb.**

John, the believer in the Self is saying to an aspect of the Self that
there is already awareness, understanding and knowledge of this process of stilling the mind.

The great tribulation is an undisciplined mind that experiences conflict within the Self. Those who have come out of the conflict, the tribulation, have developed a disciplined mind through concentration, meditation and breathwork.

The disciplined mind is the key to knowledge of Self.

Enlightenment is built upon the foundation of a disciplined mind.

Robes are clothing. Clothing symbolizes one's outer expression.
To wash your robes and make them white symbolically indicates the
one who has practiced mental discipline until the mind is stilled. The
blood of the Lamb is the truth and life force that is built in the Self as
one practices and applies concentration, meditation and breathwork in
the life.

Breathwork, or pranayama as it is known in India, provides one
with much more life force from Superconscious Mind. You can actually learn to draw greater amounts of life force into your very being! It
requires will and attention which are built through the practices of concentration and meditation.

Concentration, meditation and consciously breathing life force are
three of the great keys to knowing Self, quickening one's soul growth
and gaining enlightenment.

**15 Therefore they are before the throne of God, and
serve him day and night in his temple; and he who
sits on the throne shall shelter them.**

One who, through discipline of the mind, gains a still mind can
consciously and with attention exist in Superconscious Mind. The throne
of God symbolizes attention in Superconscious Mind.

To serve day and night in the temple is to cause the conscious and
subconscious mind to align and then attune to superconscious mind.
Then one can serve with both the aggressive quality symbolized by

day and the receptive quality symbolized by night. Then the superconscious awareness and perception will shelter and protect the receptive one.

To sit on the throne is to have built the still mind and to direct the aspects of Self from a superconscious perspective.

> **16 They shall hunger no more, neither thirst any-**
> **more; neither shall they be stricken by the sun nor by**
> **the heat.**

Food symbolizes knowledge. Water symbolizes conscious life experience. One who develops a disciplined mind is then capable of receiving permanent and lasting soul knowledge from each and every experience of the conscious waking life. Such a one is capable of living in the present moment, fully receiving the learning, knowledge and awareness in that experience. The life experiences, symbolized by water, become more and more satisfying and fulfilling as one disciplines the mind and receives the High Knowledge. Therefore, such a one does not thirst anymore, for such a one is receiving life from each experience. The sun symbolically represents superconscious awareness. The inner urge to know Self and to be like the Creator is present in each one of us. In some, this urge is stronger than in others.

The one with a disciplined and still conscious mind is able to fully receive this inner urge consciously. Such a one, therefore, functions according to the Divine Plan of Creation held in Superconscious Mind. This kind of evolved person does not have a conscious mind or brain that is in conflict with superconscious mind.

When the conscious mind is disciplined to work in harmony with the aggressive and receptive principals in superconscious mind, then one is not stricken. Rather than have something strike you there is the capability of receiving all of creation.

> **17 For the Lamb who is in the midst of the throne**
> **shall shepherd them and shall lead them to fountains**
> **of living water. And God shall wipe away all tears**
> **from their eyes.**

The Lamb is the one committed to becoming a Christ. Water symbolizes conscious life experience. Eyes symbolize perception. When the one committed to the quickening of soul growth has stilled the mind then can all aspects be directed to becoming the enlightened Christ.

The one with such a high consciousness shall receive abundant conscious life experiences that provide greater motion to awareness, understanding and high consciousness. Then the ability to create, symbolized by God, will remove any emotional impediments or obstructions to the higher perception. Higher perception is necessary to be able to learn the higher lessons of life and consciousness.

Summary of the Inner Meaning of Chapter 7 of the Book of Revelation
The Self, the disciplined one, becomes aware of all 144,000 aspects of Self. It is one's duty to unite the 144,00 aspects into the Knowing One, which is I AM.

Chapter 8 of Revelation

Few Word Essence of Chapter 8 of the Book of Revelation

The first and highest level of Mind

Brief and More Expanded Essence of Chapter 8 of the Book of Revelation

The disciplined one receives awareness of the first and highest level of Mind, Christ consciousness.

Chapter 8

New Symbols & The Interpretation of Chapter 8 of Revelation

1. space - the still mind, the space between thoughts

2. time - the measurement of motion

3. trumpets - quickening of chakras

4. prayers - thought forms given to I AM

5. saints - aspects in harmony with Universal Law

6. hail - rigidity in one's conscious life experiences

7. ships - vehicles of life experience

8. lamp - awareness

9. one third - the conscious mind

10. eagle - motion in the third level of Mind

Chapter 8

**1 And when he opened the seventh seal, there was
silence in heaven for about the space of half an hour.**

Opening the seventh seal is the movement in consciousness from
the first level of Mind to I AM.

Heaven symbolizes Superconscious Mind. Silence in Heaven or
Superconscious Mind is achieved by one who masters the still mind.

The space of about half an hour symbolizes the length of time between thoughts, the space between thoughts. There needs to be a time
or space of no thought in the conscious mind. This is because as long as
the conscious mind is caught up in thoughts it is incapable of listening
or receiving the thoughts or messages from superconscious mind.

**Only the still mind is capable of experiencing the silence in
heaven.**

Each individual needs to cultivate and build the still mind, the state
of no thought. Only the still conscious mind is capable of aligning with
subconscious mind and attuning to superconscious mind.

Strive to go without any thoughts for at least half an hour each day.
(See diagram 11)

**2 Then I saw the seven angels who stood before
God, and seven trumpets were given to them.**

The seven angels are the seven messengers for the seven levels of
Mind. They come from I AM. I AM is a developing creator.

The seven trumpets symbolize the ability to consciously activate
and quicken the seven major chakras. The chakras are the energy transformers not only for the physical body but also for all of consciousness.
As one grows in consciousness the chakras are quickened.

The seven churches symbolize the chakras in the normal state and
function of recycling used mental energy back into Subconscious and
Superconscious Mind.

The trumpets indicate one whose life is being given to enlightenment both for Self and others. This is a life of service and discipline.
This focus and direction for a life produces a world server. Such a one

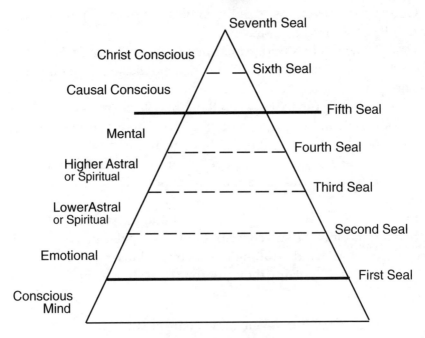

Opening of the seals to the Mind and
higher levels of Consciousness.

Diagram 11

can become a world teacher.

The seven trumpets signify one who has received or is receiving the High Knowledge and is practicing and applying this Knowledge in the life fully to transform the consciousness of Self.

> **3 And another angel came and stood at the altar, and he had a golden censer; and abundant incense was given to him, that he might offer it with the prayers of all saints upon the golden altar which was before the throne.**

The altar symbolizes one's attention in Superconscious Mind. It signifies one who has practiced concentration and meditation and has developed a disciplined mind. This disciplined mind gradually or quickly develops into a still mind.

The still conscious mind is necessary before one can choose to be either aggressive or receptive with the conscious mind. An aggressive conscious mind creates thoughts. A receptive conscious mind stops thinking, stops thoughts and instead receives. A receptive conscious mind consciously receives the thoughts of others as well as the messages coming in through the senses. A receptive conscious mind is capable of receiving superconscious awareness. A still mind must be achieved before the receptive conscious mind can be fully utilized.

A disciplined, aggressive conscious mind can align the conscious and subconscious minds. But only a receptive conscious mind can attune the aligned conscious and subconscious minds to superconscious mind.

The golden censer indicates the value of receptivity. A censer being a vessel symbolizes the ability to receive. A bowl, a vase, a jar or a censer all can receive and hold whatever is put into them. Gold symbolizes value.

Incense gives off smoke which rises to the sky. Jesus who became a Christ, an enlightened being, often referred to his Father in Heaven or to his Father in the Sky. The incense takes the place of a sacrifice upon a golden altar. It signifies giving one's attention and thoughts to superconscious mind and I AM. The golden altar represents the high value of placing one's attention in Superconscious Mind.

The throne indicates one who can direct all aspects of Self. The altar is the ability to have singular attention on giving to and receiving from Superconsciousness and I AM.

Saints are any and all aspects of Self who are completely understood and known. Such aspects align with subconscious mind and attune to superconscious mind. These aspects are in harmony with Universal Law and Universal Truth. The prayers of all the saints are thoughts that are fully attuned to fulfilling the Divine Plan of Creation held in Superconscious Mind.

> **4 And the smoke of the incense which came with the**
> **prayers of the saints ascended up before God out of**
> **the angel's hand.**

Ash and smoke are produced from a fire. Smoke rises to the sky. Ash returns to the ground in the form of minerals. Just as smoke rises to the sky, so do prayers rise to God.

Smoke symbolizes the permanent remains of the experience called understandings. Smoke is those thoughts that aid one to attune conscious and subconscious to superconscious mind.

Hand symbolizes purpose. Being an angel's hand, this purpose can bring one into attunement to the Divine or Perfect Plan of Creation held in Superconscious Mind. Saints are those aspects that are understood. They, therefore, manifest Superconscious awareness in the conscious mind.

> **5 And the angel took the censer and filled it with**
> **fire of the altar and cast it upon the earth; and there**
> **were voices and thunderings and lightnings and an**
> **earthquake.**

The quality of fire is expansion. The altar symbolizes one who has stilled the mind to enable the attention to attune to Superconscious Mind. That the fire was cast upon the earth indicates one whose attention is in Superconscious Mind is now capable of receiving the higher awareness in the conscious mind. This movement and shifting in one's consciousness is presented as thunderings, lightnings and an earthquake. The voices referred to symbolize one who is able to listen and hear the vibration of the Higher Mind.

> **6 And the seven angels who had the seven trumpets**
> **prepared themselves to sound.**

The seven angels, which are the seven thought forms or messengers from I AM, will soon bring about a quickening of the chakras. This quickening of the circular motion of the chakras will be accompanied by a quickening and increase in the vibration of the individual.

A part of preparation to receive higher consciousness is receptivity. Receptivity is expectant non-action. It possesses a drawing quality. The disciplined individual is gaining in the ability to have a still mind and thereby chooses to receive. Until one has a disciplined and somewhat still mind there is a little free will. For conscious choice proceeds from a disciplined mind. A still mind can choose either to receive or to give, to think a thought or to be receptive.
(See diagram 12)

> 7 The first angel sounded, and there followed hail
> and fire mingled with water, and they were poured
> upon the earth; and a third part of the earth was
> burnt up and a third part of the trees was burnt up
> and all green grass was burnt up.

The first angel sounded symbolizing the quickening of the root chakra located at the base of the spine. Although not physical, the root chakra corresponds to this area of the physical body.

The quality of energy transformation associated with the root chakra is physical creation. Fire symbolizes expansion. Water symbolizes one's conscious life experiences. When the root chakra quickens, there is an expansion of one's conscious awareness. The conscious mind begins to be transformed.

The earth, trees, and green grass symbolize that the way in which one learns is expanding. One's ability to produce permanent learning or understandings has expanded and quickened. The ability to learn how to learn is being gained. The conscious mind is learning more about the true purpose of life as symbolized by the angel's hand, given in verse 4.

> 8 Then the second angel sounded, and as it were a
> great mountain aflame with fire was cast into the sea;
> and the third part of the sea became blood;

The second angel functions in conjunction with the spleen chakra. The quality of the spleen chakra is physical power.

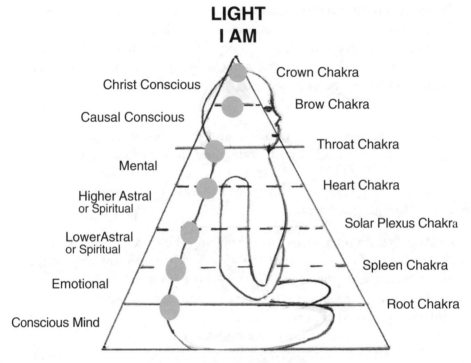

LIGHT
I AM

Christ Conscious — Crown Chakra

Causal Conscious — Brow Chakra

Mental — Throat Chakra

Higher Astral
or Spiritual — Heart Chakra

LowerAstral
or Spiritual — Solar Plexus Chakra

Emotional — Spleen Chakra

Conscious Mind — Root Chakra

Levels of Mind and their
relationship to the Chakras

Diagram 12

The great mountain symbolizes an obstacle or challenge. The mountain is cast into the sea which represents one's ability to overcome this challenge or obstacle. Since the great mountain was aflame with fire there is the indication that by overcoming this obstacle in one's own consciousness, great expansion of consciousness occurs.

Blood symbolizes truth and life force. This movement of the spleen chakra enables one to receive greater truth from every experience, thus aligning with Universal Truth. From this alignment with Universal Truth greater life force is received within the Self.

9 And the third part of the creatures which were in the sea, and had life, died; and the third part of the ships were destroyed.

The creatures symbolize one's habits and brain pathways. The quickening and conscious use of the spleen chakra enables one to begin to have power over one's habits in the brain and conscious mind.

The ships indicate that one's ways of functioning in the structures of the outer world are changing. The way one functioned previously no longer works. The Self has the power to create new ways of receiving learning, knowledge and awareness. The Self transforms the learning in order to accelerate one's soul growth.

10 And the third angel sounded, and there fell a star from heaven, burning as though it were a lamp, and it fell upon the third part of the rivers and upon the fountains of waters;

**The third angel functions with the solar plexus chakra.
The quality of the solar plexus chakra is balance.**
A star symbolizes new awareness in the conscious mind.

The star fell from heaven which indicates there is new superconscious awareness received in the conscious mind.

Light shines forth from a lamp. Light symbolizes awareness. The greater awareness from superconscious mind that comes to such a one raises the awareness of one's whole waking life experiences.

The solar plexus is the seat of the conscious and subconscious mind. As such, it is very important for the aligning of conscious and subconscious minds. In this verse the conscious mind is waking up to the true purpose and reason for existence in a physical body.

> **11 And the name of the star is called Wormwood;**
> **and the third part of the waters became wormwood;**
> **and many men died of the waters, because they were**
> **made bitter.**

Wormwood is a plant known for its bitter, tonic, and stimulating qualities and bitter feeling. Wormwood indicates the bitterness or pain that is often a part of physical experiences. The third part being referred to is the conscious mind. The Conscious Mind is one of the three divisions of Mind. The other two divisions being Subconscious and Superconscious Minds.

When the third chakra, the solar plexus chakra quickens, one's perception of physical life is never the same. Physical life and physical experiences seem to lose their meaning. Life may seem purposeless. One may become bitter over past experiences. This is because there is a need for a higher and greater purpose. Experiences without purpose seem shallow and bitter. By aligning with one's soul in subconscious mind this bitterness begins to be remedied.

The statement that men died indicates the consciousness is changing. The disciplined being is shifting from physical thinking to mental thinking. The old ways of thinking and the old ways of experiencing must change. The illusion of temporary satisfaction or happiness is wearing off. The soul encased in a physical body desires to know the essence of truth that can be received in each experience and every moment.

> **12 And the fourth angel sounded, and the third**
> **part of the sun was eclipsed and the third part of**
> **the moon and the third part of the stars, so that**
> **the third part of them was darkened, and the day**
> **was darkened for a third part of it, and the night**
> **likewise.**

In one third of Mind, the Conscious Mind, everything is in a state of change and flux for the heart chakra has been quickened. This is presented as the fourth angel that sounded.

The quality of the heart chakra is understanding.

The sun symbolizes superconscious awareness.

The moon symbolizes subconscious awareness.

The stars symbolize conscious awareness.

The day and night symbolize cycles of being aggressive then receptive. The day indicates the aggressive quality. The night symbolizes the receptive quality.

Because the conscious mind of the disciplined one is becoming more still the consciousness is becoming more receptive.

> **13 And I beheld, and heard an eagle, having a tail red as it were blood, flying through the midst of heaven, saying with a loud voice, Woe, woe, woe to those who dwell on the earth, by reason of the other sounds of the trumpets of the three angels which are yet to sound!**

The first four chakras mentioned open up the Self to more fully receive the energies of the seventh, sixth, fifth, fourth and third levels of Mind. The eagle symbolizes the third level of Mind.

The next chakra's quickening will open up the energy transfer movement from the third to the second level of Mind. With the second level of Mind, the energy of the Superconscious Mind becomes more directly involved in the consciousness and life of the individual.

Blood, signifying truth and life force, indicates that the one accomplishing this chapter and verse within the Self will and must become more honest and truthful in order to align with Universal Truth. Such a one will receive a higher energy and a higher vibration. The statement 'woe, woe, woe' means there is resistance to the quickening of consciousness because the habitual brain and conscious mind view this as change. There often exists fear of change in the conscious mind, a fear of losing something or a fear of annihilation. Yet Superconscious awareness is something to be received joyfully and gladly. Surrender, and the resistance in mind is gone. When the resistance in mind departs, one may experience, **Being**.

Summary of the Inner Meaning of Chapter 8 of the Book of Revelation
Access to the Highest Level of Mind, the first level, Christ Consciousness has been achieved by opening the seventh seal. Now one must learn to master one's own mind in order to permanently receive the Christ Consciousness.

Chapter 9 of Revelation

Few Word Essence of Chapter 9
of the Book of Revelation

The unconscious part of the brain

Brief and More Expanded Essence of Chapter 9
of the Book of Revelation

Six chakras are quickened and opened. All limitations and restrictions in consciousness must be overcome or transformed. The way is now open to the whole Mind.

Chapter 9

New Symbols & The Interpretation of Chapter 9 of Revelation

1. fifth angel - thought form working with throat chakra

2. bottomless pit - the unconscious part of the brain

3. Key - the solution that unlocks the doorway to the mind

4. locusts - habits

5. scorpion's sting - the pain and suffering that follows habit and attachment

6. hair - conscious thoughts

7. breastplates - a closed heart

8. tails - compulsion

9. sixth angel - thought form activating the brow chakra

10. the golden altar - the value of attention in or on Superconscious Mind

11. Euphrates - Kundalini energy

12. plagues - pain and suffering which comes from the refusal to receive the higher truth

13. hands - purpose

14. idols - worshiping the temporary

15. murder - destroying the opportunity to learn

16. witchcraft - undisciplined attempt for power

17. fornication - sensory engrossment

18. theft - stealing valuable learning opportunities from Self

19. devils - egotistical ways of thinking

Chapter 9

1 And the fifth angel sounded, and I saw a star fall from heaven upon the earth; and to him was given the key of the bottomless pit.

The fifth angel sounded indicating a quickening and change in vibration of the fifth chakra, the throat chakra. The quality of the energy of the throat chakra is will.

Will is developed by mental discipline that produces a series of choices toward an ideal. Will is the key to the bottomless pit. The throat chakra returns used mental energy to the third level, the highest level of Subconscious Mind and to some degree the second level of Mind in Superconscious Mind. Superconscious Mind and the causal factor of the third level of Subconscious Mind is the key to the bottomless pit of physical thinking and unconscious thinking. The bottomless pit is unconsciousness in the brain and conscious mind. A person begins to be more conscious when the discipline of concentration is undertaken on a daily basis.

The person with an undisciplined mind isn't even aware of most of the thoughts going on in the head. You must become aware of your thoughts in order to gain the ability to choose your thoughts. The star symbolizes awareness in the conscious mind. The key to the bottomless pit of unconsciousness is the will. Will develops greater awareness in the conscious mind.

The star that fell from heaven is a new awareness in the conscious mind. This awareness connects one consciously with the Divine Plan held in Superconscious Mind. This new awareness in the conscious mind has come from superconscious mind.

The one who, through the disciplined mind, becomes aware of the thoughts begins to have control of the conscious ego, the devil and quickens the movement out of the dark unconsciousness.

> **2 And he opened the bottomless pit; and there arose
> a smoke out of the pit like smoke belching from a
> great furnace; and the sun and the air were darkened
> by reason of the smoke of the pit.**

When the bottomless pit is opened, the earnest student of the Mind notices all kinds of thoughts that were heretofore unperceptible. Such a one begins to see how these subtle and unconscious thoughts have been clouding the perception and interfering with progress in the life. Smoke interferes with one's ability to see clearly. The smoke is already in the pit of the brain and conscious mind, but you just didn't see or perceive it. Now with the will, the key to the bottomless pit, one can begin to perceive what has been obstructing or clouding one's awareness and perception. Darkness symbolizes lack of awareness. Unconsciousness is a lack of awareness.

The sun symbolizes superconscious awareness. When one begins to build will through mental discipline such as concentration one's need for greater awareness and perception becomes apparent. Once the mind is opened the Self becomes aware of all the unconscious brain thoughts that were previously unknown.

Air is full of life force. Clear air is needed for clear seeing. When the air is smoke filled the perception is obscured.

> **3 And there came out of the smoke locusts upon the
> earth; and to them was given power as the scorpions
> of the earth have power.**

Locusts and scorpions symbolize habits. Habits have power to cause pain. The Buddha said that attachment to desires is the source of misery and pain. Attachment to desires becomes a habit as it is practiced over the years as one ages unless one practices mental disciplines. Attachment to desires is often experienced as possessiveness.

Habits, brain pathways, neuron connections and compulsions are built up by repetitive, often unconscious thinking. All thoughts that arise spontaneously need to be examined in the light of awareness. Then a decision must be reached as to the productivity or lack of productivity of these habitual thoughts.

Ultimately all thoughts need to be consciously chosen or, conversely, there needs to be the choice to think no thoughts in the present moment.

4 And it was commanded them that they should not hurt the grass of the earth, neither any green thing, neither any tree; but only those men who do not have the seal of God on their brows.

The grass of the earth, trees and any green thing symbolize subconscious experience. The subconscious mind stores one's permanent understandings of Self and creation. Habits-locusts, which are of the physical brain, cannot harm or destroy one's permanent memory, one's understandings stored in subconscious mind.

The seal of God or their brows indicates the correct use of the pituitary gland, the eye of perception. The third eye, the pituitary gland, is used by the disciplined one to fully develop reasoning and to evolve reasoning into the intuitive faculty. Intuition builds upon and goes beyond reasoning.

Reasoning and intuition enable the individual to go beyond the compulsion and instinct of plants and animals.

Men symbolize the physical aspects of the Self. The physical aspects-men that do not have the seal of God on their foreheads are those aspects of Self that have not learned to reason. To reason is to know Self as the cause of one's life and one's thoughts.

To reason is to wield memory, attention and imagination to create and to learn to be a creator. To reason is to understand and know Self as connected with all beings and all things. To reason is to think mentally instead of physically. To reason is to make decisions based upon what is permanent and lasting. To reason is to see and know Self as the cause of one's life.

5 And locusts were commanded that they should not kill them, but that they should be tormented five months; and their torment was as the torment of a scorpion when it strikes a man.

At this level of awareness and learning these physical aspects are still useful. They are not yet changed. Killing and death symbolize change. However, these aspects of Self must learn to reason. Five is the number of reasoning. Five months indicate a need for greater reasoning on the part of the individual. To progress and get past the torment of unconsciously creating the same painful situations over and over again one must employ the disciplined mind to reason. Man is the thinker. A scorpion is a habit. Habits cause pain and torment for the thinker and the reasoner until conscious decisions are made to think thoughts in alignment with Universal Law and Universal Truth.

> **6 So in those days men shall seek death and shall**
> **not find it; and shall desire to die, and death shall**
> **flee from them.**

A day is a point in physical time. A day symbolizes a point or level of awareness.

From the experience of pain and torment a reasoner looks to perceive the cause. Finding the cause to be one's own thoughts and attitudes, the intelligent one desires to change. Yet without enough knowledge and experience with the will it is difficult to cause the changes one desires in the Self and the life.

The will is the key to the bottomless pit.

The will is necessary to bring about caused change within the consciousness of the Self.

The physical aspects view the self as separate from all beings and all things. This is physical thinking.

The mental aspects of the true thinker know the Self to be connected to all beings and all things. This is mental thinking.

> **7 And the shapes of the locusts were like horses**
> **prepared for battle; and on their heads were, as it**
> **were, crowns like gold, and their faces were like**
> **faces of men.**

Sometimes acting through habit may seem or appear to be the use of will.

Horses symbolize will. Locusts symbolize habits.

Locusts shaped like horses symbolize habits masquerading as will and will power.

Crowns symbolize authority. Gold symbolizes value.

The crowns of the locusts were like gold but they were not of gold. They were fake. Some people fake authority by memorizing information or by using habitual brain pathways. Pharisees in the book of Matthew are an example of this. Jesus who became Christed called the

Pharisees hypocrites because they memorized the Holy scriptures yet did not practice and apply the Universal Truths of those scriptures in their lives.

The people were always amazed when Jesus talked because he did not speak like the Pharisees. Jesus spoke with true authority. Jesus was the author or creator of his life.

The faces of the locusts were like the faces of men because faces symbolize one's identity. To have faces like men is to only have an imitation of the identity of a reasoner. These habits, these memorized behaviors, look smart and intelligent, but they are not enlightened or wise. The locusts prepare for battle which means that habits cause you to fight your environment. When you view life physically and habitually then you think you are separate from all life. This illusion produces fear which produces battles and fighting. The habitual brain of the one who fails to use the mind is afraid of change and thus fights to maintain a false sense of security.

8 And they had hair like the hair of women, and their teeth were like the teeth of lions.

Hair symbolizes conscious thoughts. The locusts have hair like women indicating the attempt to imitate the receptive quality in the thinking process of the conscious mind.

Teeth indicate the ability to begin the process of assimilating knowledge and experience.

Lions symbolize large and powerful habits.

Both verses indicate the way that habits can seem like or can imitate true and greater functions and qualities of the mind. The vast amount of people go through life habitually. Yet outwardly they appear to be normal, reasoning, human beings.

When mental discipline is practiced the true and higher qualities of will, reasoning, identity, authority, and understanding are built and created in the Self. The real replaces the false imitation. Reality replaces illusion.

9 And they had breastplates as though they were breastplates of iron; and the sound of their wings was like the sound of chariots of many horses running to battle.

The quality of the heart is understanding.

Breastplates cover the area of the heart. When presented with Truth the person who is habitual will tend to have a closed heart.

Wings indicate motion. Chariots represent one's physical body.

These habits outwardly seem to get a lot done. They produce a lot of activity. Yet, they fail to produce permanent understanding or wisdom or reasoning. The iron breastplates covering the area of the heart show that habits interfere or put up barriers to the assimilation and permanent learning in every experience.

> **10 And they had tails like scorpions, and there were stings in their tails; and they had power to hurt men five months.**

Tails indicate one who is habitual and compulsive. The stings in their tails show that habitual thinking creates pain. The pain occurs in any part of the Self that is thinking physically and that is physically engrossed in sensory experience.

These stinging habits will hurt you until you learn to reason on a higher level. You must admit that you and your thoughts are the cause of your life. Then you can change the cause of your life to something better.

> **11 And they had a king over them, who was the angel of the bottomless pit, whose name in Hebrew is Abaddo, but in Greek his name is Apollyon.**

Abaddo is a Hebrew word that means destruction. Apollyon is a Greek word that means, to destroy.

The old way of thinking and acting is being destroyed. The habitual state of consciousness is beginning to crumble and shatter. Habits and compulsions destroy one's opportunity to build permanent understandings and fulfill the true purpose of life. The one who consciously engages the throat chakra destroys habits and builds choice, will and will power. This bottomless pit of unconscious thoughts and actions is being replaced with a developed will. Habit is replaced with the conscious choice that develops into a strong will. The student of the Mind who allows habits and compulsions to rule over the thoughts finds the soul growth and opportunities of life being destroyed. A highly developed will, however, has the ability to triumph over all habitual brain pathways. The unconscious one of the bottomless pit lives life for temporary experiences. The delusion that temporary, sensory experiences or physical possessions will give one permanent happiness leaves one empty at the end of a lifetime. At the end of a lifetime everything temporary is destroyed. The physical body deteriorates.

Conscious choice brings awareness. Habits bring unconsciousness and lack of awareness.

> **12 The first woe is passed; and behold, two more woes follow after.**

The first woe enables the Self to transform used mental energy from the seventh level, the conscious mind, to the second level in Superconscious Mind. To the conscious mind and brain it seems that these changes in consciousness that are occurring are woeful. Woe indicates deep suffering or misfortune.

The brain and ego consider true change as misfortune. The sensory engrossed self living in a delusion of separateness resists the movement from brain pathways or habits to using mind with choice. Resistance to the growth in consciousness due to attachments creates pain and suffering. The solution is to embrace change as the growth in consciousness and the transformation of Self into a LIGHT Being.

> **13 And the sixth angel sounded, and I heard a voice from the horns of the golden altar which is before God,**

The sixth angel sounded which is the quickening, the greater motion of the brow chakra. The quality of the brow chakra is perception. The brow chakra functions with the pituitary gland. The pituitary gland or the third eye is the eye of perception.

In the terminology of India's literature, the brow chakra is called the anja chakra. The brow chakra recycles or moves mental energy to the first level of consciousness.

The horns of the golden altar, which is before God, is in the first level of Mind. The first level of Mind is in Superconscious Mind. The first level of Mind is the level of Mind closest to I AM.

The altar is one's attention in Superconscious Mind.

One who enters into the first level of Mind consciously has great understanding of Creation and Creator.

**14 Saying to the sixth angel which had the trumpet,
Loose the four angels which are bound by the great
river Euphrates.**

The great river Euphrates is the Kundalini energy. It is the same river Euphrates referred to in the second chapter of Genesis verse 14. The sixth angel with the trumpet is the brow or ajna chakra. The quality of the brow chakra is perception.

The four angels are the thoughts in alignment with Superconscious Mind and I AM that produce a quickening of the chakras and one's soul growth. The conscious and subconscious minds are subordinate to the superconscious mind. Thus, the sixth angel directs the four lower angels or thought forms that quicken and initiate a greater motion of the lower chakras.

The stimulation and quickening of the brow chakra also brings about an activation of the Kundalini energy. The Kundalini energy then begins its ascent up the spinal column. It follows the path of the tube inside the spinal column called the Shushumna.

**15 And the four angels were loosed, those which
were prepared for that hour and for that day and for
that month and for that year, so that they might slay
the third part of men.**

When the Kundalini energy is activated and raised, the conscious mind must change. The third part of men is the physical thinking in the conscious mind. This physical thinking of Self as separate and the illusion of engrossment in sensory experiences must change.

When the Kundalini is raised and activates the four lower chakras, the hour, day, month, and year for one's greater enlightenment have arrived. The four angels are the thoughts that direct the chakras through the use of the will, symbolized by horses.

The four lower chakras are 1) the root or muladhara chakra, 2) the spleen or svadhisthana chakra, 3) the solar plexus, navel or manipura chakra, and 4) the heart or anahata chakra.

When these four lower chakras are awakened to a greater movement, one's awareness increases. The intelligent being awakens to a greater LIGHT and a higher awareness of the true reality.

16 And the number of the army of the horsemen was two hundred thousand thousand; I heard the number of them.

The number two hundred thousand thousand is 200 million. **The number two symbolizes the receptive principle of creation.**

The number one symbolizes the aggressive principle.

Zero symbolizes the power that comes from completing a cycle of learning with understanding.

The sounding of the sixth angel is the vibration of the Superconscious Mind now manifesting or moving into the receptive conscious mind. The number two indicates the conscious mind is receptive. A receptive conscious mind is needed and required in order to receive superconscious awareness and understanding.

Two hundred million is made up of the number two followed by eight zeros. Eight zeros represents tremendous power and understanding. This number indicates mastery of the receptive principle of creation.

Two hundred thousand thousand is made up of eight zeros.

The number eight symbolizes value. Eight is made up of two squares, one on top of the other. Squares are made up of four sides. Four is the number of stability. True and lasting value is built when one builds on stability. It is as Jesus the Christ said, *"To build my house on rock and not on shifting sand."*

The number 200,000,000, or two hundred million shows one has completed many cycles of learning and gained permanent understanding from this. Thus, such a one has great power inherent in the whole Self. This power is stored in one's subconscious mind or soul as permanent understanding.

The number two followed by eight zeros indicates one who has almost mastered receptivity. Receptivity is the yin referred to in the Chinese classic the **Tao Te Ching**.

To hear a word is to still the mind and listen. One who has achieved this point of awareness as given by the number 200,000,000 has achieved a mind that has a great deal of stillness. Such a one can then choose to be either aggressive or receptive. Such a one can choose a still mind with no thought or can consciously choose to think a thought.

A still mind is necessary for full receptivity to occur. One with a still mind can listen effectively. To listen is a receptive quality.

Horsemen are riders of horses. Horses symbolize will. Will is required not only for the aggressive quality but also for the receptive quality.

An army kills people. Death symbolizes change. The overall picture of this verse is of a highly evolved individual who has developed receptivity to a very high degree and is thus able to receive a higher vibration from superconscious mind.

Meditation is a receptive act. Such a one has achieved that very deep state of meditation known as samadhi in which the attention is in Superconscious Mind and the conscious mind receives superconscious awareness.

> **17 And thus I saw the horses in the vision and those who sat on them, and they had breastplates of fiery red and of smoky blue and of sulfurous yellow, and the heads of the horses were like the heads of lions, and out of their mouths issued fire and smoke and sulfur.**

Red, blue and yellow are the three primary colors.

The breastplates cover the heart. The heart's quality is understanding. The colors of the breastplates of red, yellow and blue are the primary colors from which all other colors emerge or are made. Red is the predominant color of the root chakra. Yellow is the predominant color of the solar plexus chakra. Blue is the predominant color of the throat chakra. Purple, the color of the brow chakra, is the combination of red and blue of the root and throat chakras. Orange is the predominant color of the spleen chakra. Orange is a combination of the red of the root chakra and the yellow of the solar plexus chakra.

Green is the predominant color of the heart chakra. Green is a combination of the yellow of the solar plexus chakra and the blue of the brow chakra. Indigo is the color of the crown chakra. Indigo is a deep, slightly reddish blue. It is deep blue with a trace of red. This indicates the mental consciousness of blue has become predominant over the physical consciousness of red. All the upper chakras of heart, throat, brow and crown have blue in them. This indicates that opening the heart is the key to all the other chakras, particularly the first 5 chakras meaning the root, spleen, solar plexus, heart and throat chakras.

Sulfur is brimstone. Brimstone literally means or comes from the words, burning stone. Smoke is given off as the residual of fire. Sulfur is a burning stone. This indicates there is about to be an expansion in one's understanding. Such a one is almost ready to receive greater understanding from superconscious mind. Fire is a quality of the fourth level of mind. Lions symbolize the fourth level of Mind. The quality of the fourth level of Mind is expansion. Heads symbolize identity, meaning the understanding of the identity of the Self beginning to expand. The mouth is used for aggressive speaking and receptive eating.

The fire, smoke and brimstone or sulfur that come out of their mouths carries the quality of expansion. The whole picture is one of expansion of one's consciousness and identity.

> heart = green = 1/2 blue, 1/2 yellow
> throat = blue = all blue
> brow = purple =1/2 blue, 1/2 red
> crown = indigo = 9/10 = 90% blue, 10% red

18 And by these three plagues was the third part of men slain, by the fire and by the smoke and by the brimstone which issued out of their mouths.

When the mind and consciousness expands the disciplined student becomes aware of many physical ways of thinking and being, many physical aspects of oneself changing. To be slain is to change. The question in such a condition is, "Will you receptively surrender to the change or will you fight the change?" This decision determines the rapidity and ease with which one changes or the pain one puts the Self through.

19 For the power of the horses was in their mouths and in their tails; for their tails were like serpents and had heads, and with them they do harm.

Horses symbolize will. One's power comes from the exercise of the will to give one the experiences needed for learning and growth.

Tails indicate the compulsive use or misuse of the Kundalini, creative energy. Serpents symbolize the Kundalini, creative energy.

Kundalini is a word from India that means serpent fire in referring to the creative energy that for most people lies dormant at the base of the spine. For one quickening the movement to enlightenment as given in the book of Revelation, the Kundalini energy arises from its dormant state. The Kundalini energy then rises up the spine touching and vivifying each chakra on its upward ascent.

When one resists the expansion of consciousness that comes through receiving superconscious mind one experiences pain and suffering that seems like harm. The solution is to receive fully the present moment and thereby cease resisting change.

> **20 And the rest of the men who were not killed by these plagues neither repented of the works of their hands, that is to say, the worship of devils and idols of gold and silver and brass and stone and of wood, which can neither see nor hear,**

To repent is to feel such sorrow for sin that one amends the life and changes one's attitudes and consciousness. When reasoning is lacking, one refuses to see the cause of one's life as one's own thoughts. Often people do not change except when they are forced to do so from pain and suffering. The person wanting rapid enlightenment embraces change as a way of life. Such a one identifies limitations in consciousness and strives to relieve them by replacing them with a more productive and disciplined mind.

The aspects that did not change, which is to say did not repent, continued to allow the conscious ego-devil to control them. They remained engrossed in physical experiences as evidenced by the idols. Idol worship, metaphorically, may be explained as making the physical life and sensory experiences into one's god.

To practice idol worship is to allow your attention and value to go only to physical things. Whereas, true worship is to move the attention inward to Superconscious Mind and beyond Mind to I AM.

> **21 Nor repented of their murders nor of their witch-craft nor of their fornication nor of their thefts.**

These physically thinking aspects that refuse to change continue to destroy opportunities to learn as symbolized by murder. This is given in the 10 commandments of the Old Testament as, *"Thou shalt not kill."*

Witchcraft indicates an attempt to misuse one's mind to gain only physical results and possessions. The commandment of *"Thou shalt have no other gods before me,"* is relevant here.

Fornication symbolizes the refusal to commit the Self and the life to knowing the High Self and I AM. The relevant commandment is , *"You shall not commit adultery."* The solution is to be committed to one's soul growth and spiritual development.

Theft symbolizes the way one steals from their own opportunities for learning, growth in awareness, consciousness and understanding. *"Thou shall not steal,"* is the relevant commandment concerning theft. These four changes in consciousness still need to be caused in order for the disciplined one to be fully in alignment with Universal Law and Universal Truth.

Even though such a one has made tremendous progress in consciousness, there remains much work, much effort before the full enlightenment may occur.

Summary of the Inner Meaning of Chapter 9 of the Book of Revelation
All that is unconscious in one's brain must be illumined and brought to conscious awareness. All habits must be understood and overcome.

Chapter 10 of Revelation

Few Word Essence of Chapter 10
of the Book of Revelation

Aligning the conscious and subconscious minds

Brief and More Expanded Essence of Chapter 10
of the Book of Revelation

The seventh chakra, the crown chakra, is opened and quickened.
The Plan of Creation, held in Superconscious Mind is
received into the conscious mind awareness.

Chapter 10

New Symbols & The Interpretation of Chapter 10 of Revelation

1. book - information

2. write - bringing one's thoughts into conscious awareness

3. prophet - goal setter

4. sea - conscious life experience

5. eat food - receive and process knowledge

6. eat a little book - receive information that is intellectual and therefore not digestible

7. belly - ability to process knowledge

Chapter 10

**1 And I saw another mighty angel coming down
from heaven, clothed with a cloud; and the rainbow
of the cloud was upon his head, and his face was as
though it were the sun, and his legs as pillars of fire;**

This, the seventh angel is referenced in this chapter, verse seven. The seventh angel is also presented in chapter 11, verse 15. The seventh angel represents the thought consciousness associated with the quickening of the crown chakra.

Heaven symbolizes Superconscious Mind. The angel coming down from Heaven indicates Superconscious awareness coming into the conscious mind. Clothing symbolizes one's outer expression. A cloud is made up of water. Water symbolizes the conscious life experience. An angel coming down from heaven clothed with a cloud portrays the one whose entire field of experience is changing as a result of the quickening of the crown chakra.

The rainbow of the cloud upon his head signifies one who is ready to receive the full spectrum of consciousness.

The sun symbolizes Superconscious awareness showing that the individual can and will gain a new, different and greater identity based upon Superconscious awareness that leads to understanding.

Legs are one's foundation as well as providing motion. Pillars of fire indicate a strong, stable foundation for the expansion of consciousness.

**2 And he had in his hand a little book open; and he
set his right foot upon the sea, and his left foot on the
land,**

A book contains information. A hand symbolizes purpose. Land symbolizes subconscious experience. Water symbolizes conscious life experience. One foot on land and one foot upon the sea indicates the emotional level of consciousness. The emotional level of Mind is the connector between the Superconscious and Conscious minds.

This superconscious thought form that has quickened the crown chakra is creating a vibrational movement throughout the entire mind of the individual. This vibrational shift has moved from the first level of Mind in Superconscious Mind to the sixth level of Mind, the emotional level.

The spiritual foundation symbolized by the angel's feet connects conscious and subconscious to superconscious mind in a way that a person at this level of awareness has receptively never done before. The left foot indicates the past and the right foot the future and the aggressive factor. They meet in the present moment and the still mind.

> **3 And cried with a loud voice as when a lion roars,**
> **and when he had cried, seven thunders sounded**
> **their voices.**

A loud voice indicates the initiation of a vibrational change through all seven levels of Mind. The seven thunders are the vibrational movement through all seven levels of Mind. This greater movement of the thought form from I AM brings about movement and vibrational change through all seven levels of Mind.

> **4 And when the seven thunders had spoken, I was**
> **about to write; but I heard a voice from heaven**
> **saying, Seal up those things which the seven thun-**
> **ders uttered, and do not write them.**

To write is to move one's thoughts outward into physical existence.

The voice from heaven is one's own inner voice from I AM and superconscious mind. The first experience in greater awareness is not yet permanent. To become permanent, the greater awareness cannot be sealed up, rather it must be practiced every day.

One who has achieved the awareness presented in chapter 10 has received some superconscious awareness and a quickening of all seven chakras.

To seal these things up indicates one is to continue to practice and apply the mental discipline. Such a one is not yet ready to receive or fully manifest superconsciousness in the waking day-to-day experiences of the conscious mind and conscious life experiences.

The opening and unsealing permanently of the higher consciousness will occur in chapter 22, the final chapter of Revelation.

5 And the angel which I saw standing upon the sea and on the land raised his right hand to heaven, and 6 Swore by him who lives forever and ever, who created heaven and the things which are therein, and the earth and the things which are therein, and the sea and the things which are therein, that there should be no more reckoning of time.

The right hand symbolizes the correct, right, righteous or productive purpose.

Heaven symbolizes Superconscious Mind. Therefore, when the angel raised his right hand to heaven, it indicates any individual who aligns his or her purpose in the conscious mind with superconscious mind. Such a one has a spiritual foundation balanced and grounded in both conscious and subconscious minds.

To live for ever and ever is to have eternal life. To live for ever and ever, to have eternal life, is to have a continuum of consciousness. To swear is to make a solemn statement under oath. To swear is to utter a solemn declaration with an appeal to God for the truth that is affirmed.

The reason for the angel swearing was so that there would be no more reckoning of time. How does one bring about no more reckoning of time? A still mind brings one into the present, the eternal now. In the now, there is no past or future, therefore no physical time. There is no physical time in Heaven which is Superconscious Mind. In Superconscious Mind there is only the eternal now and that is everything.

The seventh chakra, the crown chakra, works with and recycles superconscious mind energies from the first level of Mind and from I AM.

I AM exists in the eternal now. I AM is neither past nor future. If I AM was past it would be I WAS. If I AM was the future, we would say I WILL BE. I AM exists in the eternal now. The eternal now is for ever and ever with no more reckoning of physical time. Physical time is based upon temporariness. Superconsciousness is permanent, eternal and lasting.

**7 But in the days of the voice of the seventh angel,
when he shall begin to sound, the mystery of God
will be fulfilled, as he has proclaimed to his servants,
the prophets.**

The days of the voice of the seventh angel is the quickening of the
crown chakra. Those days begin when one can perceive the crown
chakra, not just visualize it but actually perceive it.

The first time I lit up all seven chakras, including the seventh or
crown chakra, I could see or perceive each chakra very clearly. Each
chakra I perceived was bright and luminescent. Each chakra had vi-
brant colors. That was when the mystery of God began to be fulfilled
in me. This process continues to this day. I am bringing my creatorship
out into physical existence. The quality of the crown chakra is creation.

God's servants are those aspects of Self that are in harmony with
and fulfill the Universal Laws and Universal Truths. Prophets are the
aspects of the Self that create the goal or ideal of enlightenment for the
Self.

**8 And the same voice which I had heard from
heaven spoke to me again, saying, Go and take the
little book which is open in the hand of the angel
which stands on the sea and on the land.**

The vibration of the crown chakra commands one to receive the
message to create.

The information and experience that one has gathered and received
from superconscious mind is to be used to connect the emotional or
sixth level of Mind consciously to the seventh level, the conscious mind.

The one who achieves this level of openness, discipline and service
has thought forms that move freely through the emotional level of Mind
to the seventh level of physical experience. This allows such a one to
manifest desires rapidly thereby learning from this process. A person
who has attained this stage of awareness is able to learn to be a creator
from the creations manifested in the life. One who has attained this
level of awareness and understanding knows how to build permanent
soul understandings from every experience.

**9 And I went to the angel, and as I was about to say
to him, Give me the little book, he said to me, Take it**

**and eat it; and it shall make your belly bitter, but it
shall be sweet as honey in your mouth. 10 So I took
the little book out of the hand of the angel, and ate it;
and it was sweet as honey in my mouth; but as soon
as I had eaten it, my belly was bitter.**

Information and experiences provide stimuli to the brain. At the
time they may seem to make one happy. Yet all physical experiences
are by their nature, temporary. Temporary experiences taste or seem
sweet and pleasant to the five senses. Yet, experience alone does not
give permanent and lasting fulfillment.

**It is in learning and building permanent understandings of Self
and creation that one finds and builds fulfillment.**

The belly is the site of much of the digestion of food. Food symbolizes knowledge. When one goes through experience but refuses to learn
from those experiences, then one stagnates just as food stagnates when
one is not processing and assimilating the nutrition. One then develops indigestion or an acid stomach which is unpleasant and painful.

In such a way one who craves for experience after experience but
refuses to learn the Universal Life lessons contained in the experiences
finds life to be painful, unfulfilling, and full of suffering. Sensory experience is always temporary. Attachment to sensory desires can give
temporary pleasure yet pain soon follows.

Honey is a whole food and is very nutritious. Yet, eating the little
book was not honey. It only seemed like honey. One at this point of
soul understanding is not yet able to fully assimilate superconscious
code. Temporary, sensory experiences can never give lasting happiness. Maya is a word from India used to indicate this illusion. Maya is
the illusion that the physical world is all there is and that our physical
world and circumstances are permanent and lasting. They are not permanent and lasting. Physical life is temporary.

As Gautama the Buddha said, *"Attachment to desires for temporary,
physical things is the source of pain and suffering."*

**11 Then he said to me, You must prophesy again
about many peoples and nations and the heads of
nations and kings.**

People symbolize aspects of Self. Nations are made up of many people symbolizing many aspects of Self. Heads of nations and kings symbolize the ruling qualities, aspects or ways of thinking in one's consciousness. All aspects of Self must be united into one, whole, functioning Self.

The reason the believer, symbolized by John, must prophesy again is because each individual must learn and be aware of who and what they can become. In this way one can image an ideal for Self that one can become. This is an ideal for Self of Christhood and enlightenment.

Summary of the Inner Meaning of Chapter 10 of the Book of Revelation
The mystery of God is the key of Creation. To eat the Little Book is to receive superconscious experience and awareness. One has yet to learn how to digest and assimilate superconscious experience.

Chapter 11 of Revelation

Few Word Essence of Chapter 11
of the Book of Revelation

Superconscious Awareness

Brief and More Expanded Essence of Chapter 11
of the Book of Revelation

The aggressive and receptive principles of Superconscious Mind are
received into the disciplined one's conscious awareness.

Chapter 11

New Symbols & The Interpretation of Chapter 11 of Revelation

1. rod - Universal Laws

2. temple - still mind mastery of time in Superconscious Mind

3. anoint - to make whole

4. outer court - conscious mind

5. the two candlesticks - the brow and crown chakras

6. two olive trees - the brow and crown chakras

7. plagues - pain and misery created from the doubt of attachment to desires

8. wild beast - brain habits stored as memory

9. the bottomless pit - unconsciousness

10. bodies - attachment to the past and past forms

11. Sodom - engrossment in sensory experience

12. Egypt - entrapment in a physical body

13. cloud - fully receiving and using experience

14. ark of the covenant - the dwelling place of I AM

Chapter 11

**1 And there was given to me a reed like a rod; and
the angel stood, saying, Arise and anoint the temple
of God and the altar and those who worship therein.**

A reed comes from plants and plants symbolize subconscious existence. A rod is used for walking. A rod is also used for measuring. You
must measure your soul progress. Since distance is a function of space
and space determines time, this verse concerns physical and mental
time. As the mind is stilled, one's consciousness becomes attuned to
superconscious mind. The one with a still mind is in the Temple of
God.

The Temple of God is the Mind, and the altar is one's capacity to
have attention in   superconscious mind and to receive
superconsciousness.

To anoint is to consecrate, usually by use of oil.

To consecrate is to make sacred with ceremonies.

To make sacred is to make whole or Holy.

To anoint the temple of God is to connect conscious, subconscious
and superconscious into a whole, unified mind.

**2 But leave out the outer court of the temple, and do
not anoint it; for it has been given to the Gentiles;
and they shall tread the holy city under foot for forty
and two months.**

The outer court of the temple is the conscious mind.

Gentiles symbolize those aspects of Self that think physically and
do not believe in the coming of Christ Consciousness. They indicate
anyone who has physical experiences without awareness of the High
Self.

The number 4 symbolizes stability. The number 40 symbolizes stability with the power that comes from understanding. Zero symbolizes power. Two symbolizes receptivity. The conscious mind will tread the superconscious mind under until stability with receptivity is achieved. This requires a disciplined, still and humble conscious mind.

An aggressive conscious mind can never attune to superconscious mind. A receptive conscious mind is necessary to attune to superconscious mind. This is why one must still the mind and meditate in order to gain the superconscious state.

Four plus two in the number 42 added together equals 6. The number 6 is the number of service. The greatest service, the greatest giving, is teaching. The greatest teaching is of the mind and Self.

You may experience the crown chakra. You may have a temporary or brief experience of Superconscious Mind. It will not become a full part of your consciousness until you become a world server, a world teacher.

> **3 Then I will give power to my two witnesses, and**
> **they shall prophesy a thousand and two hundred and**
> **three score days, clothed in sackcloth. 4 These are**
> **the two olive trees and the two candlesticks standing**
> **before the Lord of the earth.**

The two witnesses are the aggressive and receptive principles of creativity, the yin and yang referred to in Chinese Scientific Holy books. See my book, The Tao Te Ching, Interpreted and Explained. The two witnesses are also the two candlesticks which are the two churches of Revelation 1. These two churches are the brow and crown chakras. Therefore, the two witnesses function with the brow and crown chakras. This requires mastery of the Aggressive and Receptive Principles of Creation.

To prophesy is to have an image of one's next step and to act upon that ideal. A thousand, two hundred and three score days is 1,260 days. The number one in 1,000 symbolizes the aggressive quality of one of the witnesses. The number six symbolizes service. One must gain a balance of both the aggressive and receptive qualities of creation through service in order to know and attune to the first and second levels of Mind in Superconscious Mind. Then one may also consciously use the brow and crown chakras.

The two candlesticks standing before the throne are the brow and crown chakras. The two olive trees are the brow and crown chakras. Olive trees are sacred trees. Trees symbolize subconscious experience. Olives symbolize knowledge. From olives comes olive oil. Olive oil symbolizes wisdom. The one who consciously harmonizes with and uses the crown and brow chakras knows the Aggressive and Receptive Principles of Creation.

Clothing indicates one's outward expression. This indicates the Aggressive and Receptive Principles of Creation are manifesting into one's physical existence more fully. Sackcloth was often worn in times of mourning a death, indicating change is occurring in Self and one's mind.

The two witnesses also indicate the connection between the medulla oblongata and the pituitary gland, the third eye.

> **5 And if any man desires to harm them, fire will come out of their mouths and will consume their enemies; and if any man desires to harm them, he must in this manner be killed.**

To attempt to go against the aggressive and receptive principles, yang and yin, one experiences pain and suffering. The Buddha said, *"Attachment to desires is the cause of pain and suffering."*

To desire to harm the two witnesses is to experience the pain of attachment. Pain is an indication one needs to change. Fire that consumes indicates the expansion that produces a shift, a change in consciousness.

The mouth functions to receive food and to speak truth. The fire that came out of the two witnesses' mouths is the reception of truth that causes the expansion of consciousness. Anyone who desires to be enlightened and know superconscious mind must change and must expand consciousness. The mouth is also referring to the medulla oblongata that is located at the base of the brain. The medulla oblongata is the point of entry of life force into the physical body.

When the Kundalini is raised to the brain and moves from the medulla oblongata to the pituitary, the eternal oneness of all creation is experienced as cosmic or Christ consciousness.

> **6 These have power to control the sky, so that it will not rain in those days; and have power over waters to**

> **turn them into blood, and to smite the earth with all
> plagues, as often as they will.**

The sky symbolizes superconscious mind. One who lifts the Kundalini to the pituitary and pineal experiences heaven.

The words water and rain symbolize conscious life experience. Conscious life experience is the life we experience in the conscious, waking mind. Blood symbolizes truth and life force.

When the crown chakra is opened physical experiences fail to satisfy the Self. Instead one receives truth directly from superconscious mind.

Pain and suffering, as symbolized by the plagues, occurs if one resists living higher truth in the life.

The use of the will and will power is required to function from the mind. Deliberate conscious choices must be made in the conscious mind, otherwise, the individual is locked into the physical brain and operates from compulsion. Conscious choice, moment to moment, puts one in the mind. Then the conscious mind can receive the receptive and aggressive truth from superconscious mind.

> **7 And when they have finished their testimony, the
> wild beast which ascends out of the bottomless pit
> shall make war against them and shall overcome
> them.**

The wild beast is the compulsive brain. The bottomless pit is the unconscious part of the brain. This pit is bottomless because the physical brain will never get you out of unconsciousness. Only deliberate, conscious choice to think and do something different with discipline will get one out of unconsciousness.

The Buddha said, *"More than your mother, more than your father, more than all your family, a well-disciplined mind does greater good,"* **Dhammapada** 3:42-43. The Buddha is right. Buddha was right because a disciplined mind is necessary and required to get one out of unconsciousness.

This testimony is given by the two witnesses of verse 3 of this chapter. The word testimony from the Latin word testis which means, a witness. A testimony is a solemn declaration or affirmation made for the purpose of establishing or proving some fact. Therefore, the two witnesses from superconscious mind gave witness to the conscious mind. When the conscious mind gains more control due to its attunement to superconscious mind, the physical, animal brain fights to regain control. The physical, egoic brain and body resists being spiritualized by the High Self or superconscious mind.

For awhile it may appear as if the disciplined student's old, habitual, brain habits are winning out. Yet, if one persists, one will overcome the wild beast of one's habitual thoughts and their attendant emotions.

8 And their dead bodies shall be upon the street of the great city, which spiritually is called Sodom and Egypt, where also their Lord was crucified.

The two witnesses' dead bodies represent the change that must occur within the Self and the difficulty in accomplishing this. For awhile it seems as if the old habits and animal body are winning.

Sodom symbolizes engrossment in the five senses.

Egypt symbolizes entrapment in a physical body. You are a soul or subconscious mind entrapped in a physical body.

Their Lord, that is the two witnesses' Lord, is Jesus who became the Christ. The one who attains Christ consciousness has mastered and is Lord of the aggressive and receptive principles of Superconscious Mind. Crucifixion symbolizes the one who has overcome physical, horizontal time and physical matter and now knows mental or vertical time.

The one who gains Christ consciousness has mastered the physical body, senses, life and experience. Such a one exists in the eternal now.

9 And their dead bodies will be seen by the peoples and kindred and nations and tongues for three days and a half, and it will not be permitted to bury their dead bodies in graves.

Because of the higher truth received, the conscious mind has changed. Yet, the physicalized aspects of Self have not yet accepted this change. This movement in consciousness will need to progress through the four stages of growth of infancy, adolescence, adulthood and into wisdom. This is the meaning of three and a half days.

The qualities of the stage of growth known as infancy are: openness, absorption, curiosity, innocence, trust and love.

The qualities of the stage of growth known as adolescence are: experimentation, curiosity, questioning, action and independence.

The qualities of the stage of growth known as adulthood are: productivity, security, action and maturity.

The qualities of the stage of growth known as wisdom are: peace, longevity, objectivity and identity.

The reason it is not permitted to bury their dead bodies is because the conscious mind is becoming aware of the change that has taken place. This superconscious awareness will remain as a permanent change in the conscious mind as an expansion of consciousness. No longer will the Self aware student allow the lack of attention to drift into unconsciousness.

To bury the dead means to become unconscious of the changes you have made.

**10 And those who dwell upon the earth shall rejoice
over them and make merry, and shall send gifts one
to another, because these two prophets tormented
those who dwelt on the earth.**

Once a person grows in awareness there arise temptations to slip back into the old unconscious self. This must not be allowed. If you run away from your soul assignment, you may, at first, experience a temporary relief. This relief then turns to loneliness and inner sadness.

Sometimes discipline of any kind may seem a torment. Even physical exercise may seem hard. Emotional exercise may seem a challenge.

Mental discipline requires the greatest effort. It is this effort that may seem like torment, yet, discipline of the mind is the basis for freedom.

One can rejoice when one no longer is required to do physical exercise. Yet, this rejoicing is temporary for in the long run the physical exercise helps make one healthier. Mental discipline makes one more enlightened and more fulfilled permanently.

Sacrifice the short term results for the long term lasting and permanent gains.

**11 And after three days and a half the spirit of life
from God entered into them, and they stood upon
their feet; and great fear fell on those who saw them.**

This is the same 3 1/2 days Jesus spent in the tomb after the crucifixion.

The word spirit comes from the Latin word spiritus, which means
breath, and spirare, which means to breathe. The spirit of life from God
is the breath of awareness from the Creator. Every time you breathe
you receive life force into your physical body. Life force, which is the
physical manifestation of cosmic energy, comes from Superconscious
Mind. Life force is in everything and is needed for anything to be alive.
All enlightened beings have learned how to draw into themselves great
amounts of life force. This life force enables us to raise our awareness
and aids us to know Superconscious Mind. When enough
superconscious awareness has poured into one's waking consciousness,
then the spiritual foundation, symbolized by the feet, becomes firm and
strong. From that moment on the Self will never be able to deny the
true reality.

One admits the permanence and lastingness of the Real Inner Self.
One knows the Self to be more than a temporary physical body.
One realizes the true purpose of life.

**12 And they heard a great voice from heaven saying
to them, Come up here. And they went up to heaven
in a cloud; and their enemies saw them.**

The great voice from heaven is the Superconscious Mind. To come
up to heaven is to receive Superconscious awareness into the Self and
to enter more fully into this higher consciousness and Mind. To hear
the great voice one must achieve undivided attention and a still mind.

Water symbolizes conscious life experience. A cloud symbolizes
one's conscious life experience that is raising to a higher level of awareness. The symbolic meaning of the two witnesses who went up to
heaven is that the conscious mind and conscious awareness now are
aware and know they exist in a higher state of being. Now, there exists
a part of Self that functions from a Superconscious perspective each
waking day and with each experience.

**13 And at the same hour there was a great earthquake,
and the tenth part of the city fell, and the number of
men killed in the earthquake was seven thousand; and
the survivors were frightened, and they gave glory to
God.**

A great earthquake indicates a shake up in Mind. It shows one is moving consciousness in a way that will bring greater awareness and can bring greater understanding.

Ten, as in tenth, indicates the beginning of a new cycle. In this case there is still some attachment to the old cycle.

The city referred to is Babylon. Babylon symbolizes engrossment in the five senses. Engrossment is the meaning of those making merry and rejoicing over the death of the two witnesses.

Seven is the number symbolizing control. Seven thousand indicates that the power to wield the mind has been gained. The power to change and cause greater awareness has been achieved. This great change in awareness is the recognition of Self as creator.

**14 The second woe is passed; and behold, the third
woe comes quickly.**

The first woe is given in chapter 9 verse 12.

The first woe concerns the brain and its habitual way of thinking. These habits or brain pathways restrict and limit the Self.

The second woe presents the one who overcomes the limitations in the conscious mind.

Woe is an indication of grief, sorrow, misery. *"Misery, suffering and pain are caused by attachment to desire,"* said the Buddha. Jesus said it similarly when he said, *"No man can serve two masters either. One serves God or mammon."* Mammon is physical attachment to worldliness.

Attachment causes one to resist change. Yet, change is the nature of physical existence. Rather than practice attachment, instead surrender to the present moment and receive the present moment as it is.

The third woe in chapter 12 will present the conscious ego and how to overcome it.

**15 And the seventh angel sounded, and there were
great rumblings of thunders, saying, The kingdoms
of this world have become the kingdom of our Lord
and of his Christ; and he shall reign forever and ever.**

The seventh angel that sounded is the movement and outpouring of the crown chakra.

When awareness and power of the crown chakra is received in the conscious awareness, the physical, sensory life symbolized by the kingdoms of the world becomes transformed to an enlightened life. The enlightened life is presented as the Kingdom of our Lord and his Christ.

Since Superconscious Mind is beyond time and space, one who receives Superconsciousness exists, with awareness, for ever and ever. The crown chakra brings superconsciousness, Christ consciousness, and cosmic consciousness. The crown chakra brings great movement in all of Mind as indicated by great rumblings of thunders. Rumbling and thunders indicate the movement of the vibration of creation moving forward and following greater awareness.

16 And the four and twenty elders who sat before the throne of God on their seats fell upon their faces and worshipped God,

The 24 elders are comprised of the 12 major outer aspects in the conscious mind and the 12 major inner aspects in the subconscious mind.

When awareness of and outpouring of the crown chakra occurs, the conscious and subconscious divisions of mind identify a greater power, a greater authority. The conscious mind now serves the superconscious mind more and more instead of being self serving.

Faces symbolize one's identity. The phrase 'fell on their faces and worshipped God,' indicates one who identifies superconsciousness and is receiving it into the conscious awareness.

17 Saying, We give thanks to thee, O Lord God Almighty, who is and was, because thou hast taken to thyself thy great power and hast reigned.

Lord God Almighty is I AM. I AM was, I AM is, and I AM will be. Yet, I AM is always in the ever, eternal now.

The I AM reigns when the awareness in the conscious mind receives all of mind into the Self.

When all of the mind is stilled, aligned, and attuned, then can I AM make itself known and manifested to one existing in the world.

This verse offers mental pictures, an image of one who has gained experience of superconscious mind and yet still has much to receive and understand before the full enlightenment is fulfilled in the Self.

**18 And the nations were angry, and thy wrath has
come, and the time of the dead, that they should be
judged, and to reward thy servants, the prophets, and
the saints and those who revere thy name, small and
great; and to destroy those who corrupt the earth.**

Those aspects of Self that still were not fully understood and in alignment with Universal Law are angry. Anger is a violent, revengeful pas-
sion or emotion excited by a real or supposed injury to one's Self. Nations indicate many aspects of Self. Those aspects of Self that are built
around the false notions of separateness and non-change think something is being taken away when the Self evolves. At these times one
gets angry and tries to justify this anger. This anger is a signal, a sign
that one is approaching a time of judgement. This judgement or judg-
ing is a time of decision or choosing what is productive and what ways
of thinking are unproductive, what is lasting and real and what is temporary, what is of the Light and what is of the darkness. Anger indicates the need to discipline and still the mind while moving more and
more into the present moment.

The prophets are servants because setting goals and giving the mind
direction serves the Self by aiding one to move forward productively.
The saints also are servants because they are aspects that are completely
understood that are in alignment with Universal Law and Universal
Truth. The time in one's awareness has come to change and transform
those aspects of Self that are not productive.

**19 And the temple of God was opened in heaven,
and there was seen in his temple the ark of his
covenant; and there were lightnings and thunderings
and voices and an earthquake and a great hailstorm.**

When the Superconscious Mind is opened, then is perceived the
dwelling place of I AM.

The Ark of the Covenant is the dwelling place of the Lord who is I
AM. The Ark is the Holy of Holies. The still mind opens this temple.

To perceive Self as I AM changes everything about the way one sees
and views life, Self and all of Mind. New awarenesses occur as one's
whole consciousness shifts and moves. More powerful consciousness
moves rapidly into one's waking life experiences.

Summary of the Inner Meaning of Chapter 11 of the Book of Revelation
The two witnesses are the two candlesticks that are the two churches
known as the crown chakra and brow chakra. They function through
the Aggressive and Receptive Principles of Creation. The awareness
and understanding of Self as I AM is beginning to be known.

Chapter 12 of Revelation

Few Word Essence of Chapter 12
of the Book of Revelation

The birth of enlightenment

Brief and More Expanded Essence of Chapter 12
of the Book of Revelation

The dragon-ego is the adversary. The dragon-ego attempts
to stop the disciplined, conscious mind from bringing
forth the full Christ Consciousness.

Chapter 12

New Symbols & The Interpretation of Chapter 12 of Revelation

1. woman - conscious mind

2. moon - subconscious awareness

3. child - new idea

4. born - birth of a new idea

5. all nations - all aspects of Self

6. wilderness - part of mind that is yet to be tamed

7. Michael-archangel - superconscious thought form from I AM

8. serpent - conscious ego in infancy

9. devil - conscious ego in adolescence

10. satan - conscious ego in adulthood

11. dragon - conscious ego in old age, the conscious ego that overtly opposes the disciplined conscious mind

12. Christ - Christ consciousness, enlightenment

13. wings - the ability to produce forward motion in the life and consciousness

14. great sign in the sky - the Divine Plan of Creation in Superconscious Mind

Chapter 12

1 And a great sign was seen in heaven, a woman clothed with the sun, with the moon under her feet and upon her head a crown of twelve stars;

This verse indicates the one who has received conscious, subconscious, and superconscious awareness. The crown of 12 stars on her head indicates such a one has received awareness of all 12 major aspects of Self.

The woman-conscious mind whose outer consciousness receives and expresses superconscious awareness has mastery of the subconscious mind and the 12 major aspects of Self.

A crown symbolizes authority. Authority means one is the author of one's life. To be the author of one's life is to be the creator of one's life awareness and enlightenment.

The great sign in the sky is awareness of the Plan of Creation held in Superconscious Mind. The one who has disciplined the conscious mind through concentration, meditation and conscious breath has achieved the still conscious mind that is able to receive the Divine and Perfect Plan of Creation held in Superconscious Mind. Superconscious radiance appears in such a one while the conscious mind has as its foundation all the permanent understandings stored in subconscious mind, the soul.

2 And she being with child cried, travailing in birth, and pained to be delivered.

The conscious mind, while receiving superconscious awareness, births the new idea of full Christ Consciousness. The conscious mind, being very disciplined from the practice, application and teaching of concentration and meditation, achieves a more still conscious mind. Such a one identifies more and more with the true reality, the interconnectedness of all beings and all creation and the eternal nature of the Real Self. This new idea is foreign to the conscious mind. The conscious mind and physical brain have been trained to view life only through the information and experiences received through the five senses. The senses give the illusion that physical life is both discon- nected and permanent. This is incorrect. The true nature of reality is connectedness in a permanent stream of consciousness. This verse ful- fills Genesis 3:16, *"To the woman the Lord God said, 'I will greatly multiply your pain and your conception; in pain you will bring forth children, and you shall be dependent on your husband, and he shall rule over you.'"* The pain occurs due to attachment to desires and attachment to the past.

> **3 And there appeared another sign in heaven; and behold, there was a great fiery dragon, having seven heads and ten horns, and seven crowns upon his heads.**

The second sign in heaven is of a great dragon. The dragon sym- bolizes the conscious ego that has grown strong and powerful because, from mental discipline, the conscious mind has grown powerful. The superconscious mind-sky perception enables the disciplined student with a still mind the ability to more clearly perceive the conscious ego- dragon as the adversary to further enlightenment.

The seven heads symbolize the way in which the identity of the individual must move through the seven levels of Mind. The Self must master the ego on all seven levels of Mind.

The ten horns symbolize ten chakras. One chakra for each of the seven levels of Mind plus the ego, I AM, and LIGHT chakras.

The seven crowns upon the dragon's heads indicate the need to master one's authority and identity in each level of Mind and with each chakra.

> **4 And his tail cut off a third of the stars of heaven and cast them to the earth; and the dragon stood before the woman who was ready to be delivered, so as to devour her child as soon as it was born.**

The third of the stars in heaven is the awareness in the conscious mind. The conscious mind is one of three divisions of Mind. The ego reacts to this great, new superconscious awareness within the Self. The conscious ego which has heretofore manipulated and controlled the person subtly and cunningly finds its control lessening. Satan, the conscious ego, is the great deceiver and the Father of Lies. The primary or main weapon of the conscious ego-Satan is the power to deceive. When the conscious mind is disciplined and stilled so that the individual knows all thoughts, then deception and subtle lies no longer work to control.

Therefore, the conscious ego-Satan now becomes the direct, forceful dragon that tries to overpower the idea in the conscious mind that you can become a Christ. The ego, desperate for control at all costs, now rears its head trying to destroy the new idea and experience of higher consciousness. The ego must be faced, identified and conquered. Otherwise it will continue to rule one's life while deceiving, destroying and limiting the achievement of one's full potential.

The mind must be disciplined in order to still the thoughts. To whatever degree the conscious mind is undisciplined the conscious ego will interject subtle thoughts into the brain and conscious mind to keep the Self engrossed and entrapped in physical existence. The ego is afraid but pretends strength and logic. The ego is cunning but it is not reasonable. The more one develops the higher reasoning, the more one can see through the childish, yet powerful, controlling games of the ego. The dishonest ego will attempt to blame others for one's problems. The disciplined, honest conscious mind in alignment with Universal Law and Truth will accept full responsibility for Self as the cause of one's life as it is. The conscious ego's duty is to motivate the brain. However, this motivation is strictly physical. To develop the motivation to achieve the Divine Plan, purpose is needed. The conscious ego resists this higher motivation because it does not know subconscious and superconscious mind. The conscious ego only knows that which is temporary. Christ consciousness is permanent and lasting.

> **5 And she brought forth a male child, who was to shepherd all the nations with a rod of iron; and her child was caught up to God, and to his throne.**

This male child factor is the birth of the Christ child within us. Jesus, who became the Christ, was the offspring of the Holy Spirit and the Virgin Mary. The male indicates the aggressive factor of creation, the ability to create forward motion in the life, the ability to act and to give.

The Holy Spirit is the whole mind and the Holy breath or life force that enters into the physical body through the medulla oblongata.

The Virgin Mary is the still conscious mind, that is because of the stillness, capable of consciously choosing receptivity. Only the disciplined and still conscious mind is capable of receiving superconscious awareness.

The rod of iron symbolizes Universal Law. To shepherd all the nations means this birth of the new awareness of High consciousness will align with Universal Law.

The birth of the new awareness of Christ Consciousness, the male child, now begins to integrate itself into one's consciousness. This new idea is destined to shepherd all the nations which means the outcome will be that anyone who achieves this birth will gain mastery of all aspects of Self.

> **6 And the woman fled into the wilderness, where she had a place prepared by God, that they should feed her there a thousand and two hundred and three score days.**

The child is caught up to God in heaven while the woman-conscious mind goes to the wilderness to develop a more peaceful, still mind. In the book of Matthew chapter 4, verse 1, Jesus was carried away by the Holy Spirit into the wildernes to be tempted by the devil. Now, in Revelation, this woman fled into the wilderness while the child is caught up to God.

The wilderness symbolizes that part of mind that is still wild and untamed. Being wild there is need for more discipline in the conscious mind. The mind is not yet fully stilled and able to receive I AM. This still mind and mastery of discipline will be necessary to prepare for the coming of the mature, male, Christ child as the full Christ consciousness.

Food symbolizes knowledge. The number 1,260 adds together or digits down to a 9. Thus, $1 + 2 + 6 + 0 = 9$. The number nine symbolizes completion of a level of growth in consciousness. The meaning is that one who has achieved such a level of awareness will need to receive much more knowledge of Self through experience. This is possible because of a developed, still mind. This still mind is the key to defeat the conscious ego and live the higher truth. The number 60 indicates a great deal of service is necessary to master the conscious ego.

> **7 And there was war in heaven. Michael and his angels fought against the dragon; and the dragon and his angels fought 8 But did not prevail, neither was their place found any longer in heaven.**

Michael is an archangel. An archangel is a leader of angels and has the highest rank. The superconscious awareness has brought to the Self greater awareness and experience of I AM. Michael and his angels symbolize the thought forms and awareness above the Dome. Above the Dome of Mind is located Superconscious Mind, I AM, and LIGHT.

This superconscious awareness proves invaluable in recognizing the cunning and subtle machinations of the conscious ego, the dragon. This higher awareness enables such a one to gain a foothold in heaven. Such a one can now recognize the conscious ego when it arises. Therefore, one may still continue to battle one's egoic reactions. Yet it is a winnable battle, for now one can see, recognize and perceive one's opponent.

After I had raised the Kundalini through all the Chakras, including my crown chakra, and had learned to still my mind, only then was I able and capable of fully perceiving and being aware of the conscious ego. Before I used to think it was <u>my</u> conscious ego. Now I know the conscious ego is not mine at all, I do not possess it. Now, I know that it is <u>the</u> conscious ego.

> **9 Thus the great dragon was cast out, that old serpent, the ancient one, called the Devil and Satan, who deceives the whole world; he was cast out on the earth, and his angels were cast out with him.**

That old serpent, called the Devil or Satan is the conscious ego. The devil, Satan, the conscious ego deceives you. The conscious ego will deceive you until you achieve a STILL MIND. Only then will you see the subtle, cunning, animalistic thoughts that lie below most peoples' level of awareness. Only then will you be able to sort out your houghts from the conscious ego's thoughts. Then it will no longer be <u>your</u> conscious ego, it will be <u>the</u> conscious ego.

> Serpent - conscious ego in infancy
> Devil - conscious ego in adolescence
> Satan - conscious ego in adulthood
> Dragon - conscious ego in old age

Genesis 3:1, *"Now the serpent was more subtle than all the wild beasts that the Lord God has made."* This means that as long as you have an undisciplined mind, the animal body, the brain and the serpent-conscious ego will control you. This is because the serpent-ego is more subtle and cunning than any brain and physical, wild, beast body. Wild beasts symbolize your brain and physical body.

1. The number one subtle and "cunning" tool, technique or trick the ego uses to deceive a person is subtle, repetitive thoughts.

2. The number two technique the Devil-conscious ego uses is to place what <u>sounds like</u> reasonable or right thoughts in your head. However if you will practice saying all your thoughts out loud you will find some thoughts to be unreasonable or dishonest or even childish. Some of these thoughts when heard out loud sound like a scared, little child. These seemingly reasonable or right thoughts, when heard and seen in the Light of day do not align with Universal Law, Universal Truth and the true nature of reality which is connectedness.

3. When the number one and two techniques do not work the Satan-conscious ego tries offering worldly power and control to distract one from the real, permanent purpose of Life.

4. The conscious ego being encountered in this chapter of Revelation has now matured into stage 4 — the Dragon. The stage 4 ego-Dragon tries lashing out and destroying one's opportunities for Christ consciousness. To do this it applies fear, anger, rage, hatred and other negative thoughts and emotions.

An individual reaches this chapter of Revelation in the Self because of mental discipline and the commitment to Know the Self. From this comes the still mind, which enables one to see the subtle and cunning thoughts and ways of Satan-devil-conscious ego.

Then in a last ditch effort the conscious ego-serpent-devil-Satan becomes the Dragon in an attempt to reassert control. Yet the disciplined one committed to Christ Consciousness and I AM will quickly or gradually prevail. The cunning serpent of Genesis 3 became the tempting devil and adversarial Satan of Matthew 4. In Revelation 12 the conscious ego has matured into the destroying dragon.

**10 And I heard a loud voice in heaven saying, Now,
from this moment on, the deliverance and the power
and the kingdom of our God and the power of his
Christ have been accomplished; for the accuser of our
brethren, who accused them before God day and
night, is cast down.**

The loud voice in Heaven is the same voice from superconscious
mind that one hears or receives in deep meditation. It is the creative
word of John 1:1, *"The Word was in the beginning, and that very Word was
with God, and God was that Word."* One must practice regular, daily,
consistent meditation and concentration every day until the mind is
still and the thoughts are quieted. Only then can one receive and hear
the voice of one's High Self coming from superconscious mind.

When this high level of stillness is achieved then not only can one
receive from superconscious mind consciously, then one can also hear
the subtle, habitual, ego thoughts. Then and only then can one truly
choose. For without awareness, one cannot consciously choose. You
cannot choose that which you are not aware of. Awareness leads to
greater options and choices.

The accuser of our brethren is the conscious ego-devil. The conscious ego tries to find fault with every aspect of Self and everyone in
one's environment.

**Anyone who is able to cast down their conscious ego-Dragon by
achieving a still mind has begun to feel the power of Christ consciousness.**

**11 And they have conquered him by the blood of the
Lamb and by the word of their testimony; and they
did not spare themselves even to death.**

Michael and his angelic thought forms from superconscious mind
conquered the Dragon-ego by truth, will, love and mental discipline.

Blood symbolizes truth and life force. The blood of the Lamb is the
one who receives, follows and lives the commitment to Universal Truth
in the life. The conscious ego-Satan- serpent is a liar. Overcoming the
conscious ego requires Truth and life force.

The word of the archangel Michael's testimony comes from
superconscious mind. The testimony of Michael relates what has oc-

curred and what has been witnessed in superconscious mind. The word is the creative vibration of AUM manifesting through all levels of Mind in order to bring one into attunement to Superconscious Mind. Superconsciousness is required to overcome the conscious ego and a still mind is required to receive superconsciousness.   Michael and his angels symbolize the reception of superconsciousness into the waking life while still in the physical body.

> 12 **Therefore rejoice, O heavens and you who dwell in them. Woe to the inhabitants of the earth and of the sea! For the <u>Devil</u> is down there with you now; and is full of trememdous anger, because he knows that his time is short.**

Heaven, which is superconscious mind, rejoices and is fulfilled when a disciplined individual develops the still mind, receives superconscious awareness and thereby defeats the couscous ego by being able to perceive and know the conscious ego.

The inhabitants of the earth and sea are the conscious mind and conscious life experience. The conscious ego-devil was cast down to earth and sea which means that this conscious mind must face and overcome many more challenges in order to completely free the Self of the controlling conscious ego. Then the conscious ego-devil will be replaced by I AM, one's true identity.

Now, however, Satan-the conscious ego can no longer hide. The conscious ego shows itself as the Dragon. Gone is the conscious ego's cunning and subtlety. Now the disciplined mind knows what it is facing. The conscious mind will no longer be tricked and fooled. Now the enemy is clearly seen and can be fought in the open field. Now the conscious ego can be directly engaged in the battle for supremacy of one's own mind-thoughts and consciousness! Once the disciplined student of the mind gains the ability to see, perceive and identify the conscious ego and its manipulations there is little time left for the ego.

> 13 **And when the dragon saw that he was cast down to the earth, he pursued the woman who had given birth to a son.**

The exposed conscious ego, symbolized by the dragon, seeing that cunning manipulation no longer succeeds against a disciplined conscious mind, now decides to attack overtly and directly the productive aspect of the conscious mind. This is the part of the conscious mind that can now imagine Christ consciousness in the Self. The conscious mind now images and thinks thoughts of Self becoming enlightened. This enlightened awareness, this enlightened thought-image is becoming more and more one's waking consciousness. As you think, so you become. This statement is based upon the Universal Truth stated thusly, "As above, so below," or thoughts are things. "Therefore, image yourself as becoming a Christ."

The conscious ego is not able to destroy the new idea of enlightenment symbolized by the son born to the woman. Neither is the conscious ego able to destroy the conscious awareness and understanding that birthed this idea of Self enlightenment.

> **14 And to the woman were given two wings of a great eagle, that she might fly from the presence of the serpent to the wilderness, into her place, where she would be nourished for years and months and days.**

The conscious ego is not able to destroy the new idea in the conscious mind because the conscious mind has been disciplined. This disciplined mind has developed into a still mind. The still mind has then reached to heaven and received superconscious mind.

Wings symbolize one's ability to produce forward motion in one's life and consciousness. Wings indicate the ability to rise above physical thinking and engrossed consciousness and instead receive ideas and insights from higher levels of Mind. Now the Self is capable of being nourished, which is to receive from the Subconscious and Superconscious divisions of Mind.

Three and one half years symbolizes the cycle of change. The first cycle is infancy, the second is adolescence, the third is adulthood and the fourth is wisdom. The one who is progressing rapidly needs to assimilate the previous learning in order to complete the fourth stage of growth called wisdom. Three and one half years equals 42 months, $4 + 2 = 6$. The number six indicates service.

> **15 Then the serpent sent a flood of water out of his mouth after the woman, so that he might cause her to be swept away by the flood.**

The serpent-conscious ego of such a one believes it can regain control of the conscious mind. This is symbolized by the flood of water. Water being conscious life experience. The egoic person can react and say angry thoughts aloud. The egoic brain can become extreme in the way it reacts in the waking, conscious life experience. Yet the one who retains a disciplined conscious mind is able once more to thwart the dishonest, subtle or forceful conscious ego.

16 But the earth helped the woman, and the earth
opened its mouth and swallowed up the water which
the dragon had spouted out of his mouth.

The subconscious mind, symbolized by the earth, comes to the aid of the conscious mind. This occurs because the conscious mind is disciplined. This discipline aligns the conscious and subconscious minds. Therefore, the subconscious mind absorbs or swallows the experiences in the conscious mind enabling the assimilation of the essence of the learning.

The ego-dragon spouted water out of its mouth and the earth opened its mouth to receive the water. This completes a cycle of learning. This is the in breath and the out breath of God, Brahman. The disciplined one who has aligned conscious and subconscious minds is able to choose thoughts and where to place the attention. Therefore, such a one is not overcome by engrossment in the sensory experiences. Instead, the conscious mind is disciplined moment to moment.

17 And the dragon was enraged at the woman, and
he went to make war with the rest of her children,
who keep the commandments of God and have the
testimony of Jesus.

The conscious ego has still not been destroyed or completely defeated. Yet now the disciplined one realizes he can recognize the cunning, subtle, ego thoughts that arise in consciousness.

Anyone who escapes the ego-dragon's snare can overcome egoic temptations and live in harmony with Universal Law and Truth. Therefore, the ego withdraws to see if it can control, influence or affect other aspects or new productive ideas of Self. The ego attempts to directly attack aspects of Self that are in alignment with Universal Law and

Truth because these are the aspects of Self that cannot be controlled subtly.

The conscious ego is a cunning deceiver. The more the mind is disciplined to live in harmony with Universal Law, the less power or control the ego-dragon has over the conscious mind. Genesis 3:13-16, "*13 And the Lord God said to the woman, What is this that you have done? And the woman said, The serpent beguiled me, and I did eat. 14 And the Lord God said to the serpent, Because you have done this thing cursed are you above all beasts of the field; on your belly shall you go, and dust shall you eat all the days of your life; 15 And I will put enmity between you and the woman, and between your posterity and her posterity; her posterity shall tread your head under foot, and you shall strike him in his heel. 16 To the woman he said, I will greatly multiply your pain and your conception; in pain you shall bring forth children, and you shall be dependent on your husband, and he shall rule over you.*"

What was begun in Genesis between the woman-conscious mind, and the serpent-conscious ego find its culmination in the Book of Revelation.

The conscious mind must grow in strength, understanding and awareness so it can defeat and overcome the conscious ego-dragon. The birth of the Christ within will overcome the Serpent-Devil-Satan-Dragon.

Summary of the Inner Meaning of Chapter 12 of the Book of Revelation
The conscious mind is aligned with subconscious mind and both are attuned to superconscious mind. This produces the Christ child within the Self. The Christ child within is the new idea of the Christed Self, the Christ Consciousness.

Chapter 13 of Revelation

Few Word Essence of Chapter 13
of the Book of Revelation

The brain, memory, imagination and reasoning

Brief and More Expanded Essence of Chapter 13
of the Book of Revelation

The limitations of brain-memory-habits and
brain-fantasy-imagination must be overcome and transformed.

Chapter 13

New Symbols & The Interpretation of Chapter 13 of Revelation

1. wild beast - habitual memory

2. horns - chakras

3. war - mental conflict

4. saints - aspects that are fulfilling the Divine Plan

5. book of life - the Plan of Creation

6. another, the second beast - habitual brain fantasy, imagination

7. mark of the beast - misuse of memory and imagination on purpose

Chapter 13

1 And as I stood on the sand of the shore, I saw a wild beast rise up out of the sea, having ten horns and seven heads, and upon his horns ten crowns, and upon his heads blasphemous words.

The sand of the shore symbolizes the emotional or 6th level of Mind. The shore is a place where water and earth come together. Water symbolizes the conscious life experience. Earth symbolizes subconscious mind substance.

The wild beast symbolizes the unproductive arising of memories in the brain. A beast is an animal. Animals symbolize brain pathways, habits or compulsions. The sea symbolizes physical, conscious, day to day life experiences. These brain pathways or habits arise then in the conscious mind or conscious life experience. The way to use brain memories productively is to draw them forth consciously. Brain memories that arise in a seemingly spontaneous manner are usually being employed by the conscious ego-Satan-Serpent-Devil. Therefore, consciously and deliberately choose your thoughts.

The ten horns symbolize 10 chakras. The seven heads symbolize one's identity in seven levels of mind. Ten crowns indicate the authority or directive ability of memory.

Blasphemous words are expressed thoughts that run counter to the true nature of reality. The true nature of reality is connectedness. Blasphemous is blame. Blame is wrong thinking because one who blames believes Self to be separate from everything and everyone else. Admitting Self as cause of one's life is living the true reality. Blaming others and acting the victim is disconnectedness or separateness.

Because of this, blasphemy or blame is, in effect, denying your purpose in life. Your purpose will always relate to greater connectedness.

> **2 And the wild beast which I saw was like a leopard,**
> **and his feet were like the feet of a bear, and his**
> **mouth like the mouth of a lion; and the dragon gave**
> **him his power and his throne and great authority.**

People who have a lot of information stored in their brain some-times speak like they know a lot about everything. When in fact, they know little about Subconscious mind, Superconscious Mind or I AM from direct experience.

Leopards, bears, and tigers are all animals. Animals symbolize habits and compulsions. Leopards have motion yet this motion is habitual. A bear can stand on its hind feet like a human Yet it is not human. Some habits may appear to be like a reasoner or human but they are not. They lack higher purpose. Habits are of the animal brain. A lion roars. Egoic reactions relying on the animal brain may sound fierce and ex-press loudly like a lion. Yet, they are of the animal brain.

The conscious ego can use habits, compulsions and repetitive un-conscious ways of thinking to try to control. It is a false sense of power. It is the dragon giving power to the first beast. A big fat ego and a lot of memorized skills and information may appear to have authority and control. However, it is a facade. It is all compulsion. Very little free choice or conscious choice is involved.

> **3 And one of his heads was as though mortally**
> **wounded; but his deadly wound was healed; and all**
> **the world wondered about the wild beast.**

The head symbolizes identity. One of the beast's heads appeared mortally wounded because the evolved and disciplined soul is gaining control of his mind and thereby changing his identity. This deadly wound to the ego-Dragon was caused by conscious choice in the con-scious mind. The disciplined, awake being overrides compulsion and habits by the still mind.

The wound was healed because the conscious ego has decided to draw forth old memories in new ways to distract and control the in-dividual. Each lifetime the personality is formed around these tem-porary habitual thought memories. Whereas true individuality is formed around what is permanent and lasting.

All the world represents the aspects in the physical life. The individual wonders because it appears that these old memory thoughts have great importance and value in the life, particularly for healing. What appears to have value can attract and distract the conscious mind.

> **4 And they worshipped the dragon because he had given power to the wild beast, saying, Who can prevail against him to fight against him?**

The conscious ego reasserts a degree of control in the life of the one attempting to become enlightened. This is accomplished by the conscious ego getting one enmeshed in old memory images of pleasure, pain, control, power or sensory delight. At this point it seems as if old memories are controlling Self. Fortunately, by the time you have reached this point in your soul growth and spiritual development you are able to choose your thoughts.

The difficulty arises because this old, memory, thought beast that the conscious-ego dragon causes to arise in the brain is so tempting. These experiences were pleasurable in the past and these memories seem pleasurable in the present. It is this pleasure, this temptation that is worshipped because it is the focus of one's attention. For this very reason it is difficult to defeat the conscious ego and the brain memories together. The conscious ego-dragon cunningly uses the brain memories around which one's personality is built.

> **5 And there was given to him a mouth, that he might utter boastful things and blasphemies; and power was given to him to make war for forty and two months.**

Forty two months equals three and one half years. Three and one half years or 42 months is the length of time the woman was nourished in the wilderness as given in the previous chapter, verse 14. Since the dragon-ego cannot defeat the conscious mind-woman that has birthed the Christ consciousness, the ego-dragon went to make war on the rest of the woman's children as given in the last verse of chapter 12. The ego-dragon uses brain memory to try to control and deceive aspects of Self.

The mouth is the tool or vehicle for experiencing or speaking thoughts. The conscious ego at this point is misusing memories to make the conscious mind think that the old ways are good and enticing. These old brain images make you long for the good old days. Yet, this is a lie, for the good old days weren't as good as the present. The good old days do not even exist anymore. To try to live in the past is to live in memories. To live in memories is not to live at all. It is slow death and slow change.

Four is the number of stability. Two is the number of duality or the aggressive and receptive. Add four and two together and the total is six. Six is the number of service. Service to others through teaching of mind, Self and mental discipline is necessary to come to understand how to defeat one's conscious ego and tempting brain memories. The beast makes war on the conscious mind until one becomes more stable in the use of the Aggressive and Receptive Principles of Creation.

To receive higher awareness and understanding, one must first give fully of what one has learned and received. The highest form of teaching is of the Mind and Self. This is the greatest service to Self and others.

The sooner you decide to dedicate your life to enlightenment for yourself and others, the sooner you will master the brain and the ego.

> **6 And he opened his mouth in blasphemy against
> God, to blaspheme his name and his dwelling place
> and those who dwell in heaven.**

The mouth of the reasoner is to be used properly to receive food as nourishment for the body. The mouth is also to be used to speak truth.

Truth can only be spoken to the degree one has gained or received truth.

The first beast is the conscious ego's attempt to distract by using memories in the brain. This can only work while the woman is in the wilderness being nourished for 42 months.

Blame is a shortened form of the word blaspheme. To blame or blaspheme is to think and say that the cause for your life is outside of yourself. To blame someone else for you life and circumstances is to refuse to admit the power of the present moment and the power of your own thoughts.

True power resides in the present moment. All creation occurs in the present moment. The still mind causes one to value and know the present moment.

The only good use for memory is to draw forth brain images or

memories of the past that can and will be used effectively in the present.

The only good and productive use of imagination to give the mind direction is the present so that one can use the present more productively.

To allow memory images to arise somewhat spontaneously rarely gives one the productive use of the mind in the present. Without a use for the imaginings in the now, the present, one is merely day dreaming.

To blaspheme is to speak injurious words. Since one cannot injure God, to blaspheme against God is to refuse to admit and practice one's creative ability. It is to destroy instead of create. It is to wrongly think the physical world is all there is. The conscious ego does not know the eternal. The conscious ego-dragon only values what is temporary and therefore, gives a distorted perception to the individual who is entrapped in a physical body.

The misuse of memory brings one to the point of thinking he or she is alone and separate. This is what gives the first beast, the wild beast, power. The conscious ego is able to misuse these old memories to keep one engrossed in partial memories of the past and physical thinking.

> 7 And power was given to him over every tribe and
> kindred and tongue and nation, and it was given to
> him to make war with the saints and to overcome
> them.

When a concerted effort of mental discipline is initiated and sustained through concentration and meditation, the cunning ego-Satan tries to use decoys. It seems for a while as if the conscious ego will triumph by misusing memory and old brain images.

In the quest for enlightenment one becomes more aware. In becoming more aware of everything one becomes more aware of brain memories. It is this heightened awareness of brain memories that the conscious ego misuses to try to restrict, distract and maintain control. This is the secret meaning of the connection between the dragon and this wild beast. This wild beast is the first wild beat for there is another beast yet to come.

In the quest for enlightenment one can become fascinated, engrossed or caught up in memory fantasies. However, the one with the disciplined, still mind, the one with commitment and purpose will prevail.

8 And all who dwell upon the earth shall worship him, even those whose names are not written in the book of life of the Lamb slain from the foundation of the world.

To worship is to give attention. Whatever you give most of your attention to is what you worship. You worship that which you deem has worth. Your attention is drawn to what you deem has value. The first part of the word worship is related to the word worth.

When memory becomes so important to you that you give an inordinate amount of attention to it then you are worshiping memory, which is the first beast.

As one progresses in the quickening of enlightenment the brain is literally lit up. This is because one is becoming more enlightened. When the brain is lit up memories then become more available. The dragon-conscious ego attempts to misuse this new found ability.

The Book of Life is a record in Superconscious Mind of one's progress in fulfilling the Divine or Perfect plan of Creation. The foundation of the world is given in Genesis, chapter one, the first book of the **Bible**. The Lamb was slain at the foundation of the world indicating one must continually change and upgrade one's consciousness and commitment to the High Self and enlightenment. One must build one's spiritual or mind foundation in order to change, grow and expand one's consciousness. The Lamb slain at the foundation of the world occurred when God said, "Let there be LIGHT." This is the first separation from our Creator. This was the first change and death symbolizes change.

9 If any man has ears, let him hear.

To hear one must be quiet and listen. To be quiet and listen one must have a still mind. To have a still mind one must have a disciplined mind. To have ears indicates one who has grown or developed the ability to receive mentally, that is, with the mind. To receive this understanding of the wild beast, the first beast, one must practice a disciplined and still mind.

The disciplined mind grows the mental ears.
The still mind develops the mental hearing.

10 He who leads into captivity shall go into captivity; he

**who kills with the sword must be killed with the sword.
Here is the patience and the faith of the saints.**

Captivity is restriction and loss of the ability to choose. The greatest captivity is our own entrapment. To lead into captivity is to choose to dwell in the old, brain memories. Dwelling in brain memories is restrictive because one can only create in the present. The past no longer exists and memories are of the past.

The sword symbolizes a tool for change. If you want change do not destroy. Destroy just to change is not the way of the reasoner nor an enlightened being. A reasoner changes by creating. The hallmark of reasoning as an adult thinker is to add to what is already present. It is to produce more that you consume.

Saints symbolize those aspects that are completely understood and in alignment with becoming a Christ. The patience of the saints is one who continues creating and producing in the present moment. The faith of the saints is to imagine enlightenment and to work toward it in the present moment.

> **11 And I beheld another wild beast coming up out of
> the earth; and he had two horns like a lamb, and he
> spoke as a dragon.**

Another wild beast is the second beast. The first wild beast rose up out of the sea while the second wild beast came up out of the earth. The sea symbolizes conscious life experience. The earth symbolizes subconscious mind substance.

The two horns like a lamb are the brow and crown chakras.

The second beast symbolizes the habitual misuse of imagination. Imagination, this image making ability, must be employed in order to activate the brow and crown chakras more fully. The productive use of the imagination comes about after one has learned to discipline the mind.

The first beast symbolizes the misuse, unproductive or incorrect use of memory. This incorrect use or misuse of memory keeps one locked up in the past. The past no longer exists.

The misuse of imagination is to fantasize. Fantasy keeps one's attention out of the present moment. The present moment is the time and place to know I AM. I AM exists in the now, the present moment. The second beast misuses imagination thereby engrossing one in fantasy.

The more powerful use of the imagination gives more power to the conscious ego, symbolized by the dragon. Egoic thoughts at first blush seem reasonable. Yet on further examination are found to be excuses that are not in alignment with Universal Law. The conscious ego will use or misuse imagination to attain physical results. However, the highest use of imagination is for enlightenment. Commitment to the whole Self as symbolized by the Lamb must be maintained and built in order to overcome the ego-dragon, the brain memory and brain-fantasy-imagination. The mind when properly engaged by the disciplined will can use memory and attention correctly while the brain by itself cannot.

> **12 And all the power of the first wild beast before**
> **him was exercised by him, and he caused the earth**
> **and those who dwell therein to worship the first**
> **beast, whose deadly wound was healed.**

Imagination can be misused. The egoic person can take memory thoughts in the brain and imagine or fantasize about how the past could have been different, or selfish experiences that may or may not ever arrive. We can ask, "What if, the past had been different!" The past is not different. This is a misuse of both the memory and imagination by the conscious ego. To worship the first beast is to allow the conscious ego-the dragon to motivate you to live in habitual memories and fantasies.

The only productive use of memory is to apply it in the present moment to create and learn the principles of creation from the creation.

The only productive use for memory is to be productive in the present moment.

The only productive use of imagination is to be productive in the present moment. Whatever you give your attention to, that is what you worship.

> **13 And he performed great wonders, to such an**
> **extent that he could even make fire come down from**
> **heaven on the earth in the sight of men,**

This second beast looks and seems like commitment to the ideal of becoming a Christ, but it is really just brain imagination-fantasy.

Fire symbolizes expansion of consciousness.

The use of the imagination enable one's thoughts to manifest in one's life. This is the method by which goals, ideals, desires and dreams are manifested in one's life. A directed image making ability focused towards goals enables the physically minded person to achieve a physical objective or goal.

Through the power of the directed mind one can achieve riches, fame and accumulate physical objects. This feeds the conscious ego and may impress the brain and conscious mind. Yet, it is all temporary. The one determined to know the whole Self will still the mind and thus perceive beyond the temporary to embrace permanent and lasting soul growth.

14 Beguiling those who dwell on the earth to make an image-statue to the wild beast who was wounded by the sword and yet lived. 15 And he had power to breathe life into the image-statue of the wild beast, and to cause all those who would not worship the image-statue of the wild beast to be killed.

In Genesis 3:13, the woman said, *"The serpent beguiled me, and I did eat."* The serpent is still beguiling in Revelation.

One who is beguiled is deceived or fooled. All aspects of Self that are undisciplined and engrossed in physical, sensory experience can be deceived. The undisciplined mind thinks it is making decisions when in fact, it is the conscious ego misusing brain memories that is directing the person.

The ego, after misusing memory to cause one to be engrossed, now resorts to the misuse of the imagination. One can get lost in the imagination, or fantasy, for years or a whole lifetime. Imagination is used correctly when used as a part of the creation process. Imagination is misused when no productive, creative action is taken on the mental image.

The conscious ego-dragon of one who has come this far in soul awareness now attempts to misuse the imagination, the image making faculty to stimulate or tempt the disciplined one to get distracted once again by old memory images from the past.

As one's ability to hold the mind still improves, the disciplined one finds there is a temptation to review the past, imaging or visualizing various possible outcomes.

For example, one may think of an experience from one's past. One may wish to have a different outcome or result, so one imagines different variations on this past experience. Yet, this person remains locked in an imagined past that never occurred and never will occur. Therefore, there is no creation and no creative process. Neither is there permanent learning or permanent understandings being built.

The first beast, which is the misuse of memory, was changed as symbolized by the sword and the wound. So the ego next attempts to use imagination and memory together to beguile and distract the individual from the true purpose of life which is to know the whole Self.

This is how the second wild beast-imagination gives power to the first wild beast-memory.

Where your attention is, that is where and what you worship. So if your attention is engrossed in memory or imagination, that is where you worship. Undisciplined memory and imagination will allow the conscious ego-dragon to keep you engrossed and entrapped in physical thinking and the world of temporary, physical experiences.

Graven images in the **Bible** are statues that people worshipped as gods. The second beast-imagination then brought memory to life. The disciplined one must be vigilant during this stage in order to keep from getting engrossed or entranced in old memories by thinking, "What if things had been different?" The past is over. Therefore, do not worship old memories. *"Let the dead bury the dead,"* as Jesus the Christ said.

> **16 And he compelled all, both small and great, rich and poor, freemen and slaves to receive a mark on their right hand or on their brow-forehead. 17 So that no man might buy or sell unless he who had the mark of the name of the beast or the code number corresponding to his name.**

When you get to an advanced stage of soul growth you discover that the old ego motivations and sensory experiences no longer hold much value for you. You long for the inner truth. Service to others becomes your greatest motivating force.

Hands symbolize purpose. Brow symbolizes the reasoning capability and the intuitive ability.

This verse means that only those who learn to consciously create a higher purpose for life and only those who develop the higher state of reasoning will be able to know and understand their true and high value.

When something is bought or sold it has value. Someone recognizes value in an object in order to buy it. Someone wants to receive value from an object in order to sell it. The hand symbolizes purpose. The human, animal body is the only body that has a hand that can make a fist. Purpose is personal benefit. The highest benefit to the Self is permanent understandings of Self and creation which is called enlightenment.

Reasoning and the intuitive faculty are located in the third eye. The third eye is the gland of perception. The third eye is located in the area between the eyebrows, inside the head. This verse is a reference to Ezekiel 9:4. In this passage a mark is set on the foreheads of those who sign and are tormented on account of the evil things done by others in their midst. The advanced and evolved soul must maintain a commitment to the Universal Laws and Truths and to I AM.

> **18 Here is wisdom: Let him who has understanding decipher the code number of the beast; for it is the code number of the name of a man; and his number is six hundred and sixty-six.**

The woman was in the wilderness for 42 months, $4 + 2 = 6$. The first beast was given the power to make war for 42 months. Thus, six, the number of service, is the key to nourishing the inner Self and to mastering brain memories.

The number 666 is made up of three sixes and indicates sacred, selfless service. Sacred, selfless service is time, attention and energy given to aid others in the quickening of Soul growth and spiritual development.

The code number of the beast is 666. Therefore, the code number of imagination is 666. In other words, memory and imagination are to be used productively in the present moment through the giving of service.

This code number represents the Aramaic letters 100, 60 and 200, which add to 360.

Three hundred sixty is the number of degrees in a circle.

Thus, the number 360, which adds to 90, indicates one who goes around in circles never getting anywhere. This number, 360, shows clearly that one who has accepted the mark of the beast lives the life for what is temporary, such as the pairs of opposites of pleasure-pain and the accumulation of physical possessions.

However, the one who accepts the mark of the <u>Lamb</u> instead of the mark of the <u>beast</u> lives a disciplined life devoted to building permanent understandings of Self and creation while aiding others to do the same. The one with the mark of the Lamb gets off the <u>circle</u> of 360 degrees and achieves higher <u>cycles</u>, higher levels of Mind and the higher chakras.

The word 'man' comes from the Sanskrit word 'manu,' which means thinker. In the first chapter of Matthew of the **Bible**, the 23rd verse says, *"Behold, a virgin will conceive and give birth to a son, and they shall call him Immanuel,"* which is interpreted, Our God is with us.

> Im-manu-el
> EL=God
> Manu=the thinker

Therefore, I'm-manu-el = the I AM who is the thinker-god within each individual.

Each soul, each individual being made in the image and likeness of God has like attributes. We are to learn to demonstrate those God attributes even as Jesus the Christ did.

To develop the god-hood within Self, one must use the imaging making faculty. Imagination is the like attribute the makes us like the Creator. Therefore, any mind image or thoughts created by the Self are to be used to further one's Godhood, one's Christhood, one's enlightenment.

Six is the number of service. The number 666 indicates service to all three divisions of Mind, the Conscious, Subconscious, and Superconscious.

The numbers 6 + 6 + 6 adds to 18. The numbers 1 + 8 = 9. Nine is the number of completion of a cycle of soul awareness.

The book of 1 Kings 10:14 states, *"Now the weight of gold that came to Solomon in one year was six hundred and sixty-six talents."* Gold represents value. Solomon was the wisest man in the **Bible**. Thus, 666 talents indicates that the wisdom of giving service produces value. The meaning is that to reach completion one must practice and learn service, symbolized by the number 6, and creation, symbolized by the number 3.

To gain perception and enlightenment one must create, through mental discipline, permanent understandings in the Self. One must also practice the service of teaching others what one has gained.

Any true thinker will understand that thought is cause. Such a one will know he or she creates the life based on the degree of discipline and direction one has with one's thoughts.

Permanent value does not come from physical, sensory objects or experiences. Real, lasting value comes from the ability to still the mind and receive the essence of the learning in every experience.

In a still mind is the highest service given.

Summary of the Inner Meaning of Chapter 13 of the Book of Revelation
The limitations of memory and imagination in the brain become apparent as limitations in the individual. The Self must develop and master reasoning. Reasoning is composed of memory, attention and imagination. Sacred Selfless Service is the Key.

Chapter 14 of Revelation

Few Word Essence of Chapter 14
of the Book of Revelation

The choice of entrapment or enlightenment

Brief and More Expanded Essence of Chapter 14
of the Book of Revelation

Thought forms continue to pour forth from Superconscious Mind
and are received with awareness in the conscious mind. A
greater commitment is made to live in the present moment.

Chapter 14

New Symbols & The Interpretation of Chapter 14 of Revelation

1. Mount Zion - all obstacles to Superconscious Mind have been overcome

2. harps - harmony in the mind

3. everlasting gospel - the true nature of reality

4. statue - attention on memory

5. sickle - ability to receive knowledge from each experience

6. grapes - knowledge of Self and creation

7. winepress - ability to extract the essence of the learning in every experiences

8. horse's bridles - ability to direct the will

Chapter 14

1 And I looked, and lo, the Lamb stood on mount Zion, and with him a hundred and forty-four thousand in number, having the name of his Father written on their brows.

The Lamb indicates the one committed to the full enlightenment, of Christ consciousness. Mount Zion represents the challenge one accepts to overcome any limitations in consciousness in order to achieve and receive superconscious mind.

The number 144,000 is the number of minor aspects of Self. There are 12 major outer, or conscious mind aspects of Self and 12 major inner aspects of Self. These 144,000 aspects of the one committed to quickening soul growth have the name of the Lamb-Father written on their brows.

The Father's name is I AM. Jesus often referred to his Father in Heaven. The Father in Heaven is I AM and is referred to as Jehovah or Yahweh in the original Hebrew language.

To gain this level of enlightenment one must purify the nervous system through concentration, meditation and breathing exercises or disciplines.

The 144,000 are the nadis or subconscious aspects of the Self. This subconscious energy is received from superconscious mind and then moves into the physical body. One half or 72,000 nadis are associated with the pingala or aggressive energy on the right side of the spine. The other half or 72,000 nadis or aspects of the Self are associated with and work through the left side of the spine. They function with the ida or receptive energy on the left side of the spine.

To know the superconscious mind and as a prelude to Christ consciousness, one must raise the Kundalini up the central channel of the spine called the sushumna.

The 144,000 aspects then function primarily through the ida and pingala which in turn controls the sympathetic nervous system.

The cleansing or purification of the mind leads to the cleansing of the channels the subconscious mind and subconscious aspects use to

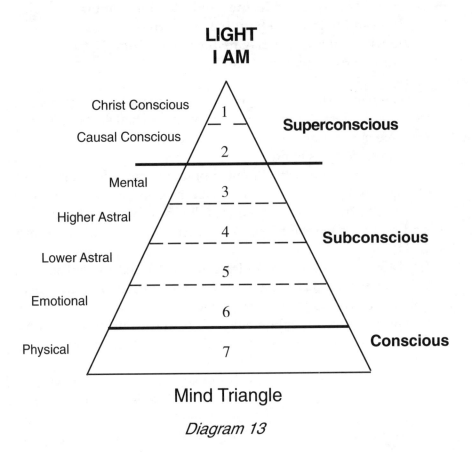

Mind Triangle

Diagram 13

activate greater consciousness in the individual. Therefore, these are the 144,000 aspects of the mind of Self. *(See diagram 13)*

To have the name of the Father written on one's brow is to have activated the brow chakra and thereby receive superconscious awareness. It is the total commitment to Self to use reasoning correctly, with discipline. It is to know the truth that "thought is cause" with no blame. It is the alignment of conscious and subconscious minds attuned to superconscious mind.

In Genesis chapter 3, verse 19, the Lord God speaking to Adam says, "By *the sweat of your brow shall you bring forth fruit, until you return to the ground; out of it you were taken; for dust you are and to dust you shall return.*"

When the name of the Father is written on the brow, one is learning how to learn from observation. One is gaining knowledge, awareness and understanding of how to receive permanent understanding from earthly, physical experiences. Compare and contrast this with chapter 13, verse 16 of Revelation. The brow is mentioned in each case. In chapter 13 the second beast compelled all to receive a mark on their brows.

In chapter 14 those with the Lamb have the name of the Father written on their brows. Instead of being <u>compelled</u>, they now <u>have</u> the mark on their brows. Instead of misuse of imagination or fantasizing, as symbolized by the second beast, we have commitment to enlightenment as symbolized by the Lamb.

Perception, reasoning and the interpretation of energies are all developing in the disciplined, committed student. The keys to the rapid quickening of soul growth are the productive use of the image making ability-imagination and commitment to the imaged ideal of becoming a Christ.

> **2 Then I heard a voice from heaven, like the sound of many waters and like the sound of a great thunder; and the voice I heard was like the music of many harpists playing on their harps;**

The voice from heaven is the communication from the superconscious mind to the conscious mind of the individual.

As one practices concentration and meditation every day, consistently, the conscious mind begins to become still. When the conscious mind ceases to generate thoughts and becomes still only then can it

receive the thoughts from superconscious mind into conscious awareness.

Once the disciplined individual begins to receive from
superconscious mind, one's whole consciousness shifts. Consciousness
expands and life takes on greater meaning and purpose. This is the
voice from heaven and the many thunders.

The reason the voice heard was like many harpists is because the
disciplined, still conscious mind becomes aligned to the subconscious
mind, and the two become attuned to superconscious mind. Then one
perceives harmonious vibration that seems like music. Such a mind is
like the strings of a harp that have been tuned to make melodious music together. To make a voice the vocal cords must vibrate. This requires air or breath. Thus, the one who masters life force through
breathwork or pranayama will receive the high voice of
Superconsciousness and I AM.

> 3 And they sang a new song before the throne
> and before the four animals and the elders; and
> no man was able to learn that song except the
> hundred and forty-four thousand who were
> redeemed from the earth.

A song is music and words to be sung in harmony. The new song
before the throne can only occur when one has aligned the conscious
and subconscious minds and attuned them to superconscious mind.
Only one who has stilled the mind and received the full awareness in
each moment can receive and achieve this. Only the one with a still
mind can hear this new song. Only the still mind is capable of receiving this higher vibration.

The 144,000 who are redeemed from the earth are those aspects of
Self that are known, understood and are following the Perfect and Divine Plan of Creation held in Superconscious Mind. The 144,000 are
identified in the physical body as the 144,000 nadis which are the minor energy transformers for the body.

> 4 These are those who were not defiled with
> women, for they are pure. These are those who
> follow the Lamb wherever he goes. These were
> redeemed by Jesus from among men to be the
> first fruits to God and to the Lamb.

The phrase, 'not defiled with women' indicates aspects of Self that are no longer engrossed in physical experience. The word defiled can also be interpreted as polluted. To be defiled is to forget who you are as a soul and become engrossed in physical, sensory experience. Sensory, physical experience defiles, pollutes and engrosses the conscious mind. The still mind is unpolluted by sensory experience. Instead, the disciplined, still conscious mind receives the essence of the Universal Life Lesson in every experience. This Universal Life is then received from the conscious mind to the subconscious mind, or soul, as permanent understanding of Self and creation. One who is pure has aligned conscious and subconscious minds and attuned them both to superconscious mind. To achieve purity of consciousness, one must have developed a still mind.

Aspects that have gained freedom from entrapment follow the Lamb. To follow the Lamb is to have made full commitment to gain the Christ consciousness.

To redeem is to buy back, to purchase, to ransom or to obtain. To be redeemed by Jesus from men is to be disciplined with the mind until one develops Self awareness, Self knowing and Self understanding.

Fruit is food and food symbolizes knowledge. The one who moves out of engrossment in the brain and five senses develops the ability to obtain permanent understanding and knowledge of Self and creation. Such a one begins to know Self as a son of God who has attained the full commitment.

5 And in their mouth was found no deceit; for they are without fault.

The mouth is a place for both giving and receiving. We receive food into the mouth. Food symbolizes knowledge.

We also speak by using the mouth. What we say indicates our level of awareness, understanding, knowledge and wisdom or lack thereof. One who practices and speaks deceitfully has little knowledge or Self understanding. One who lives by the truth has no defect or deceit. To have fault is to have deceit. One who lives truth aligns with Universal Truth. Such a one progresses rapidly in soul awareness and understanding.

6 And I saw another angel fly in the midst of heaven, having the everlasting gospel to preach

> **to those who dwell on the earth, and to every**
> **nation and kindred and tongue and people.**

An angel flying in the midst of heaven is a thought from I AM existing in Superconscious Mind. The individual is receiving this thought into conscious awareness as indicated by the statement that the angel preached to those on earth.

Gospel originally comes from the combination of two words, 'Gos' meaning good and 'spell' meaning history. The gospel of Revelation is good history. It is a good story of how to gain enlightenment and the experiences one encounters along the way. The everlasting good story is the detailed explanation of the steps to enlightenment that Revelation offers.

The phrase, 'Every nation, kindred, tongue and people,' symbolizes all the aspects of Self.

> **7 Saying with a loud voice, Serve God and give**
> **glory to him; for the hour of his judgement has**
> **come; and worship him who made heaven and**
> **earth and the sea and the fountains of waters.**

To serve the Creator one must demonstrate it in the life by serving and aiding others. If you would be greater you must serve something greater than yourself. If you would become the greatest you must first become the least. Service is the key.

The hour of your judgement is when the mind has been disciplined and stilled and the Self is in alignment with Universal Law and Universal Truth. Judgement has to do with law. God's judgement is in regard to Universal Law. This angel delivers the thought of the new and greater commitment into the consciousness of Self.

To worship is to give attention to someone or something. Therefore, give attention to knowing all aspects of Self, all divisions of Mind. Raise your consciousness to know Christ consciousness and I AM.

Heaven, earth and sea symbolize respectively the Superconscious, Subconscious and Conscious Minds. Fountains of waters are one's own experiences in consciousness.

> **8 And another angel, a second, followed him, saying,**
> **Babylon has fallen, that great city which made all na-**
> **tions drink of the wine of the passion of her whoredom.**

Engrossment in physical, sensory experiences, symbolized by Babylon, has fallen. Babylon has fallen represents one who has disciplined the mind to overcome engrossment in sensory experience. Overcoming sensory engrossment means disciplining the mind to know the Self in every experience. The sensory engrossed person forgets who they are in the experiences.

Becoming drunk on wine indicates the misuse of the conscious mind and a refusal to exercise one's will. Whoredom symbolizes the refusal to use one's creative energy for the uplifting of one's consciousness and the enlightenment of the whole Self.

Babylon has fallen indicating one who has learned to direct the creative urge upward through the chakras and up the central channel of the spine. The Kundalini is being raised for higher consciousness. In India this central channel of the spine is called the Shushumna. The channels on either side of the central channel are called the Ida and Pingala.

> **9 Then another angel, a third, followed them,**
> **saying with a loud voice, If any man worships the**
> **beast and his image-statue and receives his mark**
> **on his brow or on his hand, 10 He also shall drink**
> **of the wine of the wrath of God, which is mixed**
> **with bitterness in the cup of his anger; and he**
> **shall be tormented with fire and brimstone in the**
> **presence of the holy angels and before the throne;**

The Ten Commandments are given in Exodus chapter 20. The second commandment given by God, whom in Hebrew is called Yahweh or Jehovah, is, *"You shall not make for yourself any graven image."*

Graven means 'to carve or to dig.' To engrave means to scrape or to make an imprint in or on. The second commandment as given fully in the 4th, 5th and 6th verses of Exodus 20:4-6 is, *"4 You shall not make for yourself any graven image, or any likeness of anything that is in heaven above or that is in the earth beneath or that is in the water under the earth; 5 You shall not worship them nor serve them; for I, the Lord your God, am a zealous God, visiting the offenses of the fathers upon their children to the third and fourth generations of those who hate me. 6 And showing mercy to thousands of generations of those who love me and keep my commandments."*

Therefore, an image, a graven image is a statue or imitation of the real thing. To make a statue or graven image requires some memory of what one is imitating and some imagination as to how to make the imitation look like the real thing.

The second beast, indicating a habitual or compulsive use of imagination with memory, fools people into thinking they have real power. God gave this commandment to keep his people from being fooled and deceived by false imitations of enlightenment. It is amazing how many people mistake a good memory or good imagination for enlightenment.

Instead of receiving the mark of the beast and his image on the hand or brow one is to strive to have the name of the Father-Superconscious Mind written on one's brow chakra-pituitary gland.

The beast's image is the misuse of imagination. Memory and imagination are required in order to build a statue, a graven image. The second beast and his image is the conscious ego deceiving one into living in the fantasized future instead of the eternal now. The first beast deceives one into living in imagined memories of the present.

To let the beast-memory or his image-undisciplined imagination control the mind of Self will cause difficulty and pain in attempting to learn in and through the experiences.

To have the name of the Father written on one's brow is to have gained a disciplined mind and full commitment to know the whole Self. The name of the Father written on one's brow is the key to mastering the conscious ego-Devil-Satan-Dragon. The wrath of God is the violent anger one experiences in the Self when one becomes engrossed and willess in one's physical experiences. It is the responsibility one has to accept and practice if one is to be a Christ. The undisciplined person will always be emotionally out of control. Discipline of the thoughts brings discipline of the emotions. Since one's consciousness must expand the emotional resistance creates pain until one develops a still mind and learns to live in the present moment.

> **11 And the smoke of their torment will rise for ever and ever; and those who worship the beast and his image will have no rest day or night.**
> (*See diagram 14*)

As one resists the expansion and growth in consciousness, one experiences pain. The one with the disciplined mind learns to accept change as a part of the temporary, physical existence. This is accomplished with a still mind in the eternal now.

The difference between having the mark of the beast on one's forehead and having the name of the Father on one's brow are herein given. Comparison of the mark of the beast chapter 13, verse 16-17,chapter 14, verse 9-11, and the mark of the Father in heaven chapter 14,verse 1.

Mark of the Father in Heaven Chapter 14:1	**Mark of the Beast** Chapter 13:16-17
Name of the Lamb's Father written on their brows.	Compelled to receive mark on right hand or brow No one would buy or sell unless they have the mark of the beast or the code number of his last name. The code number is 666.
Man stood on Mount Zion	
144,000	
Sang a new song before the throne and the 4 animals and elders. Not defiled by women. They are pure. Follow the Lamb. Redeemed by Jesus as the first fruits of God. No deceit, no fault	Chapter 14:9-11 Mark on his brow or on his hand. Drink of the wine of the wrath of God mixed with bitterness in the cup of his anger. Tormented with fire and brimstone. Smoke of their torment will rise forever. They will have no rest day or night.
I AM	Conscious Ego

Six is the number of service. Scared, selfless service enables one to give and receive value from and into the Self despite the conscious ego-Satan being present.

However, those who have developed the disciplined and still mind no longer have the conscious ego controlling them. These aspects are gaining freedom from sensory engrossment. They have aligned conscious and subconscious minds and attuned them to superconscious mind. These are the knowing aspects in Self. These aspects live in alignment with Universal Truth.

Diagram 14

The smoke of one's torment arises when one resists what is. The key is to become present. To become present one must have a still mind in the present moment. To choose a still mind is to cease creating new thoughts. Then after a while, from the reference point of a still mind, one may consciously choose a creative thought.

Remember wherever you give your attention that is where and what you worship. If you live in memories of the past or fantasize about an imagined future you are not present. Your attention is not in the present moment.

Only the still mind in the present moment can give rest and peace. A busy, restless mind never finds peace or rest.

> **12 Here is the patience of the saints; here are they who keep the commandments of God and the faith of Jesus.**

To have patience is to possess calmness, steadfastness, composure, quietness and endurance. It is the still mind existing fully in the present moment. This is what makes one a saint.

The commandments of God are instruction for harmonizing one's thoughts and consciousness with Universal Law and Universal Truth. The second commandment, *"You shalt not make for yourself any graven image,"* is especially important in this stage of one's soulful develop- ment.

Faith is the assent of the mind to the Truth of what is declared by another. Faith is a word of Latin origin.

Belief is the assent of the mind to the Truth of what is declared by another. Belief is a word of Anglo-Saxon origin.

The faith of Jesus is the full commitment to know the whole Self. To keep the faith of Jesus is to continually hold in mind the ideal image of the enlightened, Christ-Self one can become and is becoming rather than the physical image of a goal or desire.

> **13 And I heard a voice from heaven saying, Write, Blessed are the dead who die in the Lord from henceforth. Yes, says the Spirit, that they may rest from their labors, for their works will follow them.**

A voice from heaven is the superconscious instruction one receives when the mind is stilled and the breath is mastered. When the conscious mind exists in a state of no thought then one is capable of hearing the higher vibration-voice from superconscious mind.

To write words, such as a story on paper, is to receive a thought-picture-image which is then translated into words and inscribed on a physical piece of paper. It is the physical manifestation of a thought.

The voice comes from the Spirit. Spirit is Mind. The Mind of Heaven is Superconscious Mind and the Breath of Heaven is the animating force behind all actions.

To be dead is to cease to live. It is to cease to function. It is to cease to have an effect. Yet, to die in the Lord-I AM is to go beyond Mind, to I AM, and to exist in a state of motionless, omnipresent consciousness. It is the state of pure being. The old limited, restricted Self can die or change to be transformed into the unlimited Self of:

1. infinite being,
2. infinite energy,
3. infinite manifestation, and
4. infinite intelligence.

To rest is to be neither aggressive nor receptive. To rest is to have a still mind.

> **14 And I looked, and lo, I saw a white cloud, and upon the cloud sat one resembling the Son of man, having on his head a crown of gold and in his hand a sharp sickle.**

A white cloud symbolizes one's own consciousness rising to superconscious mind above the Dome of Mind. The man represents the thinker. The Son of Man is the one who has mastered thinking and now is making strides to go beyond thinking. Such a one is attempting to become a son of God. A son of God is brought about by the still mind. Jesus who became the Christ frequently referred to himself as the Son of Man. The Son of Man is the offspring of the thinker. The aggressive offspring of the thinker is the one who consciously chooses thoughts that are in alignment with knowing I AM.

A crown of gold indicates one who directs all aspects of Self with wisdom and thus gains value into the Self.

The sharp sickle symbolizes the ability to reap the harvest of one's own experiences thereby receiving truth, understanding and the high knowledge into the Self. A sharp sickle is used to harvest grain such as wheat. Grain is food. Food symbolizes knowledge.

> **15 And another angel came out of the temple,**
> **and after he cried with a loud voice to him who**
> **sat on the cloud, 16 He thrust his sickle upon the**
> **earth, and the earth was harvested.**

The fourth angel came out of the temple meaning a thought came from the superconscious mind. This vibrational thought form will reach the conscious awareness of the one with a still and disciplined mind. The one with a disciplined and still mind is capable of gathering and receiving the essence of the learning in each experience. Such a one, therefore, is capable of rapidly gaining permanent and lasting understanding of Self and creation.

> **17 And another angel came out of the temple which**
> **is in heaven; and he also had a sharp sickle. 18 Then**
> **out from the altar came another angel, who had**
> **power over fire, and cried with a loud voice to him**
> **who had the sharp sickle, saying, Thrust in your**
> **sharp sickle and gather the clusters of the vineyards**
> **of the earth, for her grapes are fully ripe.**

This, the fifth angel or thought form, comes out of Superconscious Mind adding to one's ability to accelerate soul growth by receiving truth and LIGHT in all experiences.

The sixth angel has power over the expansion of consciousness symbolized by fire. The sixth angel is connected and in communication with the fifth angel for now one can gather and receive not only knowledge, but also wisdom from the experience gained in physical life. The knowledge-grapes are fully ripe. Therefore, for such a one the knowledge of Self and creation one has accumulated can now be turned into the wine of wisdom. This wisdom is achieved by passing on what you know as Universal Truth.

> **19 And the angel thrust his sickle into the earth and**
> **gathered the vineyards of the earth, and cast the**

grapes into the winepress of the wrath of the great God. 20 And the winepress was trodden until the juice which came out reached even to the horse bridles, and the circumference of the winepress was a thousand and six hundred furlongs.

The conscious use of will is needed to transform knowledge-grapes into wisdom-wine. Horses symbolize the will. Horses that are directed by bridles and used for a specific purpose with the winepress symbolize the conscious use of will power. The conscious use of will power is necessary to discipline the mind and to achieve a still mind. Then the restless thoughts cease.

One thousand six hundred indicates the power of the aggressive quality given in service. The two zeros in the number 1600 indicate the power of understanding the higher truths.

It is only through the disciplined mind, given in service through teaching others, that one comes to master the ability to receive permanent understandings in every experience.

In the **Bhagavad Gita**, chapter 3, verses 6-7, Krishna, who symbolizes I AM says, *"Those who abstain from action while allowing the mind to dwell on sensual pleasure cannot be called spiritual aspirants. But they excel who control their sense and through the mind, using them for selfless service."*

Summary of the Inner Meaning of Chapter 14 of the Book of Revelation
The Self, the disciplined one, has gained partial freedom from engrossment in the senses and entrapment in the physical body.

The limitations of the brain, brain memory and brain imagination are clearly perceived. Now the Self understands how to receive the essence of the universal learning and Universal Truth in every experience. Thereby, one knows how to transmute or transform the knowledge of direct experience into permanent wisdom and understanding.

Chapter 15 of Revelation

Few Word Essence of Chapter 15 of the Book of Revelation

Receptivity in the conscious mind

Brief and More Expanded Essence of Chapter 15 of the Book of Revelation

The still mind enables the disciplined one to overcome and transform all limitations in consciousness so that one may receive in Superconsciousness.

Chapter 15

New Symbols & The Interpretation of Chapter 15 of Revelation

1. plagues - misuse of the energies or incomplete use of the energies of each of the 7 levels of Mind

2. sea of glass - still mind

3. song of Moses - fulfillment of Universal Laws and Universal Truths

4. tabernacle - ability to perceive, receive or enter into Superconscious Mind

5. golden bowls - ability to fully receive the present experience

Chapter 15

1 And I saw another sign in heaven, great and marvelous, seven angels having the seven last plagues; for in them is fulfilled the wrath of God.

The seven angels are the seven messenger thoughts from I AM that come to create a change or transformation of consciousness in each of the seven levels of Mind.

The wrath of God is the greater responsibility needed to know the whole Self and the whole Mind. The word wrath is akin to writhe. The word wrath means to writhe or twist. When one twists the truth one experiences anger. Wrath is often seen as violent anger. Yet anger of itself is not creative and can be, when misused, very destructive. God is the Creator. Within each person God is the creative part of Self for we are sons and daughters of the Creator. When the Hebrews of the Old Testament failed to keep Gods commandments, he would show wrath and would bring about some misfortune on the people. This indicates we have a choice.

1. Each person can choose to discipline the mind, the thoughts, the Self and be in harmony with Universal Law, or

2. A person can remain undisciplined and become more enamored or engrossed in sensory experience.

This choice is symbolized by Babylon and the Harlot in Revelation. This choice or refusal to use the will productively leads to pain and suffering. It is wrong thinking according to the Buddha.

The word writhe is from the same root word as worth. Writhe is to twist with violence and to distort. The wrath of God is one's need to stop distorting the facts, to stop living in the illusion of physical experience in order to know the true worth of the Self and the present moment. It is the need to exist in the true reality of higher consciousness and connectedness. The five senses falsely tell the Self that he or she is separate from others and everything. For example, the sense of sight informs you that you are separate from the person you see. The senses give the illusion of distance and therefore time. The true reality is connectedness in the ever present NOW that leads to oneness.

> **2 And I saw what looked like a sea of glass mingled with fire; and those who were victorious over the wild beast and over his image-statue and over the number of his name were standing on the sea of glass and had the harps of God.**

What looked like a sea of glass is the consciousness of one who has stilled the mind. When there are no more thoughts, the mind rests in the peace of stillness. When Jesus stilled the waters of the sea of Galilee as given in the Book of Matthew, it was because he had stilled his own mind.

Water symbolizes conscious life experience. Turbulent water such as that caused by a storm symbolizes one whose mind is untamed, undisciplined and out of control.

Fire symbolizes expansion. A 'sea of glass mingled with fire' symbolizes one who has disciplined the mind, stilled the mind and therefore created an expansion of consciousness.

The one who disciplines and stills the mind can be, will be, and is victorious over the wild beast, his image and the number that accepted his name on their forehead.

The first wild beast is the misuse of the memory by the conscious ego.

The second wild beast is the misuse of the imagination to fantasize about a past that is different from that which one actually experienced. The misuse of the imaging faculty also occurs when one expects the worst or imagines what one does not want to occur.

Rather than having the mark of the beast on our brows, which is 666 or 360, we need to earn, through discipline and service, the name of the Lamb's Father on our brows. This is the choice between the conscious ego and I AM. It is the choice between the selfish, separate, fearful, egotistical self, or the enlightened connected, LIGHT filled, loving, enlightened, I AM Self.

> **3 And they were singing the song of Moses, the servant of God, and the song of the Lamb, saying, Great**

**and marvelous are thy works, Lord God Almighty; just
and true are thy ways, O King of Ages.**

The song of Moses is the productive harmony that is created in mind
and Self when one uses the imagination and Kundalini-creative energy
wisely to live in harmony with Universal Law.

Moses was an enlightened being who followed God's commands.
The story of Moses is given in the book of Exodus in the Old testament
of the **Bible**. Moses received the vision from the Lord-I AM to lead his
people, the Hebrews out of bondage in Egypt. Egypt symbolizes entrapment. For it was in Egypt that the Hebrews, aspects of the Self,
were in slavery-bondage which symbolizes entrapment in the physical
body.

The 'song of the Lamb' is the harmony created as one is committed
to Christ consciousness. Lord God is I AM. It is each person's duty to
harmonize with Universal Laws and Universal Truths to come to know
I AM. The practice of being just, that is justice, aligns with Universal
Truth.

**The 'King of Ages' is the master of time. The master of time is the
one who has achieved the still mind and exists in the ever present,
eternal NOW.** Such a one exerts a Kingly rule over all 144,00 aspects of
Self in the eternal present moment, the NOW.

> **4 Who shall not revere thee, O Lord and glorify thy
> name? For thou only art holy. All nations shall come
> and worship before thee; for thy righteousness hast
> been revealed.**

To revere is to be in awe. To revere is to give one's full perception
and love.

To master the mind and the conscious ego, one must give attention
and perception to the Real Self, I AM. I AM is whole. In the conscious
mind we perceive Self only partially. Therefore, we perceive aspects or
parts of Self. The more one comes to know Self the more one knows
others. As one comes to know more of Self, one becomes whole or
Holy. As the conscious mind is disciplined and comes to align with
subconscious mind, one knows more aspects of Self.

As one next achieves the still mind, one gains oneness with all aspects. Oneness overcomes the illusion of separateness and one becomes

whole and Holy. One is righteous because one is doing, accomplishing and being productive as one gains enlightenment. To worship I AM is to give full attention to knowing the whole Self and all of Mind. Where you direct your attention is where you worship.

5 And after these things, I looked and behold, the temple of the tabernacle of the testimony in heaven was opened;

The full opening in one's consciousness is achieved. This allows the reception of superconscious awareness into one's waking state. This higher awareness flowing into one's consciousness initiates a series of changes and transformations within one's being.

The word temple comes from the Latin word meaning time. To know the temple one must know time. To know time one must achieve the still mind and exist in the eternal now. The Superconscious Mind is opened to the rest of Mind. This joins all aspects of Self into a mighty oneness of Christ consciousness. The Superconscious Mind is no longer separated from the Subconscious and Superconscious Minds in the disciplined being.

The word translated as testimony can just as well be translated as witness. When I realized this, I aligned conscious and subconscious minds and attuned to superconscious mind by stilling my mind. Then I received the realization that this witness was related to the two witnesses of chapter 11. A witness is one who is present at an event or during an experience, who receives or perceives the experience and who gives testimony of that experience. Such is the witness of the temple of the tent in heaven. This is achieved by having a still mind that then consciously chooses Holy thoughts that create enlightenment.

This tent-tabernacle is the first level of Mind in Superconscious Mind. A witness receives an experience through perception. One who disciplines and stills the Mind is able to receive and observe Superconscious Mind. The two witnesses discussed earlier come from Superconscious Mind.

Most people are cut off from their superconscious mind. Whereas Enlightened people are connected and openly receive superconscious mind, they have overcome the illusion of separation. Enlightened beings have also dispelled the illusion of physical time.

In the temple of Superconscious Mind, there is no physical time of seconds, minutes, hours, days, weeks, months or years. There is only the fulfillment of the Perfect Plan in the ever present, eternal NOW. This is the eternity of duration. The attunement to superconscious mind brought about by the disciplined, still mind gives one the mastery over the illusion of past and future. Then one exists in a higher purpose in the present moment.

A tabernacle is a movable habitation such as a tent. The still mind attunes to Superconscious Mind. The tent-tabernacle of Superconscious Mind is opened and one exists continually in the temple of time. Such a one learns to receive the higher consciousness in the true reality of Now, the ever present moment. For such a one, the tabernacle gives wherever one goes.

> **6 And the seven angels having the seven plagues came out of the temple, clothed in pure and fine linen and having bands of gold encircling their chests.**

The seven angels carry the message of a higher consciousness throughout all levels of Mind.

The seven plagues indicate the changes and transformations in consciousness one encounters in gaining the Christ consciousness. The seven angels that come out of the temple of Superconscious Mind represent the thought consciousness available to the one who has opened up the Self to receive Superconscious Mind.

Pure and fine linen indicates that the consciousness of such a one is coming into full harmony with Universal Law. This high consciousness is being given outwardly in the daily life.

The area of the chest indicates the heart chakra. The quality of the heart chakra is understanding. Gold symbolizes value and wisdom. The one who achieves this chapter of Revelation in consciousness is now building permanent understandings of Self and creation and is teaching this to others. Such a one uses every moment and every experience to build soul understandings and teaches others how to do the same. When this stage of Revelation is achieved in the Self, the heart is open to love and understanding and compassion. Such a one has the wisdom to pursue greater enlightenment and to aid others to do so as well.

> **7 And one of the four animals gave to the seven angels seven golden bowls full of the wrath of God who lives for ever and ever and ever.**

The four animals symbolize the four levels of Subconscious Mind.

Seven golden bowls indicate one who has developed, through mental discipline, the still mind and therefore can choose to be receptive to all seven levels of Mind. Such a one has developed the responsibility to be able to handle, wisely, such awesome power. Such a one lives for ever and ever indicating the mastery of time. Such a one has mastered time with mental discipline and a still mind. The disciplined, committed person can fully receive the higher consciousness for the disciplined mind has achieved the still mind. The still mind may receive fully the present moment. Now, one's conscious awareness is capable and able to receive all seven levels of consciousness simultaneously.

> 8 And the temple was filled with smoke from the glory
> of God and from his power; and no man was able to
> enter into the temple, until the seven plagues of the
> seven angels were fulfilled.

Temple means time. Thus, time was filled.

Smoke comes from fire. Fire symbolizes expansion of consciousness. After each initiation in consciousness there follows a period of adjustment. This period of adjustment is like a newborn baby learning to see, to focus and to perceive what is in the environment. Then one must fully integrate the change, the transformation of consciousness, into one's whole being and conscious awareness. This must occur in one's waking, conscious state.

After this transformation is complete one is able to enter into the temple of Time. Such a one has mastered and overcome physical time for such a one lives for ever and ever in an eternal continuum of consciousness. Such a Son is Awake to the ever present, eternal now.

Summary of the Inner Meaning of Chapter 15 of the Book of Revelation
The still mind enables one to live in the present moment. The present moment is the true reality. The sea of glass is the still mind.

Chapter 16 of Revelation

Few Word Essence of Chapter 16
of the Book of Revelation

Kundalini and the conscious ego

Brief and More Expanded Essence of Chapter 16
of the Book of Revelation

The Self continues to receive more Superconscious understanding, thus overcoming limitations. All seven levels of Mind are received into conscious awareness.

Chapter 16

New Symbols & The Interpretation of Chapter 16 of Revelation

1. Euphrates river - Kundalini energy

2. east - third level of Mind

3. frogs - habits

4. Armageddon - the battle between the soul and the conscious ego

5. air - motion in the Mind; the third level of Mind

6. hail - conscious life experience that has slowed down and is rigid

Chapter 16

**1 And I heard a great voice from the time-temple saying
to the seven angels, Go your ways and pour out the
seven bowls of the wrath of God upon the earth.**

The ability to hear a great voice requires a disciplined and still
conscious mind that then chooses to be receptive. This voice that produces a vibration, this great voice is one's own Real Self called I AM. I
AM exists above and beyond Mind. The seven angels are seven messengers coming from I AM to the seven levels of Mind. This indicates
one's own mind is about to be transformed as Self gains a greater ability to respond to the creative urge to be enlightened.

The seven bowls symbolize one's ability to receive the higher
message of truth and understanding. Only a still and disciplined mind
is capable of receiving to this great degree. Only the still mind is capable of permanently receiving the higher consciousness. This higher
understanding will move all the way out into the conscious mind and
physical body. This state of spiritual and mental evolution enables the
spiritualized being to learn through still minded observation. For eons
entrapped souls have learned in and through work, or as Genesis says,
"By the sweat of your brows shall you bring forth fruit." The cycle of reincarnation is coming to an end for anyone who attains chapter 16 of
Revelation within the Self.

**2 And the first one went and poured out his bowl
upon the earth; and there came a severe and malig-
nant sore upon the men who had the mark of the
beast and upon those who worshipped his image-
statue.**

The disciplined one who desires greater enlightenment comes
to realize that any remaining attachment to physical desires will cause
pain.

Memory and imagination are to be used for greater things than just achieving physical goals. They are to be used to build permanent understandings of Self and creation at an accelerated rate. Reasoning is to be used for more than just physical success. Reasoning is to be practiced as a foundation for the intuitive faculty. The brow chakra is to be used for commitment to enlightenment rather than only physical glorification. Accepting the mark of the beast means one is using reasoning just to achieve physical pleasure or possession or power. This physical thinking leads to anger (sores) and suffering.

3 Then the second angel poured out his bowl upon the sea; and the water became as the blood of a dead man and every living soul died in the sea.

The second messenger poured this greater awareness into the sea of consciousness of the enlightened being. Everything in one's physical consciousness and existence will change-die, because the nature of the physical existence is change.

Blood symbolizes truth and life force. The greater truth arrives in the consciousness of such a being. This greater, higher Universal Truth creates change in one's conscious awareness. This change is the beginning of a higher transformation of consciousness for the one with the disciplined mind.

The thinker will need to adjust the thinking. The thinker will need to think less and have a still mind more. Awareness in the conscious mind undergoes a radical change for anyone who reaches this, the 16th chapter of Revelation in their own consciousness.

4 And the third angel poured out his bowl upon the rivers and fountains of waters; and they became blood.

The third messenger from I AM affects all motion in the conscious life experience of the disciplined individual. The individual who has reached this level of awareness now perceives each activity, each motion as an experience in truth, particularly Universal Truth.

This reception of superconscious and I AM awareness into the waking consciousness of the conscious mind enables such a one to know higher truth. This universal, higher truth poured into the conscious awareness of the individual, enables the Self to exist with a higher consciousness.

Life force of the disciplined being is increased. This greater conscious use of life force-prana raises the vibration of the whole Self.

5 Then I heard the angel who has charge over waters say, Thou art righteous, O Holy One, who is and was, because thou hast condemned them.

Now, the I AM messenger, who is in charge of conscious life experience, identifies the conscious mind that is productive and right in thoughts and decisions. Such a one knows thought is cause. Living this Universal Truth is righteous and correct.

The Holy One is the I AM who is whole. I AM exists beyond Mind and time. Therefore, I AM who is in the present, who was in the past and will be in the future, exists more and more in one's waking consciousness.

Such a one's conscious awareness has developed to such a high degree that the Self is beginning to function more and more as I AM in the waking life rather than as a conscious ego. The committed one, the devoted one, more and more experiences the Real Self.

To condemn something is to pronounce it to be utterly wrong or to punish. When you reach this level of wisdom and high knowledge, you will clearly recognize and know the unproductive. You will choose the productive in word, thought and deed.

6 For they have shed the blood of saints and prophets, and thou hast given them blood to drink; for they deserve it.

Any thoughts, attitudes, or aspects of one's conscious mind that restrict or distract the Self from the goal of enlightenment are those aspects that have shed the blood of prophets and saints. You must learn to choose truth in all your thoughts to know the truth of this chapter of Revelation.

Prophets and saints symbolize those aspects of Self that are aligned with enlightenment and are committed to Christ consciousness. Therefore, those aspects of Self that continue to be engrossed in physical, sensory experience need a good dose of High Truth. They need to receive Universal Truth and so it is given. This Higher Truth is received into the waking consciousness and conscious mind.

**7 And I heard another out of the altar say, Yes, O Lord
God Almighty, true and righteous are thy judgments.**

The still mind receives the voice, the vibration and further instruction from superconscious mind. The altar symbolizes one's attention in Superconscious Mind. In Superconscious Mind one can receive
great awareness of I AM as symbolized by Lord God Almighty. In the
original Hebrew language God Almighty is given as El-Shadai. El-
Shadai is the one who fills our emptiness. Therefore, we must still the
mind until it is empty in order to receive the fullness of the Lord God
Almighty. Just like a bowl must become empty in order to receive water from a pitcher, rain, a stream, a river or an ocean.

Mind is the vehicle to know the Real, Whole Self as I AM. I AM,
being above and beyond Mind, is therefore true and correct concerning
the proper use of Mind. One who would know Self as I AM must come
to align one's consciousness with Universal Truth and Universal Law
which is 'The Righteous.'

To judge is to pronounce right. I AM pronounces and indicates
the correct and right use of Mind needed to gain Christ Consciousness.

**8 And the fourth angel poured out his bowl upon
the sun; and it received the power to scorch men
with its fire. 9 And men were scorched by intense
heat, and they blasphemed the name of God, who
has power over these plagues; and they did not
repent to give him glory.**

The sun symbolizes superconscious awareness. Fire symbolizes expansion of one's consciousness. Men symbolize physical aspects
of Self or aspects that have a limited, physical, sensory type of thinking. This physical thinking must change and expand in order for the
Self to grow in consciousness because physical thinking is based upon
the false notion of separation. The fourth angel brings the power of
understanding of the heart chakra into one's being. Then the whole
Self can be filled with love and can build permanent understanding in
every experience.

To blaspheme is to speak injury. To blaspheme is to blame. To
blaspheme the name of God is to blame God or Creation or something
outside yourself for your life. To think physically is to see or think
yourself to be separate from your environment, all people and all Cre-

ation. Therefore, to have physical thinking is blasphemous and blame thinking.

To think mentally is to perceive the true nature of reality which is connectedness.

To continue to blame is the refusal to accept your own power. For the power to expand your consciousness is the power of connectedness.

10 And the fifth angel poured out his bowl on the throne of the wild beast; and his kingdom was darkened; and men gnawed their tongues from pain.

The wild beast symbolizes the misuse of memory. The misuse of memory leads to habits that are compulsive and limiting brain pathways. Men symbolize physical aspects. Physical aspects and physical thinking occur when thoughts and consciousness are caught up in separate thinking.

The statement, 'an angel poured out his bowl,' indicates one has become more receptive to the Higher Truth and the messages from the higher levels of Mind.

Pain seems to appear or be present when one needs to change or transform in order to move to the next higher stage of evolution, soul growth and enlightenment. For example, childbirth may sometimes seem to involve pain, yet in this process a new life begins.

When the time arises for a quickening of one's consciousness, any part of Self that still thinks separately and physically will experience pain. This is because physical, separate, blame thinking does not harmonize with knowing the whole Mind, and whole Self and the true Reality.

The fifth angel brings the power of the throat chakra into one's awareness. This is the power of conscious choice that produces will power. The will enables one to override brain memories and exist in the present moment.

In Subconscious, or Universal Mind, universal connectedness is perceived and known.

In Superconscious Mind, oneness of Self and all of Mind-Creation is known.

The wild beast's kingdom was darkened is a clear description of one's experience when one has been thinking physically and now needs to elevate one's consciousness. Sadness or darkness sometimes occurs right before the dawn of a new awareness.

The phrase "men gnawed their tongues from pain" indicates the aspects of Self that are still engrossed in physical, wrong thinking and therefore refuse to receive and process the higher knowledge. These aspects are the parts of yourself that think physically, which is to view yourself as separate from all Creation.

11 And blasphemed the God of heaven because of their wounds and sores, and did not repent of their deeds.

To blaspheme is to blame. To blame the God of heaven because of one's wounds and sores is to refuse to see how you have caused your life to be the way it is. Blame thinking is separate thinking and is, therefore, non-reasoning.

True reasoning is connected thinking.

Reasoning begins in connectedness. Thought is cause and your thoughts cause your life. Every negative or limiting thought has a limiting and painful effect in one's life.

To repent is to re-do what is creating or causing pain. To continue blaming others for the conditions of your life is to refuse to re-do the cause of your misery and pain. The cause of misery and pain is thoughts, attitudes and actions of separation. Attachment to desires is separatist thinking. This is why attachment to desires creates pain and suffering.

The true nature of reality is connectedness leading to oneness. Therefore, the one living the false delusion of separateness is fighting against the true nature of reality. This creates pain, misery and suffering.

All habits must be replaced with a still mind and conscious choice.

All memories must be chosen instead of allowing the memories to arise habitually.

Remember the wild beast, the first beast, is connected to the dragon, the conscious ego. If you refuse to discipline the mind and instead allow memories to arise, the conscious ego-dragon will misuse the memories in the brain to keep you engrossed in those memories. These memories that seem to arise spontaneously are actually brought forth cunningly and subtly by the conscious ego, serpent, devil, Satan.

12 Then the sixth angel poured out his bowl upon the great river Euphrates; and its waters dried up, that the way of the king of the East might be prepared.

The great river Euphrates symbolizes the Kundalini energy.

The river Euphrates' waters dried up symbolizing the change in perspective of one's consciousness. No longer does one live a physical, conscious life experience only. Now one lives a mental, higher mind, conscious life experience.

The king of the East represents the control and conscious use of all of the subconscious mind as well as conscious mind. It indicates one has realized that thought is cause. The direction of East symbolizes the third level of Mind.

Genesis 2:14 refers to the Euphrates river. The Euphrates river in Genesis indicates the potential for each person to lift up their creative potential to know enlightenment and Christ consciousness. The sixth angel opens the Self up to receive and perceive through the brow chakra. For such a one the Kundalini has moved up and through the brow chakra.

13 And I saw three unclean spirits like frogs coming out of the mouth of the dragon and out of the mouth of the wild beast and out of the mouth of the false prophet. 14 For they are the spirits of devils, who work miracles which go forth to the kings of the whole world, to gather them to the battle of that great day of God Almighty.

The three unclean spirits are the spirits of devils. Spirit is breath. The unclean spirits come out of the mouth of the dragon-ego. Frogs are animals and as such symbolize habits.

Spirits of devils symbolize misusing one's life force and breath to promote one's own egotistical ways. The wild beast symbolizes the misuse of habitual memories. The false prophet, the second beast, indicates the misuse of imagination, the imaginative faculty, to fantasize and thereby become entrapped in an imagined future that never comes. These verses indicate the way in which one may become egotistical and misuse one's mind and brain.

Miracles are something wonderful. Storing more and more information may seem wonderful, but that information stored in the brain as memory will die when the physical body dies.

Any physical habits or habitual thinking in regards to one's conscious ego-dragon, memory habits-first wild beast or brain-fantasy-imagination-second wild beast are about to be transformed by the disciplined mind. The misuse of memory to fantasize and daydream may seem wonderful, yet it is only temporary. Being egotistical to get your way may seem great yet the results are also temporary.

That battle of the great day of God Almighty is the battle within Self to determine if one will live a physically engrossing life or a disciplined, still mind, enlightened life.

15 Watch out I come as a thief. Blessed is he who stays awake and keeps his garments-clothes on, lest he must walk naked and they see his shame.

A thief comes unexpectedly. The 'I' referred to is I AM, the same great voice referred to in the first verse of this chapter.

What does it mean that one might have his garments stolen? Garments, being clothing, symbolize one's outward presentation and expression. Clothes symbolize the way one presents the Self to the world. To keep one's garments is to be building permanent understanding of Self and of Christhood that is reflected in one's experiences with others. This occurs when one teaches to others the Universal Truths of Mind and Self that one has learned. To have permanent garments instead of going naked with shame, one must learn to give and radiate outward to others and the world the love, LIGHT and truth one has received into the Self. In Genesis 3:7, *"And the eyes of them (Adam and Eve) were opened and they knew they were naked (without experience) and ashamed."*

The one who watches out and stays awake has achieved the still mind.

The one with a still mind consciously chooses all thoughts. The one without a still mind is a victim of brain thoughts that compulsively arise or are brought forth by the devil, the cunning, subtle conscious ego. Only the still minded individual truly knows his or her own thoughts.

The undisciplined minded one thinks he knows his own thoughts when, in fact, they are only brain-conscious ego thoughts. The animal brain and conscious ego are not the Real Self. They are temporary.

Not only must one learn the Universal Secrets of Mind one must also teach it to others. Then one will go clothed in white rainment which is the Master Teacher and Christ consciousness. It is the one whose chakras have been turned outward to radiate the golden white LIGHT of enlightenment.

16 And he gathered them together in a place which in the Hebrew tongue is called Armageddon.

The 'he' that gathers them together is I AM. The battle is in a place called Armageddon. Armageddon is the Mount of Mageddo.

The battle of Armageddon is the same place and battle referred to in the Bhagavad-Gita as Kurushetra, the Plain of Kuru. The **Bhagavad Gita** is a great spiritual text from India. It is the battle within the Self to determine whether physical thinking and physical aspects will control one or if mental thinking and I AM will win out.

The field of Kuru in the **Bhagavad Gita** is the Mount of Mageddo, the Armageddon of Revelation.

The armies of the Pandus verses Kurus in the **Bhagavad Gita** are the same as the armies of the kings of the whole world verses the armies of the Lord in Revelation.

It is the battle within Self to determine if one will gain Christ Consciousness this lifetime or if one will remain entrapped in a physical body and engrossed in the physical senses. Armageddon is the battle of I AM, served by the conscious mind, against the conscious ego-Dragon.

17 Then the seventh angel poured out his bowl into the air; and there came a great voice out of the temple from the throne, saying, Now it is done.

The seventh angel is the messenger for the first level of Mind, the Christ consciousness level. This verse symbolizes the piercing of the crown chakra by the Kundalini and the opening of this chakra. This process occurred in me and I have never been the same since. Now I receive truth at a accelerated rate. To prepare for this I practiced concentration, meditation, breath work, service and teaching others for many years. When this occurred in me, immediately after the Kundalini had pierced my crown chakra, a voice came from deep inside of me that said, "IT IS DONE." This was said aloud. This came from I AM.

This was the 'voice from the temple.' When one receives from the seventh angel, one has received from all seven levels of Mind and all seven chakras.

The great voice out of the time-temple directing all of Mind is I AM. I AM says, "It is done." What is *it*? *It* is the transformation of consciousness. One has made the full commitment to still the conscious mind and to receive all seven levels of Mind into one's consciousness.

When the mind is still one knows the time-temple. One can then master time. When the mind is still, one goes beyond physical-horizontal time to know vertical, mental time and consciousness itself. One can quicken soul growth and spiritual development ten-fold or even 100-fold to become enlightened this lifetime. You don't have to wait for another 10 or 100 lifetimes to become enlightened. You can quicken your soul growth and become enlightened 10 times or 100 times faster. This is the mastery of time. The overcoming of entrapment in a physical body and freedom from the cycle of reincarnation is occurring. *(See diagram 15)*

18   And there were voices, and thunder and lightnings; and there was a great earthquake, the like of which had never happened since man was upon the earth, so mighty an earthquake and so great.

Voices are vibration in air. Thunder is a vibration in air. Lightning is an electrical vibration traveling through the air. Earthquakes are a vibration moving through the earth. All of this symbolizes the movement of vibration throughout all seven levels of Mind.

The earthquake indicates the movement and shift of consciousness in the whole subconscious mind of such a one. This is a first time experience for the thinker – man. Thinking did not cause this earthquake shift in consciousness. A disciplined, still mind with no thought caused this movement in consciousness.

19   And the great city was divided into three parts, and the cities and the nations fell; and great Babylon came in remembrance before God, to give to her the cup of the wine of the fierceness of his wrath.

The great city symbolizes the whole Mind. The great city was divided into three parts symbolizing one's ability to separate and iden-

The 7 Plagues of Revelation and the 10 Plagues of Exodus	
Exodus	**Revelation**
1. Water turned to blood	1. Severe and malignant sores – boils on those who accepted the mark of the beast *(cunning separate thinking)*
2. Frogs came up out of thewater and covered the land	2. The sea became as blood, every living soul died in the sea *(conscious experience produces inner Truth)*
3. Lice – dust of the earth turns into lice.	3. Rivers and fountains of water become blood *(Motion is used to produce truth)*
4 Flies – swarms of flies	4. Poured his bowl on the sun and scorched men with fire *(expansion of consciousness)*
5. Cattle – all the cattle died	5. Poured his bowl on the throne of the wild beast and his kingdom was darkened *(will overrides compulsion)*
6. Boils and sores on men	6. Poured his bowl on the great river Euphuates and waters dried up to make way for the kings of the East (*Kundalini energy enables one to receive superconscious awareness*
7. Hail and flaming fire mingled with hail	7. Poured his bowl on the air, a great voice from out of the temple said, 'It is done." *(All seven chakras are opened).*
8. Locusts	
9. Darkness	
10. Death of the first born	

tify the Conscious, Subconscious and Superconscious divisions of Mind. Such a one now functions with superconscious awareness.

Only the disciplined and still mind can know and consciously receive the Divisions of Mind.

The cities of the nations symbolize all physically thinking aspects of the Self. They fell indicating the Higher Mind is taking over. Babylon symbolizes engrossment in sensory experience.

The cup of the wine of the fierceness of God's wrath symbolizes the power of the fullness of the experience that is moving through one's emotions to become a full part of one's higher consciousness. Then one obtains the greater responsibility to achieve wisdom and the complete openness of receptivity.

> **20 And every island fled away, and the mountains could not be found. 21 And great hail, about the size of a talent, fell out of heaven upon men; and men blasphemed God because of the plague of the hail; for the destructive force of the hail was exceedingly great.**

Islands symbolize isolated areas of consciousness that one needs to emote or move through the emotional level. Otherwise one continues to over-react emotionally. The islands fled away indicating there is no more emotional separation between one's conscious and subconscious minds. No mountains could be found shows that for such a one, superconsciousness is now. There are no obstacles to superconscious mind and no separation between the divisions of Mind. The conscious, subconscious and superconscious are fully connected in an unbroken, connected stream of consciousness.

Mountains symbolize obstacles or challenges to one creating the higher consciousness. Plagues represent the pain of denial that occurs right before a transformation in consciousness. When one accepts Self and one's thoughts as the cause of one's life, obstacles such as blame, doubt, fear, worry and guilt cease to control or limit one's consciousness.

Hail is made up of water. Water symbolizes life experience. Hail indicates the physical, rigidly structured thinking when one believes that Self is separate from the universe. The physical aspects lack of movement in consciousness causes pain. To become fixed, stubborn cold, rigid and attached like ice instead of yielding and flowing like water creates pain, suffering and misery.

The quality and benefits of yielding and flowing are given in chapters 8 and 22 of the **Tao Te Ching** and also in Isaiah 55 and Revelation 22.

Chapter 8 of the Tao Te Ching

The best way to live is to be like water
for water benefits all things
without competing or going against anything
flowing in places others reject and avoid
This is why water is like the Tao
Dwell close to the Earth
still the mind thoughts and go deep
Give with kindness
speak truth and honesty
govern peacefully
be responsible when serving others
when causing movement be timely

Such a one does not go against the nature of things. Therefore, things do not go against such a one.

Chapter 22 of the Tao Te Ching

Yield and become complete
Bend and become straightened
empty and become full
Wear out and be renewed
Have little and gain much
Have much and be confused

Therefore, the Sage embraces the One unity
and thus becomes an example to the world
not showing off he shines forth
not promoting himself he is distinguished
not boasting he gains continual merit
not being conceited his greatness leads

*Because he does not compete
no one can compete against him
The ancients who said yield and become complete
were not just saying empty words
Becoming whole and complete depends on yielding*

The **Tao Te Ching** is one of the great Holy Books of the world revered and studied by billions of Chinese. I have interpreted and explained the **Tao Te Ching** to make it understandable to the western mind and the world in my book titled, The Tao Te Ching, Interpreted and Explained.

Physically thinking aspects still blaspheme, which is to blame. To blame is to falsely believe Self is separate from the universe including everyone else. Someone else or something outside of you is not to blame for your pain and suffering. Attachment to physical desires produces your pain and suffering.

The Dhammapada Chapter 1, verses 1 and 2

*1 Twin verses
Our life is shaped by our mind; we become what we think. Suffering follows an evil-dark-separate thought as the wheels of a cart follow the oxen that draw it.
2 Our life is shaped by our mind; we become what we think. Joy follows a pure thought like a shadow that never leaves.*

Suffering is the pain of limitation. The Dhammapada is a collection of the teachings and sayings pf Gautama the Buddha. It is revered worldwide as one of the great Holy Books of the world.

Summary of the Inner Meaning of Chapter 16 of the Book of Revelation
The one with a disciplined and still mind is prepared to identify, change and transcend all limitations in the brain, the conscious mind and the thinking.

Chapter 17 of Revelation

Few Word Essence of Chapter 17 of the Book of Revelation

Engrossment in sensory experience

Brief and More Expanded Essence of Chapter 17 of the Book of Revelation

The full awareness of one's engrossment in sensory experience is realized. This will be overcome.

Chapter 17

New Symbols & The Interpretation of Chapter 17 of Revelation

1. beast - habit

2. bottomless pit - unconsciousness

3. hills - obstacles to higher consciousness

4. Lord - I AM

5. heart - understanding

Chapter 17

1 Then came one of the seven angels which had the seven bowls and talked with me, saying, Come, I will show you the condemnation of the great harlot who sits upon many waters. 2 With whom the kings of the earth have committed adultery, and the inhabitants of the earth have been made drunk with the wine of her adultery.

To condemn is to pronounce to be utterly wrong. The harlot symbolizes that part of self that is engrossed in sensory, material existence and has refused the commitment to the whole Self. The harlot sits on many waters indicating the unproductive, sensory engrossed conscious mind. The gluttony of the harlot symbolizes sensory engrossment. The harlot symbolizes a complete disregard for any type of commitment to the soul, one's subconscious mind.

However, the disciplined one who achieves this level of awareness is waking up to the true nature of reality and is therefore, realizing the futility of allowing temporary, sensory pleasures to distract one from the permanent and lasting truth. The five senses cannot give fulfillment. The five senses give temporary experience. It is up to us to draw the essence of the learning from every experience.

The kings of the earth are the five senses. These five senses give the illusion that everything is separate. This illusion gives rise to physical thinking. This physical thinking is based on temporary experience and adds little or nothing to the soul.

To be drunk is to give up one's will and reasoning. When one allows the five senses to be in control the Self becomes a shallow thinker. Such a one thinks mostly with the brain and very little with the mind. Often people think they will be deep thinkers if they think more thoughts. This is not true.

A deep thinker is one who stills the mind in order to receive in-

tuitive awareness and higher reasoning from the deeper Subconscious and Superconscious Minds.

However, the one who has reached this chapter in awareness of Self has recognized key limitations in consciousness. Such a one, whether in male or female body, identifies the need to overcome engrossment concerning certain aspects of Self. The Self chooses to cause the attention to be in the present moment while deciding to place the attention where permanent learning is rather than only where sensory experiences reside. To this end the Self chooses a greater commitment to the whole Self.

> 3 So he carried me away in the spirit into the wilderness; and I saw a woman sitting on a scarlet, wild beast inscribed with many words of blasphemy and having seven heads and ten horns.

The scarlet, wild beast having seven heads and ten horns is the first beast of Revelation 13:1. In both instances the beast is described with 7 heads and 10 horns.

Therefore, the harlot rides the first beast of Revelation 13:1. The harlot-sensory engrossment rides the habitual, bestial use of memory. What is the meaning? People become habituated to sensory experience. Then the ego gains control by calling forth memories of sensory experiences in the past. One can get lost in memories of the past and waste a lifetime.

The spirit, which is the pranic-breath of life force from Superconscious Mind, carries or brings one's consciousness to a greater awareness in the part of the conscious mind that is still habitual and uncommitted to soul growth and spiritual development.

The overthrow of this physical thinking part of the Self that functions in the brain is a major key to then gaining awareness and reception of the seven levels of Mind and the 10 chakras.

Thinking physically is to view life, people and the world as separate from the Self.

To think life is separate from the Self leads to blasphemy which is to blame the environment for one's troubles or limitations or pain.

The wilderness is the wild and untamed part of one's own brain that needs to be disciplined by the will, purpose and the conscious mind.

4 And the woman was arrayed in purple and scarlet, and adorned with gold and precious stones and pearls; and she had a golden cup in her hand full of abominations and filthiness of her adultery on earth.

This undisciplined, conscious aspect symbolized by the harlot woman misuses the senses to delude the brain into thinking value lies in physical, sensory, experience alone. Yet, this value is false for sensory experiences are temporary and limited.

Abominate means to hate extremely, to abhor, to detest and to be of ill omen. The cup is full of hate, anger, and thoughts that are destructive. These destructive thoughts are a product of the undisciplined mind.

The individual who desires to progress in soul understanding and enlightenment beyond this point must perceive the illusory glitter and attraction of temporary, physical, sensory sensations. "All that glitters is not gold," it has been said.

One must identify and realize that true worth and value lie in the permanent and lasting true reality of connectedness and oneness.

The woman was arrayed in purple and scarlet indicates the misuse of reasoning and the misuse of the brow and root chakras. The predominant color of the root chakra is red and the brow chakra is purple. Specifically, misuse of perception and misuse of physical creation is indicated.

5 And upon her forehead was a name written that not all could understand: BABYLON THE GREAT, THE MOTHER OF HARLOTS AND ABOMINA-TIONS OF THE EARTH.

The name was written on her forehead. Recall that in chapter 14, verse 1, the <u>Lamb</u> stood on Mount Zion and with him a hundred and forty-four thousand in number, having the name of his <u>Father</u> written on their brows. And in chapter 13, verse 16, the <u>first beast</u> compelled all to receive a mark on their right hand or on their <u>brow</u>. The harlot's forehead is similar to the first beast's brow or forehead. You can either have the mark of the Lamb which is the name of the Father in Heaven on your forehead or you can have the mark of the beast and the harlot.

The name of the Father on your brow is the full commitment needed to know Superconscious Mind. Such a one has aligned conscious and subconscious mind and attuned them to superconscious mind.

The mark of the first beast on one's forehead is the misuse of memory and the limited use of reasoning to only accomplish physical goals and physical desires. There is a heavy dependency on and misuse of memory. The misuse of memory leads to a mistrust of reasoning because reasoning is made up of memory, attention and imagination.

The mark of the harlot on one's forehead is the misuse of sensory experience to fantasize with the imagination about further sensory engrossment.

The only true and productive use of memory is in the present moment. I discovered this through years of discipline with meditation, concentration, and the body. And the brain is a part of the body.

Memory is to be consciously drawn forth and applied in the present moment.

The name written upon the forehead of the harlot concerns engrossment in physical, sensory, experience. This engrossment indicates a lack of commitment to the whole Self. It is the misuse of reasoning to lead a life devoted to the achievement of physical desires.

Babylon symbolizes engrossment as does the harlot. Engrossment means being caught up in the delusion that the physical, sensory life is one's total reality and that the physical world is all there is. It is life of separation lived for temporary, sense pleasures and pains. The harlot symbolizes habitual, sense gratification and misuse of the creative energy. The harlot indicates a lack of commitment to the High Self or to anything permanent and lasting.

An abomination is something one detests or abhors. The knower, the Christ within and I AM have their urge to aid the conscious mind to know and live what is lasting and real. The soul abhors a life lived only for the pursuit of physical desires and sense pleasure. The soul is fulfilled in a life lived for building permanent understandings of Self and creation.

> **6 And I saw that the woman was drunk with the blood of the saints and with the blood of the martyrs-witnesses of Jesus; and when I saw her, I wondered with great amazement.**

The woman, who is the harlot, is an aspect of the conscious mind. The harlot symbolizes that part of you that is still engrossed in sensory experiences and has yet to make the full commitment to know the whole Self.

To be drunk is to give up one's will and reasoning. To be drunk is to go partially unconscious. Blood symbolizes truth and life force. The saint and martyrs of Jesus symbolize those aspects of Self that are fully committed to knowing the whole Self.

The woman, the harlot was not only drunk, she was drunk with the blood of saints and martyrs. This indicates that the misuse of truth and life force until one becomes drunk with one's own power. Power to control or create sensory experience at will causes one to become more and more unconscious. This unconscious, egotistical use of power or control will corrupt one's reasoning. This corruption will interfere with one's reasoning and commitment to Christ Consciousness.

The solution is mental discipline which is discipline of the mind. Then one can wake up to a greater consciousness. Discipline of the mind creates a mind capable of receiving higher truth. A disciplined and still mind can witness or observe each experience with the mind. An undisciplined mind will receive only a partial experience.

> 7 And the angel said to me, Why do you wonder? I will tell you the mystery of the woman and of the wild beast that carries her, which has the seven heads and the ten horns. 8 The wild beast that you saw was, and is not, and is ready to come up from the bottomless pit and go to be destroyed; and those who dwell on earth whose names were not written in the Book of Life from the foundation of the world shall wonder when they behold the beast that was, and is not, and now whose end has come.

The statement, "the wild beast you saw was and is not," indicates this beast is a function of memory. The word, "was" indicates the past. Memory is of the past. The past is over and no longer exists. Memories are not the past, they are synapses firing in the brain, repeatedly in the same way. Memory is electro-chemical impulses. People are under the delusion that synapses electrically firing in the brain are the true reality. This is the meaning of the phrase, "the beast that is not." The beast that is not, doesn't exist as a true reality except as repeated electrical firing of nerves and synapses in the brain.

This beast is about to come up out of the pit of unconsciousness and be destroyed because, you, the enlightened being, are about to use the disciplined mind to realize the truth about memory. Then you will choose to live in the ever present now. The true reality.

The beast has come up out of the pit because the reasoner with the disciplined mind remains more and more in the present moment. The attention is focused in the now. The eternal now is the only reality. The past exists only as a memory. The ego-dragon misuses memory, symbolized by the wild beast, to control you and your consciousness. The beast that was, and is not and now whose end has come, is the misuse of reasoning that is coming to an end.

Since the conscious ego exists only as a reflection, a shadow, of I AM, and because the conscious ego functions though the physical body, it perceives life as physical and temporary. The experiences of the 5 senses form the ego's view of the world. It is a limited, illusory view of life as temporary existence.

The reason the wild beast is ready to come up out of the abyss, the bottomless pit, is this. The bottomless pit is one's unconsciousness. The bottomless pit is the unconscious part of the brain. When one refuses to make consistent, conscious, choices and decisions that keep one awake in the present moment, that refusal will cause one to go unconscious. To allow old memory thoughts to rise in your consciousness and then to dwell in these memories of the past in unconsciousness.

You can only be awake and conscious in the present moment.

To drift off into worry about the future is to become unconscious.

To daydream about the future with no intentions of fulfilling that daydream is being unconscious.

Memory is only used correctly when it is consciously drawn forth to apply in the present.

Imagination of the future is only used correctly when applied in the present to create that imagined future.

Only by being and doing consciously in the present moment can one be conscious and get out of the bottomless pit. The reference to 'the beast that was', is indicative of the past. The conscious ego-the dragon misuses memories of the past. The wild beast, the first beast is not, because memories are temporary. The event in the past no longer exists. Memories are images stored in the brain. The ego-dragon will use repetitive memory images over and over to control a person who is relatively unconscious. Anytime you have thoughts that you are not fully aware of , you are unconscious. Yet unconscious thoughts can and will control you. This is why and how people create pain in their lives, unconsciously.

Only by disciplining the mind to consciously choose every thought can control of memory-the wild beast and the ego-dragon be gained. When the subtle, cunning ego-dragon can no longer control you he will then attempt direct frontal assault on your consciousness. The disciplined mind is the key to overcoming the subtle ego-dragon because the disciplined mind gives one awareness of one's own thoughts. With awareness one can choose to think the same thought, think different thoughts, or think no thoughts at all.

When subtlety no longer works the ego-dragon will try rage, anger and other outward shows of false power. The ego-dragon wants to maintain control at all costs. When the ego-dragon rises from the bottomless pit of the unconscious part of the brain, it is because he knows his time for existence is running out. When the wild beast that is the first beast arises out of the bottomless pit, be aware that you now have the opportunity to be aware of all your habitual, memory thoughts. This is a powerful step in getting control of your consciousness and your life. When the subtlety of the serpent-Devil-conscious ego no longer works to control the individual them the conscious ego-Dragon appears. The Dragon attempts to use force.

Those whose names were not written in the Book of the Living from the foundation of the world are physical aspects or physical ways of thinking. Blame is an example of physical thinking.

> **9 Here is understanding for him who has wisdom: The seven heads are seven hills on which the woman sits.**
> **10 And there are seven kings, of whom five have fallen and one is and the other has not yet come; and when he comes he shall continue only for a short time.**

The seven heads which are the seven hills symbolize the seven levels of Mind.

The conscious mind needs to become totally disciplined and productive. Each experience needs to be used to build permanent understandings of Self and creation. The conscious mind must be disciplined and brought under the control and direction of the Real Self that is beyond Mind.

The seven kings are one's ability to gain mastery over the seven levels of Mind and the seven root races. The seven root races are within the Self.

> The seven root races are:
> 1. gas
> 2. mineral
> 3. plant
> 4. animal
> 5. the reasoner
> 6. Intuitive spiritual being
> 7. Still mind creator

The kings that have fallen indicate one who has mastered the first five root races and now exists as a productive reasoner. A productive reasoner understands that thought is cause. The sixth king is one who is gaining mastery of the 6th root race known as intuitive man or intuitive being.

The reason that the seventh stage will continue only for a short time is that such a one gains enlightenment rapidly. Such a one overcomes Karma and the cycle of birth and death. Such a one is no longer bound to physical existence, and therefore, no longer is restricted by physical time. Such a one functions from mental, or vertical time.

He shall continue only for a short time because when the mind is disciplined and stilled, physical time shortens or contracts into the single point that is everywhere and encompasses all of Mind and Creation. For one who has reached this level of enlightenment the time of entrapment in a physical body is drawing to an end.

**11 And the wild beast that was, and no longer is,
even he is the eighth along with the other seven
destined to be destroyed.**

The eighth king is the conscious ego. The wild beast is controlled by the ego-dragon. The ego-dragon that controls memory thoughts is destined to be transformed and will be transformed as one comes to know I AM. You will learn discipline of your mind, become aware of your thoughts and choose to dwell less in old, habitual, memory thoughts. The way one's consciousness works with or functions with the 7 levels of mind and the ego will be transformed.

The one who reaches this stage of Self awareness and understanding knows the thoughts that arise and recognizes the ego's part in bringing forth those old memory, habitual thoughts. Then it is possible to upgrade one's thoughts and choose different, more productive thoughts. Thoughts that are in alignment with the present more so than the past.

> **12 And the ten horns which you saw are ten kings who have received no kingdom as yet, but receive authority as kings for one hour with the beast. 13 These are of one accord, and they shall give their strength and authority to the beast.**

As each of the 10 chakras are activated new awarenesses rush into the consciousness of the individual. The conscious mind has insight and power as never before. Memory and imagination increase. The conscious mind begins to align with subconscious mind and attune to superconscious mind as the chakras spin faster. This is why the 10 kings are of one accord.

The mind that can direct the attention and clearly image-imagine the future is able to manifest or create that future in a physical way. Such a one is able to create physical goals and achieve them. However, this is not enlightenment.

When the kings give their strength and authority to the beast the thinking remains physically based. The ideal is to master all of Mind, the conscious, subconscious and superconscious not just the physical body and the conscious mind.

> **14 They will make war with the Lamb, and the Lamb will conquer them, for he is Lord of lords and King of kings; and those who are with him are called and chosen and faithful.**

The Lamb symbolizes commitment to the whole Self, the Real Self. This full commitment is needed in order to master the whole mind and become enlightened.

Commitment to becoming an enlightened Christ will overcome any physically minded thinking or any physically based engrossment or illusion of control. Thought is cause. The physical world is the effect of mental cause. The more one masters the mind of Self, the more one has the true power of the causal factor.

King of kings is the ultimate authority. Lord of lords is I AM. I AM is the ultimate authority. Those aspects that align with I AM are then called to know Self as a Christ. They are chosen to be enlightened. And they are faithful which is the full commitment.

> **15 Then he said to me, The waters which you saw, where the harlot sits, are peoples and multitudes and nations and tongues.**

The thought form angel, or messenger from I AM explains to the conscious mind what is being received and experienced. This is different from a physically minded person who only receives experience and information through the five senses.

Water symbolizes conscious life experience meaning one's sensory experiences gained and received through the five senses into the brain and conscious mind. The peoples and multitudes and nations and tongues symbolize those aspects of the conscious mind that have become physicalized and therefore distracted from the real purpose of life.

The temporary, physical, life of the senses is to be used to build permanent understandings of Self and creation.

> **16 And the ten horns and the wild beast which you saw shall hate the harlot, and shall make her desolate and naked, and shall eat her flesh and burn her with fire.**

As the ability to use the 10 chakras increases through the disciplined use of imagination, memory, and attention, the reasoning Self chooses to overcome and transform the part of Self that is still engrossed in sensory experiences. The true limitation of sensory engrossment is its temporariness. This is symbolized by the harlot's nakedness. Reasoning will overcome sensory engrossment. However, reasoning alone will not give enlightenment. The disciplined being can achieve superconscious awareness and thereby, understand the limitations of sensory engrossment. Such a one is using reasoning to understand connectedness.

The consciousness is now ready to expand as symbolized by the fire.

17 For God has put into their heart to do his will and to be of one accord and to give their kingdom to the wild beast until the words of God shall be fulfilled.

The heart chakra's quality is understanding.

Each individual is to choose and will the Self to build permanent understandings of Self and creation. The will, when combined with the activated chakras working in unison, enables the correct use of memory and imagination to prepare the way for a higher consciousness. Thus reasoning is to be used to build permanent understandings of Self and creation until one's whole, entire subconscious mind is filled with understandings of Self and creation. Then the words of God will be fulfilled for then the Self will be filled full of LIGHT filled understandings. God's word is, "Let there be LIGHT," as given in the first chapter of Genesis, verse 3.

18 And the woman whom you saw is that great city which has dominion over the kings of the earth.

The great city that has dominion over the kings of the Earth is Babylon. Babylon symbolizes sensory engrossment as does the woman who is the harlot. The meaning is that the conscious mind of such a one has awakened to the fact that sensory experiences are temporary and sensory engrossment brings suffering. Therefore, the reasoner engages the conscious mind in the great effort to overcome sensory engrossment which breeds attachment to desires. The one committed to the great enlightenment, the great awakening, will commit to continue this great effort until one gains control of the conscious mind and the senses. The conscious mind must be brought under the control, discipline and direction of the individual.

Summary of the Inner Meaning of Chapter 17 of the Book of Revelation
What once was unconscious in the Self has now been made conscious. Mental discipline and commitment to know the whole Self are the keys to overcoming engrossment in the 5 senses of sight, smell, taste, touch, and hearing.

Chapter 18 of Revelation

Few Word Essence of Chapter 18
of the Book of Revelation

Mastering the 5 senses

Brief and More Expanded Essence of Chapter 18
of the Book of Revelation

The disciplined Self with a still mind has overcome
engrossment and attachment to sensory experience.

Chapter 18

New Symbols & The Interpretation of Chapter 18 of Revelation

1. devils - unproductive, egotistical thoughts

2. unclean birds - habitual subconscious thoughts

3. wine of her wrath - distilled anger

4. merchants - those aspects of Self that exchange perceived temporary value

5. dust - subconscious mind substance

6. millstone - the will to transform temporary experience to permanent knowledge and understanding

Chapter 18

1 After these things I saw another angel come down from heaven, having great power; and the earth was lighted by his glory. 2 And he cried with a mighty voice, saying Babylon the great is fallen and has become a habitation of those possessed with devils and shelter of every foul spirit and the shelter of every unclean and detestable bird and the shelter of every unclean and loathsome wild beast.

The angel messenger indicates the disciplined one is awakening to the LIGHT of awareness. This greater awakeness and awareness has enabled the still minded one to identify the unproductiveness of sensory engrossment. When sensory experience loses its allure, its drawing power, its illusion, the illumined one soon knows the truth. The craving for desires only creates pain and misery, and this is exactly what the Buddha said.

Babylon, symbolizing sensory engrossment, leads to falseness of perception. When one identifies the limitation of sensory engrossment the cunning conscious ego becomes easier to identify. The disciplined student disciplines and observes the breath. Now the Self identifies all habitual ways of thinking.

'Every foul spirit' indicates the misuse of breath and life force.

'Loathsome wild beasts' symbolize one's unproductive habits.

Wrong perception coming from sensory engrossment leads to wrong thinking.

Wrong thinking is based in temporariness and separateness.

3 Because all nations have drunk of the wine of her wrath and the kings of the earth have committed adultery with her and the merchants of the earth have become rich through the power of her trade.

Nations symbolize the many aspects of Self.

The wine of Babylon's wrath symbolizes the anger one experiences when one refuses to discipline the conscious mind. When the conscious mind is undisciplined the thoughts are undisciplined due to a weak will. When the conscious thoughts are undisciplined, the emotions are undisciplined. When the emotions are undisciplined one often experiences anger at the self and others.

Accumulating possessions does not give one permanent understandings of Self and creation. The perspective of life changes from the temporary to the permanent and lasting.

> **4 And I heard another voice from heaven, saying, come out of her, O my people so that you may not become partakers of her sins and lest you be smitten by her plagues.**

Coming out of Babylon indicates the movement out of sensory engrossment. To live your life for touch, taste, smell, sound or sight is sensory engrossment. To maintain a disciplined, still mind while receiving sensory input is the movement out of Babylon.

A sin is a mistake. It is to violate one's duty. One's duty is soul growth and aiding others to do the same. The sin of the harlot is sensory engrossment. Sensory engrossment provides no greater understanding of Self and no soul growth. The productive use of the senses by a disciplined mind enables the Self to receive the essence of the learning, the permanent understanding from each experience.

The one with a disciplined, still mind will not be smitten by Babylon's painful plagues for in a disciplined, stilled mind there is no disorder.

> **5 For her sins have reached up to heaven, and God has remembered her iniquities.**

Heaven symbolizes superconscious mind. By the time one has reached this chapter, this high level of soul growth and spiritual development, one has aligned conscious and subconscious minds and attuned them to some degree to superconscious mind. Sins are mistakes or errors in thinking. The more enlightened or evolved one becomes, the more one's mistakes in thinking, action and consciousness become apparent. One has the clear perception to identify which aspects of Self are still entrapped.

Iniquity is wickedness that is harmful and unproductive. Sensory engrossment is harmful and unproductive. It creates pain and misery as well as retarding one's soul growth and spiritual development. When one reaches this level of awareness and understanding, there is the recognition of one's misery making and unproductive thoughts including sensory engrossment.

> **6 Reward her even as she has rewarded you, and return to her a double portion according to her works; in the cup which she has mixed, mix for her double.**

Babylon the harlot, indicating sensory engrossment, has created pain and misery in the individual. A double portion symbolizes the physical manifestation of the Universal Law of Cause and Effect-Karma.

The Buddha, as recorded in the **Dhammapada**, a Holy book of India, said that the cause of pain and suffering is misery making attachment to desires. This craving, this attachment, must be overcome by doubling one's efforts of mental discipline, such as concentration and meditation until one can observe the thoughts. Then one achieves balance in the Aggressive and Receptive Principles of Creation. Every time you observe sensory engrossment, attachment to desires, or craving, double your efforts of mental discipline. From this you will master your thoughts, know thought is cause, and overcome karma. Karma is indebtedness as an individual. The debt owed Self is relieved by building permanent understandings of Self and creation.

> **7 For as much as she has glorified herself and lived deliciously, give her so much torment and sorrow; for she says in her heart, Here I sit, a queen, and am no widow and shall see no sorrow.**

Sensory delight is delicious. Yet it is only temporary. Without choice and moderation misery ensues. Therefore give the harlot, Babylon, misery by practicing mental discipline. The conscious ego, the brain and the physical body resist mental discipline, yet resistance is overcome by one committed to knowing Self, the Real Self.

Double your effort. Double your mental discipline by learning to concentrate and still the mind throughout the day. Don't give in to excesses. Don't wait until your meditation time at the end of the day to practice meditation. Rather practice the still mind of meditation one half of the day throughout the day. The other one half practice choosing your thoughts deliberately and consciously throughout the day. This I have practiced for many years now.

> **8 For just that reason, her plagues shall come in one day, death and mourning and famine, and she shall be burned with fire; for mighty is the Lord God who judges her.**

A queen receives the abundance of her kingdom. However, these sensory delights are only temporary. Babylon's plagues come in one day because as soon as one recognizes, is aware of and identifies the plague in Self, which is the disastrous mistakes in thinking, the thinking can begin to change. When one changes the thinking, making the thoughts more productive, one changes the cause. Thought is cause. A productive thought is one that aligns with Universal Law and Universal Truth.

As one stills the mind and then chooses productive, truth filled thoughts and teaches this to others, consciousness expands. This expansion is symbolized by fire.

The Lord God is I AM. The one who discovers more of the Real Self identifies the limitations of sensory engrossment and physical thinking. You are I AM. Therefore, you judge your own limitations in consciousness that are created by sensory engrossment.

> **9 And the kings of the earth who committed adultery and lived deliciously with her will weep and mourn and wail over her when they see the smoke of her burning. 10 Standing afar off for the fear of her torment, saying, Woe, woe, that great city Babylon, that mighty city! For in one hour you have been condemned.**

The kings of the earth are the senses. The senses must be disciplined and trained by the individual. This is accomplished by disciplining the mind. The brain, the five senses and the physical body have enjoyed these sensory experiences and sensory stimulation. Yet, it was all temporary. Now, for the one prepared for this chapter or stage in understanding, the consciousness expands.

The kings of the Earth, the 5 senses, stand far off from Babylon, which is burning because the five senses remain even after one has overcome engrossment. The truth is, that after overcoming engrossment, one has the capacity to use the senses even better because they are used for the whole Self to produce permanent understandings of Self and creation. One hour symbolizes one who is getting closer to living in the ever present now. The word 'woe' indicates one's attachment to the old sensory desires.

> **11 And the merchants of the earth shall weep and mourn over her; for no man buys their merchandise any more.**

Merchants exchange something of value for something else of value. These merchants have traded in sensory gratifications. Sensory gratification for the purpose of pleasurable sensory gratification leaves one unfulfilled because the stimulation is temporary. The one who causes the fall or destruction of Babylon in the Self has chosen to discipline the mind and live for the permanent and lasting. These everlasting benefits are assured to those that master the senses, the body, the ego and the mind.

Man symbolizes the subconscious aspects of Self. The word man comes from the Sanskrit word manu, which means thinker. The one who has learned to reason from the point of cause, which is thought, no longer invests the time and attention in sensory engrossment. In other words, the senses no longer rule the life.

> **12 Never again will there be cargoes of gold and silver and precious stones, and pearls and fine linen and purple and silk and scarlet and every kind of aromatic wood, and all manner of vessels of ivory, and all manner of vessels of most precious wood, and of brass and iron and marble. 13 And cinnamon and perfumes and spices and myrrh and frankincense and wine, and oil and fine flour and wheat and cattle and sheep, and horses and chariots and hides and slaves. 13 And the fruits which your soul lusted after are departed from you, and all things which were luxurious and goodly are lost to you, and you shall never find them any more at all.**

Gold, silver and precious stones symbolize value; in this case the value one had previously given to sensory engrossment. The entire listing of silk, purple dye, scarlet, aromatic wood, ivory, brass, marble, iron, spices, oil, flour, cattle, sheep, chariots and slaves all indicate the ways attention is given to physical, sensory experiences. Sensory engrossment is becoming a thing of the past. Sensory experiences alone do not provide truth and understanding. This disciplined one has realized this. Purple and scarlet indicate the ways one has externalized the life and attention. Now the attention must be turned inward to know the truth.

Fruit symbolizes knowledge. One does not gain permanent knowledge from sensory experience alone. One has to learn how to derive or distill the essence of the learning in every experience. The one who has achieved this level of awareness has learned how to draw understanding from life's experiences.

Verse 12 indicates those objects that engross one through the senses of sight and touch. Verse 13 presents those objects that engross one in the senses of smell and taste.

> **15 The merchants of these things, who were made rich by her, shall stand afar off for the fear of her torment, and they shall weep and wail, 16 Saying, Woe, woe, that great city, which was clothed with fine linen and purple and scarlet, inlaid with gold, and precious stones and pearls! For in one hour these great riches are destroyed.**

The body and the senses need to be brought under the control of the individual. Once one is no longer engrossed in the five senses, one no longer wrongly believes the Self to be the experiences. Rather, one with a disciplined mind is able to separate the experience from the Self. This is the meaning of the statement, 'the merchants shall stand afar off.' Separation is afar.

To achieve this level of understanding, one must be able to give the full attention to the present moment. The hour has come for the great riches of Babylon-engrossment to be destroyed. The hour referred to is the present moment. This hour or time occurs when one develops the capability to still the mind and live in the present moment.

One's perspective on what is valuable in life and the purpose of life changes.

**17 And every shipmaster and all the travelers in ships
and sailors and all those who labor at sea stood afar off,
18 And cried when they saw the smoke of her burning,
saying, What city is like to this great city!**

The sea indicates conscious life experience. The shipmaster and
sailors symbolizes aspects of the Self that use one's conscious mind.
Ships travel on the surface of the sea and therefore indicate those parts
of Self that, up to now, have remained rather surface in the thinking.
These aspects have not served in developing a deeper awareness of
Self. These aspects tend to view life in a physical or superficial way.
This is that part of Self that has thought physical, temporary experiences to be more valuable than the inner life. These aspects of Self are
becoming aware of expansion of consciousness symbolized by the smoke
and burning.

**19 And they threw dust on their heads and cried,
weeping and wailing, saying, Woe, woe, that great
city, where all who had ships on the sea were made
rich by reason of her preciousness! For in one hour
she is destroyed.**

Their heads symbolize identity. Dust symbolizes subconscious mind
substance. The shipmasters and sailors threw dust on their heads symbolizing aspects of one's conscious mind that are becoming aware of
the subconscious mind, soul. These aspects are admitting the truth that,
'There is more to life than meets the eye.' The physical things that
seemed so valuable to such a one are now seen to have little or no value
because they are temporary. For in one hour she, meaning Babylon-the
Harlot, is destroyed. One hour means a certain point or period in time.
One hour symbolizes an individual who has achieved the still mind in
order to know oneness in the ever present, eternal now.

**20 Rejoice over her, O heaven and angels, apostles
and prophets, for God has avenged you on her.**

Angels rejoice because the message from I AM has been received
into one's conscious awareness. The message is, you are an eternal
being rather than a temporary, physical body. An apostle is a teacher of
Mind and the Secrets of Creation. Apostles rejoice because all the Universal Truths these aspects are teaching are being more fully accepted

into the whole Self. To rejoice is to feel joy again. The prophets feel and experience joy because the second coming of Christ, the Christ consciousness, within the individual is about to be fulfilled as engrossment is overcome.

The prophets have prophesied of the coming of the enlightened Christ being. Engrossment in sensory experience is being overcome.

> **21 And a mighty angel took up a stone like a great millstone and cast it into the sea, saying, So shall that great city Babylon be overthrown with violence and shall be found no more at all.**

A stone symbolizes will. A millstone symbolizes will power.

A millstone is used for grinding grain into flour. Flour and other food symbolize knowledge. A stone like a great millstone symbolizes one's new found ability to exercise the will to produce permanent understandings from life experiences. Previously the individual had become engrossed in the temporary experiences, thus gaining little of permanent and lasting value.

The previous, engrossed, conscious, sensory life experience is overthrown by the conscious use of choices to produce a powerful will that quickens one's soul growth and spiritual development. The time of sensory engrossment and the delusion that physical life is all that exists, is coming to an end.

> **22 And the sound of harpers and musicians and singers and trumpeters shall not be heard in you again; and no craftsman of whatever craft he be shall be found any more in you; 23 And the light of a lamp shall shine no more at all in you; and the voice of the bridegroom and of the bride shall be heard no more at all in you; for your merchants were the great men of the earth; for by your sorceries were all peoples deceived.**

Harpers, musicians, singers and trumpeters all symbolize those aspects that have produced a type of harmony in the conscious mind. The meaning is that the pleasure type harmony or temporary happiness one found in temporary, sensory experiences will no longer suffice to keep one distracted from the real purpose of life. Verse 22 represents the engrossment that had occurred through the sense of hearing.

This engrossment is now being overcome. Thus, all 5 senses have been mastered by the disciplined, still mind.

Whatever activities have kept your mind busy will no longer avail you. Your craft is what keeps your conscious mind busy and brain occupied. No longer will you be committed to physical life only. No longer will such a one accept the delusion that physical experiences and memorizing information is awareness or knowing. No longer will you be deceived in this way. Now you are committed to the whole Self and using the whole mind. The true bridegroom is the High Self. No more commitment to sensory experience. Now the commitment is to I AM.

24 And in her was found the blood of prophets and of saints and of all who were slain upon the earth.

Babylon, which symbolizes physical engrossment in the senses, has kept the blood-life force and truth from fully manifesting in one's being. The one who achieves the still mind and needs a still mind more than sensory experience achieves mastery over the senses. Having mastered the senses one triumphs over the brain, memory, fantasy-imagination and the conscious ego. Thus is one's energy and life freed up to pursue the Truth.

Now that one is no longer lost in sensory experience the delusion is coming to an end. Physical experiences are used to produce a quickening of soul growth. The process of building permanent understandings of Self and creation can proceed at an accelerated rate.

Now, the High Truth is revealed.

Now, the keys of change and transformation of consciousness are revealed.

Now, the Real Self, the inner Self can come forward.

Summary of the Inner Meaning of Chapter 18 of the Book of Revelation
Now, one can perceive and identify clearly one's own engrossment in matter. No longer do sensory experiences hold the highest priority in one's life. The true value lies in what is permanent, lasting and real. The Real Self is overcoming the resistance in the brain.

Chapter 19 of Revelation

Few Word Essence of Chapter 19
of the Book of Revelation

Relieving karma, sensory engrossment and
entrapment

Brief and More Expanded Essence of Chapter 19
of the Book of Revelation

The disciplined Self with a still mind has, through
superconscious awareness, overcome all limitations of
the brain.

Chapter 19

New Symbols & The Interpretation of Chapter 19 of Revelation

1. marriage - commitment to the Real Self

2. white horse - will power, the productive use of the will

3. cloak - outer expression or presentation

Chapter 19

1 And after these things, I heard a great voice of a great multitude in heaven, saying, Hallelujah! Salvation and power and glory and honor to our God.
2 For his judgments are true and righteous; for he has condemned the great harlot who has corrupted the earth with her adultery, and has avenged the blood of his servants at her hand.

The 'harlot who corrupted the Earth by her harlotry' represents the conscious mind that became engrossed in physical experiences without a purpose for permanent learning. Hallelujah is an expression of praise, joy or thanks.

Many superconscious aspects appreciate and value the effort Self has given in the conscious mind to gain greater enlightenment. Salvation is achieved by overcoming engrossment in physical, sensory experience.

The creator within has triumphed in such a one and is now able and capable of using physical experience wisely and correctly. To use physical experience correctly is to receive the permanent and lasting Universal Truth and understanding from every experience.

The wrong has been righted. The unproductive has been replaced with the productive. The temporary has been replaced by the permanent and lasting. Engrossment in the maya of sensory illusion has been overcome by the disciplined and loving being.

3 And a second time, they said, Hallelujah! And her smoke rose up for ever and ever. 4 And the four and twenty elders and the four animals fell down and worshipped God who sat on the throne, saying, Amen, Alleluia!

As sensory engrossment and the illusion of physicality is transformed in the Self the result of that transformation moves throughout the conscious, subconscious and superconscious minds.

Smoke comes from fire. Fire symbolizes expansion of consciousness. Smoke rises into the sky indicating that the results of expansion of consciousness rises all the way to Superconscious Mind.

The four and twenty elders are the inner and outer aspects of Self. They are the 12 disciples that are the inward moving, subconscious aspects of Jesus the Christ and the 12 outward moving, conscious mind aspects symbolized by the 12 tribes of Israel. The 4 animals symbolize the four levels of subconscious mind. All of these aspects of Self direct their attention in reverence to the Divine High Self.

> **5 And a voice came out from the throne, saying, Praise our God, all you his servants and you who worship him, both small and great. 6 And I heard as it were the voice of a great multitude, like the voice of many waters and like the sound of mighty thunderings, saying, Hallelujah! For our Lord God, omnipotent, reigns.**

The voice from the throne indicates one's consciousness in the conscious mind is receiving instruction from superconscious mind. The voice indicates the right of choice. It is the power of conscious choice that builds the will into will power. The voice proclaims the use of will to direct the attention to knowing Self and becoming a son of the Creator.

This second voice is the choice to align and harmonize many aspects of Self into one voice of will and attention. This one voice is the greater recognition and knowing of Self as I AM.

Lord God is I AM. I AM is omnipotent over all aspects of Self when one recognizes Self as I AM. Once you know Self then I AM reigns, which is to rule or direct all aspects of Self.

> **7 Let us be glad and rejoice and give glory to him, for the time of the marriage feast of the Lamb has come, and his bride has made herself ready. 8 And it was given to her that she should be arrayed in fine pure linen, clean and white; for fine linen is the righteousness of saints.**

The Lamb symbolizes anyone who is committed to knowing the whole Self as I AM. The time of the marriage feast of the bride and the Lamb is the full alignment of conscious and subconscious minds and their attunement to superconscious mind.

The conscious mind, symbolized by the bride, has made herself ready for this alignment and attunement. The time of the marriage feast can only occur when the mind is stilled through mental discipline and a higher purpose.

Fine, pure linen signifies the most productive outer expression of the conscious mind. This comes about through a disciplined, stilled and committed conscious mind.

Righteousness is right thinking. Right thinking begins with a still mind. Saints are those aspects of Self fully in harmony with Universal Law and Universal Truth.

> **9 And he said to me, Write, Blessed are those who are invited to the wedding feast of the Lamb. Then he said to me, These words of mine are the true sayings of God.**

To be blessed is to receive or invoke divine care. Those invited to the wedding feast of the Lamb are blessed or under divine care because of alignment of conscious and subconscious minds and attunement to superconscious mind. When one tunes or attunes to the superconscious mind, one becomes blessed. When one's superconscious attunes to all of Superconsciousness or Superconscious Mind, one becomes divine.

The Buddha was referred to as the Blessed One.

The true sayings of God are the outpouring of the Divine or Perfect Plan of Creation held in Superconscious Mind. To write something down is to bring a thought into physical existence. The indication is that the conscious mind or conscious awareness of the individual is now receiving Superconscious awareness.

> **10 And I fell at his feet to worship him. And he said to me, Do not do that; I am your fellow servant, and one of your brethren who have the testimony of Jesus; worship God for the testimony of Jesus is the spirit-breath of prophecy.**

The feet of the one who spoke from the altar symbolize the foundation of superconscious mind. The Self is now giving full attention to an aspect of superconscious mind, the divine being of Self. This aspect of Self says do not worship or give the whole attention and consciousness to just one aspect or part of Self. Instead give your full attention to knowing the whole Self, one's whole being, that one's full consciousness may align with being a creator and with all of creation.

The one who has the testimony of Jesus, the spirit of prophecy knows the present, the now, and therefore knows the past and future. Breathe the breath of cosmic life force in the present moment.

> **11 And I saw heaven opened, and behold, I saw a
> white horse; and he who sat upon him was called
> Faithful and True, and in righteousness he judges
> and makes war.**

The one who opens heaven now has forces available to him as never before. Such a one has developed the will to the highest. When this is achieved one is able to choose the still mind and from that to choose to either think a creative thought or to be receptive with a still mind and thereby receive creation.

The one who sat on the horse has an identity of allegiance and loyalty and is in agreement and alignment with the true reality. The disciplined one is able to overcome all limiting thoughts, ideas or aspects of the Self because of righteousness. Righteousness is the ability to make right or correct choices. Right or correct choices always align with the true nature of reality which is connectedness. Right and conscious choices always proceed from a still mind.

> **12 His eyes were like a flame of fire, and on his head
> were many crowns; and he had names written
> thereon, and one of the names written, no man knew
> but he himself.**

Eyes symbolize perception and a flame of fire indicates expansion of consciousness. His head symbolizes one's growing understanding of the true identity of Self. Crown symbolizes one's authority to create. To have author-ity is to author or create one's life in order to become enlightened, a Christ.

The names written on the crown symbolize one's awareness and recognition of the Real Self. The one name that no man knew is the true, real and deepest identity of Self. No thinker can know the true identity of Self. Only the one who can still the mind, still the thoughts and empty the mind can know the Real Self as I AM. Brain thinking can never know the Mind.

The **Bible** says, *"Be still and know that I AM God,"* Psalm 46:10.

13 And he was clothed with a cloak-vesture dipped in blood; and he called his name, The Word of God.

His cloak-vesture is the outpouring of consciousness of the one growing in enlightenment.

Blood carries one's life force. The cloak-vesture dipped in blood is the living Truth. Such a one teaches the Truth and is fully becoming the Truth. The one who knows and becomes the Truth becomes the Word of God. The Word of God is OM. OM is the creative vibration that sets Creation and the universe in motion. OM is also known in its derivative forms of AUM and AMEN.

The two lettered OM has within it the Aggressive and Receptive Principles of Creation.

The three lettered AUM has within it the three divisions of Mind, the Conscious, Subconscious and Superconscious as well as the Father, Son and Holy Spirit. The AMEN is I AM encased in physical matter attempting to know all of Mind and the whole Self.

A word is creative vibration that comes out of the mouth of the one speaking. Words express one's thoughts. Creative thoughts proceed from a still mind. Destructive thoughts proceed from a busy and undisciplined mind. The Word of God proceeds from the still mind of a creator. The Word of God is the creative urge and ability of one who is becoming a Son of God.

14 And the armies which were in heaven followed him on white horses clothed in fine linen, pure and white.

White horses symbolize the development of will through mental discipline and conscious choice.

'Fine linen, pure and white,' indicates one whose thoughts and actions are fulfilling the Perfect Plan of Creation in Superconscious Mind. The armies in heaven riding on white horses and clothed in white linen are those superconscious aspects of Self that have fully developed the will to choose a disciplined life of the still mind and service to all humanity. This will create heaven on Earth.

> **15 And out of his mouth came a sharp two-edged sword, that with it he should smite the nations; and he will rule them with a rod of iron; and he will tread the winepress of the fierceness and wrath of Almighty God.**

The sharp two-edged sword symbolizes Karma, the physical manifestation of the Universal Law of Cause and Effect. It is first referred to in Genesis 3:24 as the fiery sword to guard the path to the Tree of Life.

This one comes out of heaven with his armies signifying one who has superconscious awareness. Such a one is wielding the High consciousness to change and transform all unproductive and limiting thoughts and aspects of Self. Change and growth in the consciousness of Self that previously would have taken lifetimes can now be accomplished in years, months, weeks or even days. I have practiced and taught this acceleration of consciousness and know it is possible both in myself and others.

The rod of iron symbolizes the Universal Laws. The superconscious aspect bringing superconscious awareness brings alignment of all aspects of Self. The winepress will bring responsibility and wisdom. The wrath of God is the anger that occurs within Self when one is not responsible with thoughts.

> *16 And he had a name written on his vesture-cloak and on his thigh, KING OF KINGS AND LORD OF LORDS.*

A name indicates one's identity. Vesture-cloak is the way one gives and what one gives of the Self outwardly to the world. The thigh symbolizes one's creativity.

The King of Kings and Lord of Lords is I AM. I AM is the greatest authority of one's life. This means that superconscious awareness has now moved into and been received in the conscious mind and conscious awareness of the Self. Such a one is expressing this High Consciousness outwardly and is becoming a master teacher. The disciplined one with this high level of consciousness is creating a better world for all humanity. This individual is consciously causing and creating Christ consciousness within the Self.

> **17 And I saw an angel standing in the sun; and he**
> **cried with a loud voice, saying to all the birds that fly**
> **in the midst of heaven, Come and gather yourselves**
> **together for the great supper of God,**

The difference with this angel and the previous angels is this angel is standing in the sun. The sun symbolizes awareness of Superconscious Mind. This superconscious awareness gives one the greater and higher perspective needed to know what thoughts are productive and those thoughts that are limited, unproductive and no longer needed.

The fowls or birds that fly in the midst of heaven are those thoughts one has created that are in alignment with subconscious mind and therefore have risen to attunement to superconscious mind.

Superconscious awareness is taking over and is overcoming the limited brain habits, associated memory thoughts and sensory engrossment still remaining within the Self.

> **18 That you may eat the flesh of kings and the flesh**
> **of captains of thousands and the flesh of mighty men**
> **and the flesh of horses and of those who sit on them**
> **and the flesh of all men, both free and slave, both**
> **small and great.**

To eat is to process, assimilate and transform food or substance into energy for the Self. The meaning is that one has learned how to process all the thoughts one has. Now one is capable of transforming one's thoughts, memory thoughts, associated memory thoughts, emotional attachments and attachments to desires into higher, permanent understanding of Self and all creation.

Men symbolize aspects of Self that think physically instead of mentally. To think physically is to blame others and place the cause outside of yourself. This must change and be transformed to realize that Self is connected as one with all Creation and all beings.

> **19 Then I saw the wild beast and the kings of the earth**
> **and their armies gathered together to fight against him**
> **who sat on the horse, and against his armies.**

Habitual memory, symbolized by the wild beast, gathers what control it has left over the one with a disciplined consciousness. This false author-ity, which is really controlled by the conscious ego-dragon, marshals all its forces to try to maintain control of the individual, the brain and the conscious mind.

The forces of the wild beast are memory thoughts and associated memory thoughts that keep one attached to physical desires and sensory experience. This craving controls the brain, conscious mind and life of one until, through mental discipline and Universal Truth, one raises the thoughts to a higher level.

Chapter two of the **Bhagavad Gita** states it this way, "*62 When you keep thinking about sense objects, attachment comes. Attachment breeds desire, the lust of possession that burns to anger. 63 Anger clouds the judgment; you can no longer learn from past mistakes. Lost is the power to choose between what is wise and what is unwise, and your life is utter waste. 64 But when you move amidst the world of senses, free from attachment and aversion alike, 65 there comes the peace in which all sorrows end, and you live in the wisdom of the Self.*"

Therefore, the process that keeps one engrossed in temporary, sensory experiences is the following:

1. Thinking about sense objects,
2. Attachment to sensory experiences and objects, which breeds
3. Desires-this lust of possession burns to
4. Anger-that clouds one's
5. Judgement-that keeps one from learning from past mistakes so that
6. The power to choose is lost.
7. A life is wasted.

The one who has superconscious awareness, due to mental discipline that has created a still mind, can move among the sensory experiences without attachment. Such a one no longer allows the memory thoughts to colorize or cloud the perceptions of the present experience. An enlightened being like this sees through the conscious rationalizations of the conscious ego. Such a one accepts the fact that most of the thoughts one has been thinking have been for the entertainment of the brain and conscious ego. All those many thoughts that previously you believed were so important are now found to be distractions to the goal or ideal of enlightenment.

Thoughts that arise spontaneously into one's consciousness are habit, memory thoughts. They are a misuse of memory.

Now I have greater purpose for choosing all thoughts or I choose to have a still mind. This is the correct use of will as symbolized by the horse.

> **20 And the wild beast was caught and with him the false prophet who wrought miracles before him with which he deceived the people into accepting the mark of the wild beast and those who worshipped his image-statue. These both were thrown alive into a lake of fire burning with brimstone-sulphur.**

The wild beast symbolizes habitual, memory thoughts.

The false prophet is any goal or mental image that does not direct one's consciousness to enlightenment. The false prophet keeps one's attention in a fantasized future rather than the ever present, eternal now. The present moment is the true reality. Physical goals and physical accomplishments that lack permanent soul growth are the false prophet. Both the wild beast and the false prophet are cast alive into a lake of fire because consciousness must expand. The one who has chosen to take control of the thoughts has developed a purpose. This purpose or benefit for more enlightened thoughts causes consciousness to expand.

The one who reaches this level of understanding will no longer be deceived by egoic memory images that keep one bound to sensory engrossment and memories of sensory experiences. No longer will such a one live in a survival mode. Now one lives for I AM and the Whole Being in the eternal present, the now.

> **21 And the others were slain by the sword that came out from the mouth of him who sat upon the horse; and all the birds were filled from eating their flesh.**

All limited thought and aspects are changed and transformed by the one attuned to superconscious mind. The sword symbolizes a tool for change. The sword that came out of the mouth indicates one who is now aware of all thoughts. Therefore, this one chooses to eliminate all limited thoughts and unproductive thinking. Such a one states all unproductive thoughts aloud in order to be fully aware of those thoughts. Then the cunning-subtle-ego-dragon-devil-satan-serpent-deceiver can no longer control the conscious mind by misusing a person's thoughts.

The will, symbolized by the horse, can then be used effectively by choosing to eliminate any unproductive thoughts, habits or attitudes from one's consciousness. Thus, this energy can be transformed into superconscious awareness.

Summary of the Inner Meaning of Chapter 19 of the Book of Revelation
The highly developed will has attuned one to the ideal Self, the High Self, in Superconscious Mind. Now the conscious mind aligned with the subconscious mind and attuned to Superconscious Mind can defeat and overcome all habits and limitations of the brain. The brain is part of the animal body. The disciplined Self exists in the Mind while productively using the brain.

Chapter 20 of Revelation

Few Word Essence of Chapter 20 of the Book of Revelation

The Second Death and the Book of Life

Brief and More Expanded Essence of Chapter 20 of the Book of Revelation

The great battle to fully overcome entrapment. The conscious ego is overcome and transformed.

Chapter 20

New Symbols & The Interpretation of Chapter 20 of Revelation

1. the second death - entrapment in a physical body

2. prison - restriction

3. four corners of the Earth - the four levels of Subconscious Mind

4. Gog-China - 3rd level of Mind

5. Magog-Mongolia - 4th level of Mind

6. beloved city-Jerusalem - the peaceful, still conscious mind

7. broad plain - the productive, conscious mind

Chapter 20

**1 And I saw an angel come down from heaven,
having the key of the bottomless pit and a great
chain in his hand.**

The angel from heaven is the superconscious awareness that has
power over the unconsciousness in the brain.

The bottomless pit is one's unconsciousness. The bottomless pit is
memory thoughts, memory habits and memory attitudes stored in the
brain. For the most part these are thoughts of which people are unconscious.

Only the Buddha, only the Christ is fully awake and fully conscious.
However, being aware of all your thoughts and then learning to consciously choose all of one's thoughts gives the key to the bottomless
pit.

The key to the bottomless pit is the still mind. The still mind is an
open mind. Because it is open, the still mind can receive the Light of
awareness. The Light of awareness brings LIGHT to the darkness of
the bottomless pit that is in the unconscious part of the brain. The bottomless pit, the abyss, is the old memory thoughts one received as a
child that are wrong thinking and opposite to the Universal Laws, the
Universal Truths and the true nature of reality.

The unconscious part of the brain is the bottomless pit. Some habitual and unconscious thoughts that are of the bottomless pit are the
following:

1. Thinking of Self as worthless
2. Thinking of Self as bad or wrong
3. Self disgust
4. Thinking life is meaningless
5. Fear of life
6. Thinking of Self as stupid
7. Lack of Self value
8. Meanness
9. Cruelty

Choosing to think only thoughts that are in alignment with Universal Law, Universal Truth and Universal Principles give one the power to fully use the key to the unconsciousness, the bottomless pit. From the still mind one can consciously choose thoughts with full conscious awareness. The busy mind never knows where thoughts come from or where they are going.

The great chain in the angel's hand symbolizes purpose. Purpose is personal benefit. The highest benefit for the Self is to become awake and enlightened, a Christ. Purpose enables one to direct the cause of events.

This high purpose gives such a one the motivation to want to choose either to:

1. Have a still mind,
2. Be in a receptive state of non-action, or
3. Choose a productive, light filled thought.

To choose a thought, one must first image or imagine or visualize a thought. To choose a thought and image a thought is to create a thought. This creative ability is the key to get one out of the dark, unconscious, memory images in the brain.

**2 And he seized the dragon, that old serpent, which
is the Tempter and Satan, who deceived the whole
world, and bound him a thousand years,**

Purpose gives one the motivation and desire to want to overcome the ego-dragon-serpent-Satan with its attendant sensory engrossment, engrossing memory and fantasizing-imagination. Then the tempter, Satan, can no longer cunningly tempt one to lead a physical, temporary life of sensory engrossment because one is no longer unconscious. The purpose filled mind consciously chooses all thoughts. You cannot be deceived when you are fully awake and conscious. This is why a disciplined mind is an absolute necessity to overcome the ego-Satan.

Even though the one who has achieved chapter 20 of Revelation in the Self is not yet fully enlightened, such a one as this has the motivation to find or control or limit the conscious ego-Satan so that it no longer keeps one in a state of delusion and distraction. The disciplined one has gained power over the cause of pain and suffering. The cause is attachment.

One with awareness can use time, as symbolized by a thousand years, to cause rapid, conscious soul growth and spiritual development. Such a one can master the present moment and motivate the Self to a greater discipline and a still mind. Then the Self progresses rapidly to existing more and more in the present moment. The present moment enables the Self to move through the stages of growth within the Self. The four stages of growth are called infancy, adolescence, adulthood and wisdom and are explained fully in my book, <u>The Four Stages of Growth.</u> Movement through these four stages produces completion of a cycle as symbolized by 1000 years.

1. First through concentration I learned to slow my thoughts down.

2. Next, I noticed there was a space between my slowed down thoughts.

3. Next, I realized I could consciously choose my thoughts.

4. Then I consciously chose thoughts that were in alignment with Universal Laws and Universal Truth, the permanent instead of the temporary. From this the real Self comes to choose the thoughts instead of the conscious ego-satan dragon.

3 And cast him into the bottomless pit and shut him up and set a seal over him, that he should no more deceive the nations until the thousand years should be past; after that he will be loosed for a short time.

Thus the conscious ego, the dragon-Satan, is seen for what it is; a poor reflection or imitation of I AM that is misusing the animal brain and body while fighting for control.

The conscious ego knows only the temporary, sensory, physical world. Therefore, the ego uses all its cunning and subtle techniques to try to solve physical problems in order to survive and have more pleasurable, sensory experiences.

The one that has superconscious awareness in the now is able to understand, know and be aware of unconsciousness. Therefore, the Self is able to bind or limit the ego while moving the attention out of a state of unconsciousness. The Self now understands unconsciousness because such a one is awake. One can seal up the ego-dragon-serpent-Satan so that it can no longer deceive, distract or mislead the Self.

Once the Self has received superconscious awareness and the soul or subconscious mind is filled full of understanding, the conscious ego-dragon will be examined in the light of awareness once again. This for the purpose of completely transforming the conscious ego and the whole Self to I AM and Christ consciousness. This is the meaning of the Dragon-Serpent-Tempter-Satan being released for a short time. This time is short in regards to physical time because now one is aligned with subconscious and superconscious vertical time instead of just physical, horizontal time.

> **4 And I saw thrones and those who sat upon them, were given the power to pass judgement. And I saw the souls of those who were beheaded for the witness of Jesus and for the word of God and who had not worshipped the wild beast, or its image-statue, nor had let themselves receive his mark upon their foreheads or on their hand, lived and reigned with their Christ these thousand years.**

Therefore, the factors of those aspects of Self that reign with their Christ consciousness these thousand years are:

1. beheaded for their witness of Jesus and the word of God
2. not worshipped the wild beast or its statue-image
3. not received the beast's mark on their foreheads or on their hand.

Symbolically, beheading is to change your whole identity.

To not worship the wild beast or its image is to use the disciplined mind instead of being engrossed in the brain and its memories and fantasies. It is the one whose attention is in the present moment.

To not receive the beast's mark is to use only the highest of reasoning instead of cunning logic.

All aspects that are productive and are in harmony with Universal Law, Universal Truth and Universal Principles will receive superconscious awareness. The one who is consciously fulfilling the Perfect Plan of Creation held in Superconscious Mind will receive the Truth and LIGHT of Superconsciousness into the whole being.

The thrones and those sitting on the thrones indicate conscious use of or control of the inner levels of Mind. To be beheaded for the witness of Jesus is to change and transform one's identity to know Self as a Christ, an enlightened being.

Those aspects who had not worshipped the beast or his image are those parts of Self that did not deem dwelling on old memories to be worth their attention. Such a one refuses to become engrossed in old memories that arise in one's consciousness. A one such as this also refuses to get caught up in the fantasy of what might have been. Instead, this great one exists mostly in the present moment. Therefore, he or she is able to use perception, reasoning and purpose correctly rather than giving attention to habit and compulsion.

The number one symbolizes the aggressive quality.

Zero symbolizes the empty mind and the power to create from space.

Ten = 10 symbolizes the beginning of a new cycle with the power that comes from understanding and completing the previous cycle.

One hundred = 100 indicates more power and understanding. One thousand = 1,000 represents almost complete understanding of the aggressive quality of Mind and the Still Mind.

To reign with Christ for a thousand years requires a still mind, and a still mind enables one to know time.

5 This is the first resurrection.

The first resurrection is achieved by the still mind. The still mind knows all thoughts and chooses no thought.

To resurrect is to raise from the dead or restore to life. Only one who is conscious can know life. One who is unconscious is dead to the world. The one with a still mind becomes awake and conscious and rises above engrossment in the physical brain. Just as Jesus, who became the Christ, was resurrected from the death of unconsciousness, so you can raise yourself to an awake consciousness. Mental discipline and a still mind are the keys. When the disciplined mind has produced the still mind, one is in control of Self and is capable of directing all aspects of Self. Such a one is alive and awake and therefore lives and reigns over all aspects of Self.

Then the disciplined student knows time and masters time.

6 Blessed and holy is he who takes part in the first resurrection; over such the second death has no power, and they shall be the priests of God and of his Christ, and they shall reign with him a thousand years.

Blessed and Holy is he who has a still mind. The one who has achieved the still mind is whole and is blessed, which is to be under divine care because the conscious and subconscious minds are attuned and in harmony with the Superconscious Mind. The Superconscious Mind is existence in the Divine. The Superconscious Mind holds the Divine or Perfect Plan of Creation.

The one who has achieved the still mind and therefore, the first resurrection, has power over sensory engrossment. Sensory engrossment created the second death. The second death is entrapment in a physical body. Entrapment in a physical body created the cycle of reincarnation. The first resurrection is triumph over sensory engrossment, through awareness and restriction of the conscious ego.

The Buddha was referred to as the Blessed One by his contemporaries. This is because he lived in Divine Superconscious Awareness. The superconscious aspects, those aspects that are understood and have superconscious awareness, are fully committed to the Divine and to Christ consciousness. These aspects of Self will know the still mind and master time in preparation for the full enlightenment, which is the cosmic consciousness and the Christ consciousness.

7 And when the thousand years come to an end, Satan shall be loosed out of his prison,

The end of the thousand years referred to is the full establishment of the disciplined, still mind in the Self.

As the mind is stilled, one becomes aware of the conscious ego that is Satan. Without mental discipline and the still mind, one is never able to separate out one's own thoughts from those of the conscious ego. In fact, without mental discipline and the still mind, one is not even aware of unconscious thoughts. Many thoughts lie just below the surface of one's conscious awareness.

The conscious ego, Satan, is subtle and cunning as referred to in Genesis 3:1, "*Now, the serpent (Satan-dragon) was more subtle-cunning than all the wild beasts that the Lord God had made.*" The conscious ego is more cunning than all of one's habits. The conscious ego is so subtle and cunning that only a disciplined and still mind can discover what is not the Self. Only you with a disciplined and still mind can discover that the conscious ego is not you. Only you with a disciplined and still mind can discover that the conscious ego's thoughts are not your thoughts. Until you can discover the difference between your thoughts and the conscious ego's thoughts, you will not know who you are. You will not know the Real Self.

In the disciplined and still mind, you are aware of the conscious ego and its thoughts. The subtlety of the Satan-conscious ego will no longer be effective. The light of awareness will shine in the darkness of unconsciousness. As you become more and more aware of the subtle thoughts of the conscious ego, these cunning thoughts will have less and less power over your day to day decisions. You will find that your higher reasoning will overcome the conscious ego's cunning rationalizations. When Satan's cunning manipulations no longer control you, the serpent-conscious ego changes tactics. Finding it can no longer control the individual subtly it now attempts to prepare for direct frontal assault.

This is when Satan is released from prison.

8 And shall go out to deceive the nations which are in the four corners of the earth, even to China-Gog and Mongolia-Magog, to gather them together for war; the number of them is as the sand of the sea.

China-Gog and Mongolia-Magog symbolize yin and yang, the Aggressive and Receptive Principles of Creation as they manifest into one's consciousness as the pairs of opposites. In preparation for the onslaught, the conscious ego attempts to bring together any and all aspects of the Self that are not enlightened. The conscious ego-Satan uses deception. The conscious ego seeks to control the Self in the conscious mind by deceiving, which is lying. Lies are not honest, lies are not truth. Therefore, the conscious ego-Satan is not in alignment with Universal Law and Universal Truth. To discover if your thoughts are from conscious ego, ask yourself this question, "Is this thought I am thinking in harmony with Universal Law and Universal Truth?" If the answer is no then the conscious ego-Satan has you, especially if you are aware of the Universal Laws and Truths or have read any of the Holy Books of the World.

Holy Books present whole Truth. This is what makes them Holy.

The one who would master the ego, now, in addition to having a disciplined and still mind, must have all the thoughts in harmony with Universal Truth and Universal Law. This is the test to determine if the conscious ego is deceiving you. These are the keys to winning the battle with the conscious ego.

The four corners of the Earth are the four levels of the subconscious mind.

**9 And they went up on a broad plain, and sur-
rounded the camp of the Holy Ones-saints and their
beloved city; and fire came down from God out of
heaven and consumed them.**

The beloved city is the conscious mind that is committed and devoted to knowing I AM and the Plan of Creation in Superconscious Mind. In the **Bible** the beloved city is presented as Jerusalem. Jerusalem symbolizes the use of reasoning to achieve the still mind attuned to Superconscious Mind. The still mind is the peaceful mind. Salem means peace.

The Saints-Holy Ones are those aspects committed to knowing the whole Self.

When the conscious ego of an individual recognizes it can no longer control the conscious mind with deceit and cunning, force is used. This manifests as battle going on within the Self.

This power play of the conscious ego is doomed to failure because the Real Self has developed a continual, conscious presence in the conscious mind. This means such a one is aware of all the thoughts that arise in consciousness. A developed being like this is now consciously choosing the thoughts and is improving in this capacity every day.

The fire that came down from God out of heaven is the expansion of consciousness and awareness in one's conscious mind and waking conscious awareness. Such a one is becoming more awake and aware in consciousness. A highly spiritualized being such as this is constantly aware of what is going on in the mind of Self.

The fire that consumed Satan's armies is the expansion that must occur in one's consciousness as one develops the still mind and thereby is aware and conscious of everything going on in the mind of Self. Then one is free to choose all thoughts. Such a one is capable of rejecting all unproductive thoughts that arise until no more unproductive thoughts arise spontaneously from the brain or deliberately from the conscious ego. The fire that came down out of heaven is also the Kundalini energy fire that has been raised through all the chakras and moves out the

crown chakra. The Kundalini 'fire' then descends over one's consciousness and being, destroying or casting out Satan

**10 And the devil who deceived them was cast into
the lake of fire and brimstone, where also are the
beast and the false prophet; and shall be tormented
day and night for ever and ever.**

The devil is the adolescent conscious ego. The devil-conscious ego
is not consumed by fire but rather is cast into a lake of fire to experience
the torment of expansive consciousness forever. This is because you
will always have a conscious ego, as long as you have a physical body.
Therefore, the devil will be present as long as you have a brain and a
physical body. The conscious ego goes with the conscious mind. However Satan, the conscious ego in adulthood, is destroyed. Thereby, such
a powerful, mature conscious ego can never control or deceive the enlightened one again.

When one has control of the conscious ego, its essence can be used
for expansion. The conscious ego resists this and is therefore in torment in the lake of fire-expansion. Mental discipline and a still mind
are what is needed to control and expand one's consciousness even with
the conscious ego-devil resisting.

The beast and the false prophet are also cast into the lake of fire
because misuse of memory and misuse of imagination is no longer allowed in the consciousness of the one with a still and disciplined mind.
Any misuse of habits, which is misuse of memories of the past, is not
allowed in the one who is awake and conscious every moment of every
day. Such a one chooses every thought or chooses not to think. When
memories are chosen, it is for the deliberate purpose of using them to
be more effective in the present moment. Superconscious awareness
overrides misuse of brain memory and brain imagination.

The misuse of imagination, symbolized by the false prophet, no
longer distracts the disciplined one because fantasizing by the conscious
ego can no longer distract from the goal of enlightenment. Instead, the
one with a disciplined and still mind chooses to imagine goals and images that will direct the mind to greater and greater enlightenment.
The mind is the vehicle with which to know the Self. The enlightened
one uses and directs the mind rather than allowing the mind to misuse
Self.

Discipline seems like torment to the conscious ego-devil and to the habitualized brain. Yet, discipline of one's mind and thoughts are exactly what one needs to become enlightened.

> **11 And I saw a great white throne and the one who**
> **sat on it, from whose presence-face the earth and the**
> **heavens fled away; and there was no space found for**
> **them anymore.**

A throne is a chair indicating power or sovereignty. The great white throne symbolizes the one who has stilled the mind and is thus able to direct all aspects of Self. The One is I AM. The one with a disciplined and still mind gains power over the false, illusory Self known as the conscious ego and becomes the Real Self-I AM.

White is a combination of all the colors of the rainbow, the entire light spectrum. The one with a still mind has found and knows the LIGHT of awareness and wakefulness. The One on a great white throne chooses a still mind or consciously chooses thought. Because of this wakefulness and awareness, such a one is aware of all aspects of Self. Then this high consciousness being separates the wheat from the chaff, which is to separate the productive thoughts that produce high knowledge from the unproductive thoughts. Then this one discards the unproductive while practicing and building the productive. The conscious mind is aligned with the subconscious mind and both are attuned to superconscious mind. Then one can once again build permanent understandings of Self and Creation from still mind observation just as was done before entrapment.

> **12 Then I saw the dead, small and great, stand before the**
> **throne; and the books were opened; and another particular**
> **book was opened, which is the Book of Life; and the dead**
> **were judged according to their works using those things**
> **which were written in the books. 13 And the sea gave up**
> **the dead which were in it; and death and Sheol gave up**
> **the dead which were in them; and they were judged**
> **according to their works.**

All aspects of Self of which the individual has been unconscious are now known. This occurs because one has overthrown and overpowered the conscious ego with the disciplined and still mind. The dead are those aspects that are unconscious. They are entrapped in the pairs of opposites, the small and great.

The one with the full commitment to know the Self has used the disciplined mind to overcome and master the brain memories as well as the imagination. This is because the one with the disciplined and still mind has mastered attention and thereby exists in the ever present, eternal now.

The one who has mastered thought, mastered attention and exists in the present is able to use memory and attention correctly and productively. No longer do habits or fantasy rule such a one. One only chooses memory thoughts when they will aid one to be effective in the present. One only chooses to image or imagine when the mind needs to be directed toward an ideal. When a person reaches this level of consciousness, learning is no longer a function of work, the sweat of your brow. Work without purpose is living the illusion of separation. Now the true reality of connectedness in the still mind is understood. Therefore, all aspects are now examined to determine if they will produce understanding that is permanent and lasting or if they are only temporary. The other books referred to are the Akashic records.

The sea symbolizes the conscious mind. All aspects of the conscious mind are now consciously examined to determine which aspects of Self produce permanent understandings that are eternal. All thoughts are examined and judged according to whether they produce lasting high consciousness and understanding or if they are only temporary. The Book of Life is the Perfect, Divine Plan of Creation held in Superconscious Mind and related to the Tree of Life and the River of Life.

14 And death and Sheol were cast into the lake of fire. This is the second death, which is the lake of fire.

Sheol, Hell or Hades is sensory engrossment meaning engrossment in the senses. Death-entrapment is replaced by the expansion of consciousness.

Death symbolizes change. Sheol symbolizes temporariness. Sheol has also been called Hell, Hades or the Netherworld. All temporary experiences and memory of experiences will be transformed and the energy used for the expansion of consciousness. All change will be transformed into the expansion of consciousness.

The lake of fire is the second death, the death that comes after death. The second death is the change in consciousness that produces the overcoming of entrapment. The first death is entrapment in a physical body and the cycle of reincarnation. The second death is freedom from and over entrapment and the cycle of reincarnation.

The first death was becoming entrapped in a physical body. This entrapment set up the cycle of reincarnation and karma. Karma is a word from India that indicates the physical manifestation of the Universal Law of Cause and Effect. The second death is the lake of fire and means that anyone who moves out of entrapment gains an expanded consciousness. Fire symbolizes the expansion of consciousness.

15 And whoever's name was not found written in the Book of Life was cast into the lake of fire.

Upon examination any aspect of Self that is found to be temporary is disregarded and the energy transformed into a greater expansion of one's consciousness.

The one with the still mind has mastered reasoning. This one is able to, *"separate the wheat from the chaff,"* as Jesus the Christ said. The chaff is the temporary information and experience. The wheat symbolizes the knowledge of the permanent, lasting and eternal. The identity of the physical personality and the conscious mind must expand into the individuality of Christ and cosmic consciousness in order that one knows, I AM.

Summary of the Inner Meaning of Chapter 20 of the Book of Revelation
Now, the conscious mind is stilled and therefore open to receive superconscious awareness. With this superconscious awareness the Self is able to defeat the conscious ego-serpent-devil-Satan-Dragon. Now, the Self consciously knows the Divine Plan of Creation held in Superconscious Mind.

Chapter 21 of Revelation

Few Word Essence of Chapter 21
of the Book of Revelation

I AM and Superconscious Awareness

Brief and More Expanded Essence of Chapter 21
of the Book of Revelation

Superconsciousness moves fully into the conscious mind
and conscious awareness. The full commitment to
discipline, teaching and service enables
one to know, I AM

Chapter 21

New Symbols &The Interpretation of Chapter 21 of Revelation

1. New Jerusalem - superconscious awareness

2. Aleph and Tau - the first and the last letters of the Aramaic Alphabet; in Greek these are Alpha and Omega

3. living water - the fully awake consciousness

4. fountain of living water - awakened Kundalini merged with life force-prana

5. Holy - whole, complete

6. gates - openings to the Mind

7. apostles - teacher aspects of Self that are understood

8. rod of golden reed - the value of knowing and measuring the present moment

9. time-temple - attention in Superconscious Mind

Chapter 21

1 And I saw a new heaven and a new earth; for the first heaven and the first earth had passed away; and the sea was no more.

The new earth symbolizes the alignment of conscious and subconscious minds. The new heavens indicate the aligned conscious and subconscious minds that are attuned to superconscious mind. Together they offer a picture-image of the enlightened one who can receive the essence of the soul learning in every experience without sensory engrossment. No longer will the Self need to learn through physical experiences of entrapment. Now the learning will proceed from observation of connectedness.

Thus, the first heaven, superconscious mind, and the first earth, subconscious mind, are no longer separated in the enlightened being. The conscious mind as represented by the sea is no more. This is because the conscious mind and subconscious mind have so aligned that they have become one.

Being no longer engrossed in sensory experience and having gained the still mind and mastery of the thoughts, one functions from subconscious mind observation. The subconscious and conscious mind can function together instead of as separate units. The Superconscious Mind-heaven, Subconscious Mind-earth and Conscious Mind-sea now function as one unit.

The following is a diagrammatic image of what I have just described. *(See diagram 15)*

2 And I saw the Holy City, New Jerusalem, coming down from God, prepared as a bride adorned for her husband.

The combined conscious-subconscious minds now receive fully Superconscious Mind.

The New Jerusalem coming down out of heaven, from God is superconscious awareness fully descending into one's conscious, waking aware-

Two Diagrams of Mind

Before Christhood

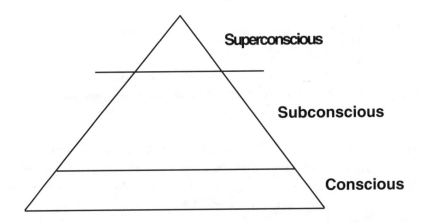

Superconscious

Subconscious

Conscious

After Christhood

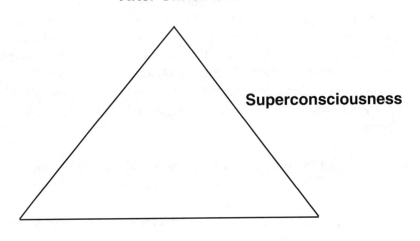

Superconsciousness

Diagram 15

ness. The still and peaceful, conscious mind is capable of receiving the high consciousness.

For such an enlightened being as this the conscious mind is no longer the bride of the subconscious mind, for the conscious mind has been merged with the subconscious mind.

Now, the new bride of the subconscious mind is superconscious awareness. The subconscious mind that has received or absorbed the conscious mind must now become receptive to receive the bride that is the superconscious mind.

> **3 And I heard a great voice from heaven saying, Behold, the tabernacle-tent of God is with men, and he will dwell with them, and they shall be his people, and the very God shall be with them and be their God;**

An enlightened being with a still mind is able to hear, which is to receive the great voice of superconscious mind. Such a one has superconscious awareness and is thus able to interpret the vibrations from superconscious mind.

A tabernacle is a movable building. Thus, the house or abode has moved to a position of availability. Before this the superconsciousness was unavailable to the individual. Now, however, superconscious awareness and perception is with one's conscious being every minute of every waking day. Superconscious enlightenment has descended from on high into the physical world. For such an enlightened being the LIGHT now dwells within and radiates outward to all the world. Such a one is a light unto all the world, unto all humanity

Just as Jesus who became the Christ dwelt with and among men, and Siddhartha Gautama who became the Buddha dwelt among men, so shall the one who achieves chapter 21 of Revelation into the Self, dwell with LIGHT and be a LIGHT among humanity.

Thus, shall one know Creation and Self as a son or daughter of God the Creator.

Now, does one know the God within.

> **4 And he shall wipe away all tears from their eyes; and there shall be no more death, neither sorrow nor wailing, neither shall there be any more pain; for the former things have passed away.**

Tears occur because one is suppressing the emotions and needs to fully understand the correct use of the emotional or 6th level of mind. Now there is no separation between the emotional level of Mind and the conscious mind. When this is achieved there is no separation between conscious and subconscious minds. The emotional level of Mind, being the level of subconscious mind closest to the conscious mind, is no longer separate. Eyes symbolize perception. One who has achieved superconsciousness has clear perception.

There will be no more death because there will be no more engrossment in the senses and no more entrapment. For such a one there is no more change. There is an eternal continuum of consciousness. There is only the further expansion of consciousness and awareness of Self and Creation. That is everything. That is cosmic consciousness.

There will be no more sorrow or wailing because the enlightened being has achieved the still mind and therefore lives in the eternal now. The statement, 'for the former things have passed away,' indicates the enlightened one lives in the present, not memories of the past. Such a one has achieved the still mind and overcome the entrapped existence of the reincarning soul.

> **5 And he who sat upon the throne said, Behold, I make all things new. Then he said to me, Write; for these are the trustworthy and true words of God.**

The one who sits upon the throne is the one who has achieved and exists with superconscious mind, which is the Christ consciousness. The one with superconscious awareness, the one on the throne, commands all aspects of Self. **Such a one makes all things new because everything is always new in the eternal now.** Only those that dwell in the past find things and life to be old.

Every moment is a new creation for the one who has learned to create and be a creator.

To write is to bring an inner awareness fully out into one's consciousness. Trustworthy means to be worth believing in. True words of God means this thought image is in harmony with all of Creation.

Such a one is fully manifesting the Divine Plan of Creation. In the enlightened one the conscious, subconscious and superconscious have become one in I AM.

> **6 And he said to me, I am Aleph and Tau, the beginning and the end. I will freely give of the fountain of living water to him who is thirsty.**

I AM is the Aleph and Tau, the beginning and the end. Each individual was created as I AM, in the image and likeness of the Creator. We each have the ability to image and create our lives. Genesis 2 says, *"And a stream was coming up out of the earth to water all the surface of the ground."*

Those who image or imagine or visualize themselves to be like Jesus or Buddha as a creator become like Jesus the Christ or Gautama the Buddha. We were made to be like God the Creator. That is what likeness means. Likeness means with like or similar attributes. When we were created as I AM we lacked experience. Those who gain enough experience of creation and the Universal Laws governing Creation become enlightened and know Self as I AM.

The fountain of living water is the ability to be fully conscious in the present moment and the present experience and receive the full essence of the permanent learning-knowledge-enlightenment. Life giving water is the experience that gives immortality. What is the experience that gives immortality? It is the experience of being fully present in the eternal now. Now, is the only time you can grow in awareness and become enlightened. Therefore, train yourself to be fully present and receive the full experience. Thereby, you will know the fountain of life giving water. The one who thirsts is the one who wants the experience and understanding that come from creating. The one who is thirsty is the one who has listened and heard the inner soul urge and realizes there is more to life than meets the eye.

When I got to the point where I said, "I have to know," meaning I have to know the Truth of Life, at that point I admitted my thirst. At that point I began my real commitment and quest for enlightenment. Knowing became more important to me than food. The Kundalini creative energy raises up the spine to merge with the life force-cosmic energy pouring in through the medulla oblongata located at the base of the brain causing and creating the fountain of living water that pours out the crown of the head. This only occurs in the enlightened one. For those yet to be enlightened, the Kundalini remains dormant at the base of the spine. The aspiring student may, however, raise the Kundalini up to touch one or more of the Chakras. The fountain of living water is connected to and related to the Tree of Life and the Book of Life.

7 He who overcomes shall inherit these things; and I will be his God, and he shall be my son.

Sensory engrossment, memory attachments and the conscious ego are to be overcome.

The one who sits on the throne of superconscious mind is I AM. In order for I AM to be your God and for you to be God's son, you will have to be a Son of God. Jesus who became the Christ is not the only one who can become a Son of God. In fact, Jesus usually called himself the son of man. The one who is using the image making ability to choose and exercise the will is creating the Self as I AM to be like God, a Son of God. Son symbolizes the aggressive movement of the will to choose soul growth. Of course, male or female can gain the Christ consciousness. The physical body is not what is referred to as a son of God or son of man.

The one who has achieved chapter 21 of Revelation in the Self is nearing Christhood.

> **8 But as for the fearful and the unbelieving and the sinful and the abominable-despicable and murderers and those who commit adultery and magicians and idolaters and all liars, their portion shall be in the lake that burns with fire and brimstone-sulfur, which is the second death.**

Fear is the misuse of imagination. Fear is imagining what you don't want to occur instead of what you do want to occur. Unbelieving is also a misuse of the image making faculty. To use believing correctly, image the enlightenment that does need to occur in the Self. Being sinful is the refusal to learn the truth in the present moment.

Murdering is destroying opportunities for permanent soul learning.

Idolaters worship sensory engrossment and therefore miss out on enlightenment.

Liars refuse to live the truth and are therefore out of harmony with Universal Truth. All soul growth must be in harmony according to Universal Truth and Universal Law.

Therefore, all limitations, real or imagined, must be transformed in order that consciousness can expand to fill one's being and the universe.

The second death is the expansion of consciousness that overcomes entrapment in the body and the cycle of rebirth.

> **9 And there came to me one of the seven angels who had the seven bowls full of the seven last plagues, and he talked with me, saying, Come, I will show you the bride, the wife of the Lamb. 10 And he carried me away in the spirit to a great and high mountain, and showed me that great city, the Holy Jerusalem, descending out of heaven from God.**

The angels are messengers from I AM that move through superconscious mind and come into one's waking consciousness. The bride, of the Lamb is superconscious awareness which is created from the full commitment to know Self as I AM.

Spirit is breath. The breath is the key to elevating one's conscious. The mind and will are the keys to maintaining the high consciousness.

The great and high mountain indicates that all the major obstacles to full enlightenment have been overcome. Consciousness is raised to such a high and expanded level as to be able to receive superconsciousness which is the Holy Jerusalem descending out of heaven.

Heaven is Superconscious Mind. Jerusalem is one's waking consciousness that previously was associated solely or mostly with the conscious mind. Holy Jerusalem descending out of heaven is superconscious awareness in the whole mind and in the whole consciousness of the individual that has achieved the still and peaceful mind. For such a one there are no divisions in Mind. Mind is one as symbolized by the Holy-whole city.

> **11 Having the glory of God, radiant as a brilliant light, resembling a very precious gem, like a jasper stone, clear as crystal.**

Superconscious mind provides the life force for all of Mind and is therefore, self radiant. This brilliant light of awareness is of the greatest value and worth. One who has achieved superconsciousness has a mind that is as clear as crystal because it is a still mind. The still mind is not murky with busy brain thoughts. The still mind exists in the eternal present and therefore clearly perceives all experiences. From this clear perception all experiences are fully received into the Self for further enlightenment.

The enlightened one radiates light. This is why enlightened beings are often pictured in paintings with a halo around the head and a brilliant aura surrounding the whole being.

> **12 It had a wall great and high and it had twelve gates, with names inscribed thereon, which are the names of the twelve tribes of the children of Israel. 13 On the east were three gates, on the north three gates, on the south three gates, and on the west three gates. 14 And the wall of the city had twelve foundations and on them the twelve names of the twelve apostles of the Lamb.**

The 12 gates are the 12 inner aspects of the Self. They are 12 gateways or portals to the soul. They are also symbolized by the 12 gods on thrones on Mount Olympus in Greek Mythology and also by the 12 apostles of Jesus.

There are three gates for each direction east, north, south and west. The directions symbolize each of the four levels of Subconscious Mind.

The wall of the city also had 12 foundations or layers of stones. On each layer or foundation there was the name of an apostle of the Lamb-Jesus. The 12 foundations with the names of the 12 apostles symbolize the 12 aspects that have gained awareness of the inner subconscious mind of the Self. These are the 12 ways we learn to master the Mind and the conscious ego.

The reason 12 is used over and over is to indicate mastery of Self. The number 12 is a combination of the numbers 10 and 2. One symbolizes a new beginning. Zero indicates that the cycle of one through nine has been completed and a new cycle has begun. This new cycle is beyond the previous cycle as indicated by the zero. Zero indicates space or placement. Ten indicates the cycle of one through nine has been completed and a new cycle has begun. This new cycle is beyond the previous cycle as indicated by the zero. Zero indicates the power that has been gained from understanding the previous cycle.

Twelve indicates the Aggressive and Receptive Principles of Creation have been mastered. The aggressive-one has been added to the receptive-2 and to the power completion-new cycle-10.

15 And he who talked with me had a measuring rod of golden reed to measure the city and its gates and its wall.

This measurement of 12 was done with the 12 tribes of Israel in Genesis and Exodus. The Exodus explains the predominant qualities of each of the 12 tribes of Israel. The angel from I AM measures the Holy City that has come down out of Superconscious Mind. To measure something is to ascertain the extent or capacity for something. A measuring rod of golden reed symbolizes one's ability to ascertain the extent of one's superconscious awareness and the value thereof. One's consciousness takes on a great new capacity and dimension when superconscious awareness is received. The 'rod of golden reed' symbolizes the great value to the individual when one harmonizes with the Universal Laws to produce subconscious understanding of time and the present moment.

16 And the city was laid foursquare, the length the same as the breadth; and he measured the city with the reed, twelve furlongs, twelve thousand paces. And the length and breadth and the height were equal.

Since the length, breadth and height were equal the Holy City, the New Jerusalem, was shaped like a cube. The New Jerusalem is shaped or laid like a cube. It has equal dimensions on all sides. (*See diagram 16*)

The cube has six sides. Each side is a square. The four sided 2-dimensional square symbolizes the physical existence which is the seventh level of Mind.

Six is the number of selfless service. Therefore, the cube which has six sides symbolizes one who has learned to think connectedly while in the physical body. Such a one is a reasoner because true reasoning requires connected thinking and connectedness is the true nature of reality. Sacred, selfless service connects one with those who are aiding, helping or serving.

The cube is the second of the sacred geometric figures or solids. The first being the tetrahedron.

The tetrahedron being the most basic straight-lined, 3-dimensional form indicates stability in physical existence with the possibility of growth and upward development.

The cube indicates the use of reasoning to cause a quickening of one's soul growth and spiritual development.

The 3-dimensional cube is built up of six 2-dimensional square sides. The cube is a very stable structure. The cube is a 3-dimensional symbolic representation of the stability of physical existence. The cube shape of the New Jerusalem indicates one who is becoming stable with superconscious awareness. Such a one has superconscious awareness all the time in the waking state. The formless New Jerusalem of Superconscious Mind, that is the Christ Consciousness, takes on form as it moves fully into one's waking consciousness.

The length is 12 furlongs. Twelve is the same number as the number of apostles of the Lamb and the 12 Tribes of Israel. Obviously, the number 12 has great significance. What is the significance of the number 12? The number 12 is a master number as are the numbers 10, 11, and 13. The numbers 1 through 9 indicate the various stages of learning as one grows and matures in consciousness. The number 10, having within it the number one plus zero for placement, indicates the beginning of a new cycle with understanding. This understanding gives one the power to cause creation. It gives one the power to cause the creation of an elevated and enlightened consciousness within one's being.

Eleven symbolizes one who initiates action on a new, consciously caused creation.

Twelve symbolizes one who has caused and is using the Aggressive and Receptive Principles of Creation on a very enlightened, evolved basis.

Such a one is close to the full Christ consciousness.

**17 And he measured the wall thereof , a hundred and forty
and four cubits, according to the measure of a man, that is,
of the angel.**

The 12 apostles of the Lamb multiplied by the 12 tribes of Israel equals 144.
12 X 12 = 144

The angel is equated with a man. Man is the thinker. A measure is a fixed
unit of capacity or extent.

One who has received superconscious awareness is able to determine the
extent of this effect in one's physical day to day life. The conscious mind is
affected by superconscious awareness and never sees the world the same again.

The power of 12 multiplied by itself is the power of 12 squared. This is the
power that comes from knowing and understanding all aspects of Self. The
numbers 1 + 4 + 4 = 9. Nine is the number of completion.

**18 And the wall was constructed of Jasper; and the city
itself was pure gold, resembling clear glass.**

Jasper is an opaque colored quartz. Jasper can be polished elegantly. Gold
symbolizes value. Clear glass is used to view the outside world. Superconscious
awareness and understanding are of the greatest value. Superconscious awareness enables one to perceive the physical world and all of mind much more
clearly than ever before.

The image of this verse is one of clear and heightened perception, great
value and the ability to reflect on all experiences until the full understanding is
achieved.

**19   And the foundations of the wall of the city were
adorned with all kinds of precious stones. The first
foundation was jasper, the second sapphire, the third
chalcedony, the fourth emerald.**

The foundation for knowing superconscious mind is will and value. Precious stones represent applying the will to discover and know one's value.

Sapphire is a precious stone next in hardness to the diamond and of various shades of blue. Sapphire represents a strongly developed will of great
value that one is able to direct mentally and spiritually.

Chalcedony is a kind of quartz. Chalcedony is the color of milk diluted
with water, somewhat opaque. Chalcedony symbolizes the ability to evolve in
order that one may receive the light of awareness.

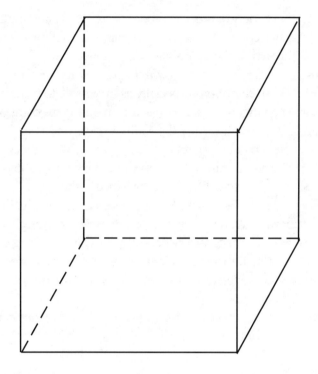

Diagram 16

Emerald is a precious stone that is usually green. Emerald represents the ability to heal all limitations while recognizing one's value and worth to do so.

> **20 The fifth sardonyx, the sixth sardius, the seventh**
> **chrysolite, the eighth beryl, the ninth topaz, the tenth**
> **chrysoprases, the eleventh jacinth, the twelfth amethyst.**

Sardonyx is a variety of precious stone consisting of alternate layers of deep red and white chalcedony. Sardonyx symbolizes the ability to learn and grow in awareness by being either aggressive or receptive.

Sardius is a variety of carnelian of a deep blood red. Sardius indicates the understanding of the emotions especially as they relate to physical creation.

Chrysolite is a greenish sometimes transparent gem composed of silica, magnesium and iron. It indicates the ability to clear one's perception by healing and growing in consciousness.

Beryl is a colorless or bluish form of emerald. Beryl symbolizes one's ability to change unproductive thoughts to productive thoughts.

The word topaz comes from a Sanskrit word meaning fire. Topaz is a gem harder than quartz often having the color yellow. Topaz represents the ability to cause the expansion of consciousness and the value of doing so.

Chrysoprases is a translucent mineral of an apple green color. It is a variety of chalcedony much esteemed as a gem. It represents the ability to improve and heal one's perception.

Jacinth, also called Hyacinth, is a mineral, a variety of zircon of a red color tinged with yellow or brown. Jacinth indicates the value of gaining control of one's emotions.

Amethyst is a violet-blue or purple variety of quartz. Amethyst symbolizes the highest devotion to enlightenment. This is why it is the last or highest stone on the wall surrounding the New Jerusalem. Purple and Indigo are also the colors associated with the brow and crown chakras.

> **21 And the twelve gates were adorned with twelve pearls,**
> **one for each of the gates, and each gate was made of a**
> **single pearl; and the great street of the city was of pure**
> **gold, as it were transparent glass.**

A pearl is a jewel produced by mollusks. Each gate is made of a single pearl symbolizing the great value and organic wholeness of superconscious awareness.

Pure gold symbolizes great value. The gold being, as it were, transparent as glass indicates one whose mind is so still as to be able to receive and perceive superconsciousness.

This verse describes the great value of coming to know the 12 major aspects of Self and the portals to awareness they provide. The 12 gates are doorways or openings to receive higher understanding and awareness into the Self. One who has mastered these 12 openings to enlightenment has achieved and received the greatest value.

> 22 But I saw no time-temple therein, for the Lord Almighty and the Lamb are the temple of it.

The Lord Almighty is I AM. The one who knows Self as I AM comes to possess the great power to create and transform.

There was no temple therein because such an enlightened being is no longer controlled by physical time. The time-temple is temporary because time is temporary. The temple is where you temporarily use time to achieve goals and learning until you achieve the still mind. Then you become the temple and go beyond time and space.

The Lord Almighty is I AM. I AM is above and beyond Mind. I AM is therefore above and beyond time and space.

The Lamb is the one committed to becoming the Christ. The Lamb is Jesus who gained Christ consciousness. Therefore I AM and Christ consciousness are the new temple of time for the enlightened being. Since such a one has received superconsciousness, the temple and therefore time is no longer outside of Self. The Self radiates the temple from within.

> 23 The city has no need of the sun, neither of the moon, to shine in it, for the glory of God brightens it and the Lamb is the lamp of it.

Superconsciousness, superconscious mind, that has been received or come down into one's conscious awareness gives its own light of awareness to every experience. No longer does one say, "Why do these things happen to me?" Now one creates the life, knows the thoughts, chooses the thoughts and lives in harmony and conscious connectedness with Self and creation.

The one who knows Self as I AM has fully integrated superconscious mind and subconscious mind into one's consciousness. There is no more separation in Self, and therefore, no divisions of Mind. Mind is one. The one who knows Self as I AM is a Self radiant being who showers the light on all. Such a one teaches all who would listen to the truth of the soul and spirit.

Such a one is a Light unto the world.

**24 And the people who have been saved shall walk by
that very light; and the kings of the earth shall bring their
own glory and the honor of the peoples into it.**

To save is to make safe and preserve from destruction. To save is to gain salvation. One who is saved is preserved, which is to transform from temporary to permanent.

Those that are saved have refused to be engrossed in sensory experiences which are temporal. Instead, those who are saved have devoted and committed themselves to the true reality that is permanent and eternal. Those who live according to Universal Law and Universal Truth and fulfill the Divine Plan of Superconscious Mind have a totally different perspective on life than those who are physical minded and sensory engrossed.

The LIGHT comes from Superconscious Mind. Those that live for the LIGHT of awareness are saved from the sin of the mistakes that cause entrapment and engrossment in physical experience.

Those that have disciplined all aspects of Self and the mind come to know this higher truth. They understand the impermanence of physical experience. Therefore, they have learned to receive and derive the essence of the permanent and lasting truth and understanding from each experience. All physical authority of such a one and all aspects that are directed by a disciplined mind will come to know the great, permanent LIGHT of awareness. Such a one will understand where the true value and worth lies, for one who has reached this great enlightenment exists in harmony with Universal Truth. The enlightened one walks and exists in the LIGHT of Superconscious Mind and the Christhood.

**25 And the gates of it shall not be barred by day, for there
is no night there. 26 And they shall bring the glory and the
honor of the peoples into it.**

Physically minded people close their mind-gates to learning. This is due mainly to fear. Fear is of the darkness. Fear comes mainly from falsely believing Self to be separate from others and the universe. For the enlightened one there is no separation, and therefore there is no fear. Therefore such a one remains open to receive the LIGHT, Love and Truth that is always available in the present moment.

There is no night in the New Jerusalem because night is of the darkness.

Darkness represents lack of awareness. The enlightened one is always aware and therefore, always walks and exists in the Light of day and awareness. The Christed one is fully awake, fully conscious forever, at all times, throughout eternity.

All aspects may now come freely into one's perception, one's awareness, and one's consciousness. The fame and truth of one's enlightenment can now spread to and be received by all aspects of Self. A great being then unites all aspects into a whole unified Self.

> **27 And there shall not enter into it anything which defiles nor he who works abominations and lies; only those shall enter whose names are written in the Lamb's Book of Life.**

The enlightened one that has reached chapter 21 of Revelation lives Universal Truth and exists in High Consciousness. Such a one can immediately perceive and know any thought, habit or feeling of the Self.

Those aspects of Self that are aligned with Universal Truth and fully committed to knowing the Real Self will achieve or receive the New Jerusalem that is Superconsciousness and Christ consciousness in the still and peaceful mind.

Any thoughts of separateness, any sensory engrossment, cannot receive superconscious awareness. The identity, symbolized by the name, must be identified with the permanent and lasting to receive superconsciousness. The temporary cannot receive superconsciousness because the superconscious mind is lasting and eternal. All is a connected oneness, unity in Superconscious Mind.

Summary of the Inner Meaning of Chapter 21 of the Book of Revelation
Superconscious awareness, enlightenment is now permanently received into such a one. Self is understood and known as I AM. The conscious mind, subconscious mind and superconscious mind are one. Self becomes a radiant being of Light.

Chapter 22 of Revelation

Few Word Essence of Chapter 22
of the Book of Revelation

Full, Complete and Continual Consciousness

Brief and More Expanded Essence of Chapter 22
of the Book of Revelation

All life force from Superconscious Mind is available to
the one with Christ Consciousness. The enlightened
one is awake in continual consciousness.

Chapter 22

New Symbols & The Interpretation of Chapter 22 of Revelation

1. Tree of Life - permanent understanding produced from every experience; Ida and Pingala

2. face - identity

3. holy - whole, complete

4. David - reasoning with commitment to know I AM

Chapter 22

1 And he showed me a pure river of the water of life, clear as crystal, gushing out of the throne of God and of the Lamb and 2 into the midst of the great street of the city, and on either side of the river, grew the tree of life, which bore twelve kinds of fruits, and each month it yielded one of its fruits; and the leaves of the tree were for the healing of the peoples.

Water symbolizes one's conscious life experiences. In other words, water symbolizes the life experiences that anyone passes through and receives through the five senses, the physical body and the conscious mind.

The pure river of the water of life is pure consciousness. It is the still mind that experiences consciousness. The busy mind's brain experiences thoughts. The disciplined and still mind has achieved pure consciousness. The one who achieves and receives chapter 22 in Revelation has gained and earned the still mind and pure consciousness.

The pure river of the water of life or life giving water is manifested in the physical body as the Kundalini energy that has awakened from its dormant state to rise up the spine and through the crown of the head. For such an enlightened one the Kundalini energy is permanently raised. It has risen from the base of the spine up through the cerebral-spinal canal and through the crown of the head enlivening and quickening each of the seven chakras, the seven churches of Asia.

The Kundalini energy now showers up and out of the top of the head and the crown chakra. This is the meaning of the water gushing out of the throne of God and of the Lamb. The throne of God and the Lamb is located at and above the crown of the head in the areas of the pituitary, the pineal and the medulla oblongata.

The one that has aligned the conscious and subconscious minds and attuned to superconscious mind, the one who exists in pure consciousness, has clear, omnipresent perception. The clear consciousness that is the eternal LIGHT gushes and shines forth from the enlightened being. Such a one radiates the LIGHT of enlightenment.

The throne of creation and the fully committed one is I AM. The water of life flows from the throne of creation into the great street of the city, the New Jerusalem. This means that I AM consciousness and superconsciousness now flows through the mind of the enlightened one. Such a one knows I AM and experiences an awake consciousness all the time, throughout all of Mind. The enlightened Self is awake and fully alive. The enlightened one experiences and knows all energies of Mind. The spiritualized being knows and experiences life force as cosmic energy and directs this fully and completely.

All energy and all consciousness is available to the Christ. Complete and full consciousness is received and achieved in the whole being of Self. In the blessed one the middle channel in the spinal column, the shushumna, as it is referred to in the Holy literature of India, is open and filled with the Kundalini energy. This is the pure river of the water of life.

In the Christ, the enlightened one, the Kundalini gushes out and radiates out from the top of the head through the crown chakra. This is the throne of God and of the Lamb.

The Tree of Life is the full and awake consciousness that uses life force and cosmic energy. Trees symbolize subconscious experience. Permanent understandings of Self and Creation are stored in one's subconscious mind. The Tree of Life is, however, a very special kind of tree. The Tree of Life indicates one who has completely filled the soul or subconscious mind full of understandings of Self and Creation. The individual can then exist with fulfillment of the Divine Plan of Creation held in Superconscious Mind.

Now exists both the pure river of water of life and the Tree of Life in the enlightened one. This means that such a one exists with conscious awareness in all Divisions and all Levels of Mind simultaneously. Such a one is fully attuned to the life pulse of the universe and all of Creation. No longer is there a separation between the Levels and the Divisions of Mind. Such a one never lacks for consciousness or conscious experiences again. Such a one is eternally and continually awake to life and all it offers. This enlightened being is no longer separate from life, but instead is consciously, intimately connected to all beings and all life.

The spring of life giving water presented in Genesis 2:6 has developed into the River of Life.

Fruit symbolizes knowledge. The fruit from the Tree of Life symbolizes the ones who have developed the capacity, awareness and understanding needed to be able to perceive the essence of the soul learning in every experience and draw that knowledge into the Self. This evolved being can see a Universal Truth or Universal Law working through and within every experience. The number 12 represents the mastery of the Aggressive and Receptive Principles of Creation. A being such as this gives freely and receives freely of LIGHT, Love and Truth.

There are 12 months of the year symbolizing the 12 aspects of Self. Thus, such a one receives knowledge, wisdom, understanding and enlightenment through the openings of all 12 major aspects of Self and has achieved mastery of these.

The leaves of the tree being for the healing of the peoples indicates the full, whole and complete understanding of every aspect of Self and of every experience. Building permanent understandings of Self makes one whole. To heal is to make whole. Wholeness is healing and health. The more one comes to recognize, know and understand aspects of Self the more one becomes whole and healthy.
(See diagram 17 and 18)

> **3 And that which withers shall be no more, but the throne of God and of the Lamb shall be in it; and his servants shall serve him;**

That which withers is temporary. Anything that dies is temporary. **The purpose of life is to separate the temporary from the permanent and then live for the permanent.**
The true reality is permanent.
The true reality is lasting.
The true reality is eternal.
The true reality is connectedness.
The true reality is oneness.
The true reality is timeless
The true reality is universal.
The true reality is unified.
Whatever is lasting, eternal, timeless and connected cannot fade

Revelation Chapter 22:1-2

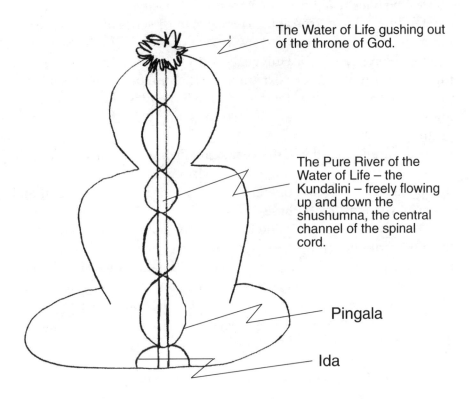

The Water of Life gushing out of the throne of God.

The Pure River of the Water of Life – the Kundalini – freely flowing up and down the shushumna, the central channel of the spinal cord.

Pingala

Ida

The ida and pingala are the Tree of Life that grows on both sides of the shushumna, the River of Life.

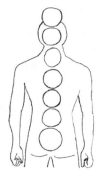

Diagram17

The Staff of Moses, The River of Life,
The Caduceus of Mercury, The Cerebro-Spinal Canal,
The Staff of Brahm and The Spinal Column

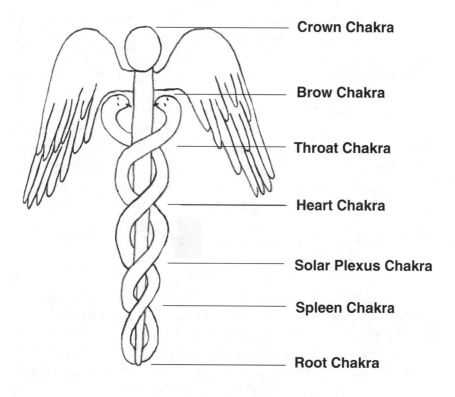

Crown Chakra

Brow Chakra

Throat Chakra

Heart Chakra

Solar Plexus Chakra

Spleen Chakra

Root Chakra

Diagram 18

away and die. It cannot wither. Therefore, make it your ideal to discover the timeless, eternal and universal lessons in every experience.

Learn the Universal Laws, Universal Truths, and Universal Principles. Harmonize with them every minute of every hour of every day. Be fully alive in the present moment. The enlightened one, the one who has become a Christ lives in the eternal, universal, timeless, one reality of connectedness.

This union within the Self and the permanent upliftment of cosmic energy enables one to fully utilize cosmic energy. This is existence in cosmic energy. The enlightened one knows Self and exists as I AM. The throne of God exists above and beyond all of Mind and directs all of Mind just as a king's throne is the place from which the entire kingdom is directed. I AM directs all of Mind. The throne of God is the abode of I AM.

The enlightened one who knows Self as I AM lives and consciously exists, awake in the permanent and lasting alive state of I AM. Such a one has transcended mortal matter and therefore never withers and dies. Such a one is always awake, aware and eternally present. Such a one, the enlightened being, is with us always, not in theory, but in fact.

The Lamb, the one like Jesus who is committed to knowing Self as I AM, will achieve this heavenly ideal. All aspects that are permanent and all the Universal Laws shall serve such a one.

4 And they shall see his face, and his name shall be on their foreheads.

Face symbolizes identity. The one who gains the Christ consciousness will know the Self's identity as I AM. The name of the Lamb is Jesus, the Knower, who became the Christ. Each individual must become the Knower with Christ consciousness.

The enlightened one who achieves chapter 22, the final chapter of Revelation has the name-identity of Christ written on the forehead. The forehead symbolizes the pituitary gland and the brow chakra. The quality of the brow chakra is perception. Perception is the ability to receive the higher awareness.

Contrast this with the mark of the beast from chapter 13, verse 16. The second wild beast came up out of the earth and forced all to receive a mark on their right hand or on their brows. This beast is connected with the Dragon who is Satan, the conscious ego. The conscious ego-

Satan will try to misuse the pituitary, the gland of perception, by practicing physical thinking that seems to be a type of reasoning but is actually logic or brain thinking. Many people think they are great thinkers and reasoners yet have very little concept or ability to cause a still mind. Without a disciplined mind that produces a still mind, one cannot be a deep thinker. A busy brain-mind can never be a deep thinker. Only a mind that is still is then capable of choosing or receiving a thought from deep within subconscious and even superconscious mind.

For such a one the Kundalini energy can enliven the pituitary gland and the brow chakra. The incarned, enlightened one, therefore, has the highest reasoning and the greatest perception. This is what enabled Jesus the Christ to reason with the Pharisees and always get the better of them. The enlightened one is filled with the Light of the Truth. To see God's face is to receive the Divine presence into your being. It is to know your own identity as a son or daughter of God. The creative impulse is thus fulfilled through the brow chakra.

> **5 And there shall be no night there; and they shall
> neither need a candle nor the light of the sun; for the
> Lord God shines on them, and they shall reign for
> ever and ever.**

Night is of the darkness. Darkness symbolizes lack of awareness. The Buddha, the awakened one, the Christ, the anointed one, the enlightened one, is never without the LIGHT of awareness. Such a one is never in the darkness of unconsciousness. The enlightened one is awake and aware.

The Lord God is I AM. I AM is above and beyond Mind. Mind is the vehicle to learn to know the Self. The one who knows the Self as I AM has evolved beyond the vehicle of Mind. Such a one has learned all the lessons of Creation and Self that mind can provide.

Now the Real Self exists as a conscious creator, a Son of God. Such a one directs or reigns beyond time, over all aspects of Self and over all mind. The enlightened being is timeless and eternal.

> **6 And he said to me, These sayings are faithful and
> true; and the Lord God who is the spirit-breath of the
> prophets sent his angel to show to his servants the
> things which shortly must come to pass.**

Faithful is being full of faith. Faith is the mind accepting and being willing to receive the truth presented by another. Faith is the firm and earnest belief in what is given forth as a revelation.

To be true is to be in alignment with the truth. The truth is that we live in a connected universe, not in a separate one. The great illusion that most people suffer under is that we are in a separate and disconnected world. The five physical senses provide us with this illusion. This is the cause of most suffering. The conscious ego-Satan promotes this delusion.

When you realize the truth that we are all connected, and everything is connected, your life changes. It is a completely different perspective and world view. When you live in a connected world you make different choices than when you mistakenly delude yourself into believing you exist in a world of separation.

In Superconscious Mind there is no separation because there is no distance. Everything is perceived, known and understood to be connected. Therefore, in Superconscious Mind, oneness, a unity of consciousness, is experienced. This is what Jesus who became a Christ meant when he said, *"I and the Father are One."* This indicates union of superconscious mind with conscious and subconscious minds.

Truth aligns with Universal Truth. Universal Truths explain and work with Universal Laws. For one to become enlightened, one must be in harmony with the Universal Laws and Universal Truths.

The Lord God is I AM. I AM is the spirit of the prophets. The word spirit comes from the Latin word spiritus and means breath and to breathe. To breathe we must inhale and exhale, we must receive air and oxygen and exhale carbon dioxide. Spirit also means life. Hence, the phrase, "the breath of life." Therefore, I AM is the breath of one who images the ideal of enlightenment for the Self. The one who would become enlightened must master the breath. Such a one masters the breath of life and is thus lifted up in spirit to the high consciousness. Breath and concentration-meditation are the king and queen, the aggressive and receptive disciplines for mastering one's own mind and consciousness. A prophet images the future. The spirit of the prophets is the breath, prana, life force and the imager, imagination, functioning together.

The one who is disciplining the mind and breath is quickening soul growth and spiritual development 10 fold. The one who adds service to this increases the soul growth even more. The one that adds the greatest service, which is teaching many others what one has learned of Self, Mind and breath, quickens and increases soul growth 100 fold or 1000 fold. It is just as Jesus the Christ said, *"For as you give, so you shall receive."* If you want enlightenment then while you are a student learning enlightenment you teach what you have learned. That is why Jesus, the Knower, said, *"These things must shortly come to pass."*

7 Behold, I am coming soon; blessed is he who keeps the sayings of the prophecy of this book.

The awareness of I AM will come quickly for the one who practices mental discipline, control of the breath-life force, imaging Christ consciousness and service to all.

To bless is to consecrate with truth. The blessed one knows the Truth and teaches a higher truth to the world. To be blessed is to be fortunate. Jesus the Christ began each be-attitude with the word blessed.

The first be-attitude given by Jesus who became the Christ was and is, "Blessed are the humble for theirs is the Kingdom of Heaven."

The meaning of this attitude of being, is that being truly humble enables one to receive and know Superconscious Mind, and exist in Superconscious awareness.

Why and how does this work? The answer lies in the fact that being humble enables one to:

1) master the conscious ego-devil, and

2) fully receive the Truth.

To keep the sayings of the prophecy of Revelation one must practice, apply and interiorize this great Truth. One must make the truth a part of one's being. In fact, the TRUTH must enter into and fill one's whole being.

To give a prophecy one must image and state what is going to happen in the future. Then when the future arrives the statement must be fulfilled. Therefore, to fulfill the prophecy given in Revelation, one must create an imagined ideal of enlightened Christ Consciousness for the Self. Then one must use the disciplined mind and breath to achieve this.

8 And I, John, heard and saw these things, and when I had heard and saw them, I fell down to worship before the feet of the angel who showed these things to me.

John symbolizes you the believer, the one reading this book who wants to be enlightened and has not yet done so. To worship is to give valuable and worthy attention. John worshipping before the feet of the angel is a picture of one who believes the Christhood can be achieved and therefore gives attention, valuable time, and worthy effort to achieving superconscious awareness.

Anyone who receives a vision or instruction of the possibility of Self becoming enlightened needs to admit that this is the beginning of building a spiritual foundation. Discipline of the Self and mind is your foundation for enlightenment, the Christ consciousness. This is why Jesus' main students were called disciples. Jesus taught the discipline of the mind and that is what he had been taught.

The feet of the angel symbolizes the spiritual foundation of concentration, meditation, conscious breath and other disciplines of the mind and consciousness needed to achieve Superconscious awareness.

> **9 And he said to me, Do not do that. I am of your fellow servant and of your brethren the prophets, and of those who keep the words of this book, Worship God.**

An angel, a messenger from I AM, is not the ultimate ideal or achievement. Let your ideal be to know I AM. Do not live in the future. Information is not the ultimate. A vision is not the ultimate. A message from on High is not the ultimate. Keep your attention on I AM. Still your mind. Quiet your restless thoughts. You will find out who you are in the space between your thoughts.

The conscious ego-serpent-devil-Satan will try to deceive you into thinking you are your thoughts. Yet this cannot be so for random thoughts are generated or arise in the brain. The brain can never know I AM. Superconscious awareness must be received into one's still conscious mind, in the space between thoughts. This must occur before one can come to know I AM.

The still mind must become empty to receive first superconscious mind and then I AM.

The empty mind can receive the higher consciousness.

The empty mind can be filled full thereby one is fulfilled.

Realize the value of a still mind. Therein lies your worth. Give your attention to the still mind and find the Real Self in the silence.

10 Then he said to me, Do not seal the words of the prophecy of this book, for the time is at hand.

Do not seal up the prophecy of this book and don't suppress this knowledge because you need to become enlightened now, this lifetime. Do not hesitate, procrastinate or wait until the future. The time to become an enlightened, whole functioning Self is now.

The hand symbolizes purpose. Purpose is personal benefit. The time is the eternal now, the present.

Now is the time to be disciplined.

Now is the time to be fully present.

Now is the time to be timeless.

Now is the time to live the true reality.

Now is the time to receive truth.

Now is the time for the still mind.

Now is the time to wake up.

Now is the time to receive the benefit.

Now is the time to become enlightened.

Now is the time to open your mind.

Now is the time to receive enlightenment.

Now is the time to receive the benefits assured to David.

Now, the present moment, is the time to experience the empty mind.

11 He who is unjust will continue to be unjust, and he who is filthy will continue to be filthy, and he who is righteous will continue to do righteousness, and he who is holy will continue to be holy.

Aspects of oneself that are unproductive are difficult to change. Therefore, instead of trying to change what is unproductive about yourself, place your attention, will and effort on what is productive. Imagine the Truth, Love, and LIGHT you desire to become. Give your full attention to this every day. Any unproductive, habitual or negative thoughts that you do not feed with your attention withers away and dies. Then the energy can be transformed and recycled into Love, LIGHT and Truth that is in harmony with Universal Law. Separate, identify and admit your own thoughts and consciousness that you may know connectedness.

Live according to what is right. To be and do what is right is righteousness. Righteousness in living and being in accord with Universal Law, Universal Truths and Universal Principles.

All is connected. Therefore, live the connected life. Holiness is the whole Mind and whole Self found in the disciplined and still mind. Therein, is found union and communion.

> **12 Behold, I am coming soon and my reward is with me, to give every man according as his work shall be.**
> **13 I am Aleph and Tau, the beginning and the end, the first and the last.**

I AM is coming soon for the one who understands and practices the inner, symbolic, deep Truth of Revelation. The one who remains committed to knowing Self in the face of all obstacles, which are limitations in consciousness, will prevail. The one who receives enlightenment has the greatest reward. All effort, no matter how great or for how long, is worth it, for what is received is of benefit forever, timeless, permanent and throughout eternity.

The thinker's duty is to discipline and still the mind in order that one may make conscious choices for enlightenment and Christ consciousness.

I AM is the beginning and the end. Therefore nothing is more important than knowing I AM. Now is the time to know Self as I AM in the connectedness of the whole being.

> **14 Blessed are those who do his commandments, that they may have the right to the Tree of Life, and may enter in through the gates into the city.**

Those who follow and practice the direction established by Superconscious Mind will know I AM. Such a one will be consecrated and will receive the Divine favor of the Divine and Perfect Plan held in Superconscious Mind. The one who lives, acts and has the consciousness in accord with superconscious mind has the correct and productive awareness to receive the knowledge and understanding of life itself.

The awakened one, the Christ who has achieved the still and empty mind, is always able and capable of receiving the lessons and Truth of Creation and Self that every moment affords.

Those who have achieved this will be able to use and know how to use the 12 gateways to superconsciousness. These ones will have Heaven-Superconscious Mind on Earth.

The greatest of the commandments of Moses, the 10 Commandments, that Jesus gave are, *"Love your God with all your heart and all your soul and all your Mind."* And the second commandment Jesus gave that he said was like unto the first is, *"Love ye one another."*

**15 For without are the vicious and magicians and the
immoral and murderers and idolaters and whoever
loves to tell lies.**

You can either still your mind, achieve no thought and receive superconsciousness, or you will be engrossed in outer, temporary, sensory, physical experiences. The still mind is used to practice Universal Love. *"For God so Loved the world that he gave his only begotten son, (Light-Christ consciousness)."*

If you allow the five senses to draw you outward into engrossment and to associated memory thoughts you will forget who you are, live for the temporary, that which is without and miss the purpose of life. Outside of the mind is the brain, sensory illusion and sensory input and the conscious ego. Do not allow sensory experiences to distract you from the ideal of Christhood. You will destroy your opportunities to quicken soul growth. You will worship or give most of your attention to sensory experiences. You will believe the lie, the illusion, that you are separate from everything and everyone and therefore fight to survive. Or you can discipline your mind, achieve the still mind of meditation and receive superconscious awareness. You can become a Christ this lifetime.

**16 I, Jesus, have sent my angel to testify to you these
things in the churches. I am the root and the offspring of David, the bright morning star.**

Jesus symbolizes the Knower. Jesus the Christ knows all of Mind, all of Creation and all of Self.

The angel that told all of these things, this truth of the evolutionary expansion of consciousness, came from Christ Consciousness in the first level of Mind in the Superconscious Mind.

The 7 churches symbolize the 7 major chakras of each individual. The one who is to achieve and receive Christ consciousness must activate, quicken and enliven the chakras until they are functioning at maximum capacity. With the awakened and raised Kundalini, such a one is giving service in raising the consciousness of all mankind by causing the chakras to reverse. Then does all the understandings, all the enlightenment of the Self, come pouring out as LIGHT.

Such a one radiates LIGHT, Love and Truth and is a Light to the world.

David symbolizes the productive use of reasoning with the full commitment. The productive and full use of reasoning enables the Self to live in the now, the eternal present. Such a one achieves the still mind and is fully in the present moment. Then the reasoner consciously draws upon memory solely for the purpose of applying it in the present. Then the reasoner images the productive future as an ideal to be practiced every waking moment.

The highly developed reasoner realizes that all is connected and therefore practices Jesus' command, *"Whatever you wish men to do for you, do likewise also for them; for this is the law and the prophets."*

The root and offspring of reasoning is the knowing Christ. The enlightened one with Christ consciousness has mastered the conscious ego-serpent-Satan-devil and has received the bright, promising morning star of conscious awareness. The sleeper has awakened.

17 And the Spirit and the bride say, Come. And let him who hears say, Come. And he who is thirsty, let him come. And whosoever will, let him drink of the living water-the water of life, freely.

The spirit is the life force that comes from Superconscious Mind. The bride is the combined conscious and subconscious mind. Together they represent the union of the whole mind, the New Jerusalem coming down out of Heaven. They represent the Christ consciousness that is Heaven on Earth. The spirit is the Holy Spirit or Holy Ghost. The bride is Mary, the blessed virgin that is unconditional love. When the Holy Spirit-Breath-Mind comes together with the disciplined conscious mind that lives in Universal Love, then is the compassion from on High revealed and the Real Self is known.

The superconscious mind and the Plan of Creation therein, is always drawing us to know the Self. Thus we will come to know the Truth.

The one who is thirsty is the being who realizes the need for a higher and greater level of experience of superconsciousness. As one continues the process of disciplining the mind to receive greater and higher levels of enlightenment, the living water of Christ consciousness is achieved. Receive the drawing power, the invitation to become a Christ.

Be the one to receive the Higher Truth of a Christ. Jesus of Nazareth, Joshua ben Joseph, received the Truth and became the Christ. You too can become enlightened. Others have, more will be. The great message of this book is that you also can become a Christ, this lifetime!

The enlightened one is continually partaking of and giving the living waters to others. The secret keys and secret code are contained herein.

> **18 I testify to every man who hears the words of the prophesy of this book, If any man shall add to these things, God shall add to him the plagues that are written in this book.**

To testify is to witness. Jesus, the knower who became Christ-enlightened, witnessed his own Christhood. Anyone who follows the same steps and process of the Truth can become a Christ and enlightened.

Man the thinker must learn to still the mind and stop thinking. With the still mind, one no longer, 'adds to these things.' Therefore, one no longer needs the plagues described in this book. Pain and suffering are the plagues described herein. Once thoughts cease, desires cease. When desires cease, attachment to physical desires cease.

When the mind stops forming attachments to physical, sensory experiences, desires and objects and becomes still, the source of the plagues, the pain and suffering, is removed.

> **19 And if any man shall take away from the words of the book of this prophesy, God shall take away his portion from the Tree of Life and from the Holy city and from the things which are written in this book.**

Discipline of the Self, the mind, and the thoughts is the only way to enlightenment. The mind is the vehicle to come to know the Self and become enlightened. Discipline of the mind is the way to learn to use the vehicle of the mind correctly to gain the Christhood. To try to take away from this book is to try to gain enlightenment without discipline of the mind. The way to gain discipline of the mind is to discipline the thoughts. Without discipline of the mind, one is unable to access the Higher Truth, the Higher Love, and the Higher LIGHT that is Life itself. To become alive one must become awake.

The Holy City is superconscious awareness. Only through mental discipline and a still mind will one receive superconscious mind. The one with the disciplined and still mind will receive the Christ consciousness described and explained in this *book of* Revelation.

20 He who testifies these things says, Surely I am coming soon. Amen. Come, Lord Jesus.

The one who believes Christ conscious can be achieved, and the one who knows there is progress being made in the Self towards enlightenment will soon receive the Christ consciousness.

As one accepts the discipline of the Self and mind, progress to enlightenment quickens. As one learns to breathe the breath of life and teach others the Higher Truth one quickens the process of enlightenment ever more. Once these things occur and are set into motion the time to enlightenment and Christhood is short.

The awareness of I AM is coming soon.

Welcome Lord Jesus.

Well come Lord Jesus.

Well come I AM the knower.

I receive this into myself.

21 The grace of our Lord Jesus Christ be with you all, all you holy ones. Amen.

To be in grace is to be in favor and to be grateful. The grace of our Lord Jesus Christ is the disciplined one who is accomplishing everything described herein.

The Holy Ones are the ones with a hole, an empty hole, whole, empty mind. They are the ones who have used the disciplined and still mind to achieve the empty mind. The one who achieves the empty mind does so that the mind and Self may be made whole and Holy and thereby be filled with the Holy Spirit which is the Christhood.

May the favor of I AM and Superconscious Mind be with you always as you practice the gratitude for all you have been given and all you will receive.

May you achieve the still and empty mind.

May the enlightened consciousness of Christ be yours.

May you receive the enlightened consciousness of Christ into your pure heart and empty mind.

So it will be.

IT IS DONE.

Summary of the Inner Meaning of Chapter 22 of the Book of Revelation
Life force flows continually, freely and unimpeded through the enlightened one. Such a one has healed all aspects and made them whole. Such a one has gained the complete and full consciousness. Such a one has received the Christ Consciousness. The Self has gained full and continual life and awareness.

Form and Structure
of Creation and Enlightenment
and the Meaning of Numbers
in the Bible

Form and Structure of Creation and Enlightenment and the Meaning of Numbers in the Bible

In my previous book, <u>The Universal Language of Mind: The Book of Matthew Interpreted</u> I gave an explanation of creation based upon one and two dimensional forms of height and width. In this chapter I will present that structure as 3-dimensional by adding the dimension of depth.

Creation, as given in Genesis 1:2, begins as a void without form, space or emptiness. This void or emptiness may be symbolized by zero.

Next comes a thought. A thought consciously chosen may be indicated by a line and symbolized by the number one. The aggressive quality of one is indicated as the Spirit of God that moved on the face of the water.

The receptive quality of the number two is symbolized by the face of the water that receives the movement.

The third line that forms a triangle is symbolized in Genesis 1:3 as God said, *"Let there be Light."*

The most basic of all 3-dimensional, straight lined figures or structures is a tetrahedron.

A tetrahedron is made up of 4 interconnected triangles. Four triangles, each three sided together total 12. Yet, in the tetrahedron the four triangles share sides. Thus, there ends up being only six sides in a tetrahedron. In other words, two triangles can be combined to form a tetrahedron.

One, 2-dimensional triangle plus one, 2-dimensional triangle equals one, 3-dimensional tetrahedron with six edges, and four sides, and four corners.

Thus from the simplest, straight line enclosed 2-dimensional figure, the triangle, comes the simplest enclosed, straight line 3-dimensional figure, the tetrahedron.

The tetrahedron is the basis of physical life. The workings of 3 and 4 together, multiplied equals 12. Twelve is the number of Jesus's disciplines and of the tribes of Israel. The three sided triangle plus the four sided tetrahedron create the possibility of the evolution of consciousness. $3 \times 4 = 12$

Three plus four equals seven and seven is also a very important number in the **Bible.**

The Meaning of Numbers in the Bible and
How Numbers Explain the Form and Structure of Creation

To draw a form or straight lined shape we start with a point or dot.

The dot or point may be considered as zero since it has neither length, nor width, nor height.

Therefore zero indicates a still mind, a mind that is empty or without thought.

Genesis, chapter one, verse 2 describes the quality of zero and the thought free state thusly, "And the earth was without form and void, and darkness was upon the face of the deep."

Zero = • or 0

The rest of verse 2 of Genesis chapter 1 describes the number one. The number one symbolizes the aggressive quality, the ability to initiate action. "And the spirit of God moved upon the face of the water."

Spirit symbolizes breath. The very word spirit means breath. The word 'moved' indicates the number one, the aggressive quality.

The number one may be indicated by a straight line that moves outward from the void, the point of zero.

Genesis, chapter one, verse 2 continues by describing the first manifestation of the aggressive and receptive principles into creation.

The receptive or feminine symbolized by 'the face of the water.' The face of the water received the aggressive movement of the Spirit or breath of God.

The receptive factor is symbolized by the number two and may be represented as another line added to the first line.

The separation of the Light from the darkness in verse 4 of Genesis 1 indicates the ability to separate and identify the difference between the aggressive quality and the receptive quality.

In verse 11 of chapter one of Genesis, "God said, Let the earth bring forth vegetation." Thus, the number three indicates the coming together of the aggressive and receptive qualities in order to create.

The number three may be drawn as a third line that connects the previous two thus forming a triangle.

Thus, we have in the triangle a straight lined, enclosed figure or form.

We now have an enclosed figure with height and width.

The next step of creation is created by adding a second triangle to the first triangle thus producing a tetrahedron. The tetrahedron is the simplest, straight lined enclosed figure.

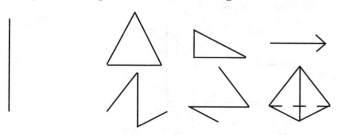

Therefore, a one sided triangle plus a one sided triangle creates a four sided tetrahedron. The four sided tetrahedron exists in the dimensions of height and width and also a third dimension of depth. The tetrahedron is made up of four triangles. Thus one triangle plus one triangle creates four triangles. This is made possible because the two triangles share lines.

Thus, the two triangles with a total of six sides existing in 2-dimensional space come together to create a synthesis of four sides existing in 3-dimensional space.

$2 \times 6 = 12, 3 \times 4 = 12$

Six is the number of service and 4 is the number of stability. Thus, from sacred service to others and to a higher ideal, is created a greater or higher from with stability.

Following the 4 sided tetrahedron comes the pyramid. The pyramid is a five sided figure consisting of a square, four sided base and four triangular sides meeting at a point.

The four sided base of the pyramid exhibits stability and the four sides also represent stability. The triangular sides indicate the one who has gained stability in the ability to create.

Following the pyramid comes the cube. The cube has six sides. Six represents the quality of service. Service to others and all of Creation is a necessary factor to gain enlightenment.

The cube continues this quality of stability because each of the six sides is a square.

Thus it is that service, caring about and giving to others, brings about the next stage of evolutionary development.

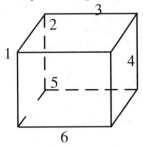

The next number is seen as implicit in two tetrahedrons placed base to base, one pointed up and the other pointed down. The seventh side being the location where the two tetrahedrons come together.

The same implicit seven factor is also seen in the circles.

Place one circle such as a coin on a flat surface. Place coins around the central coin. Six coins of the same size are always required to encircle the original coin.

For example, exactly six pennies are required to encircle the one central penny.

Thus, it is seen that service, symbolized by the number six, is necessary to know the inner Self and the secret keys to knowing the real Self.

The number eight may be seen in the octahedron. The octahedron is one of the five Platonic solids. The other four Platonic solids being the tetrahedron, the cube, the dodecahedron and the icosahedron.

The octahedron consists of one pyramid pointed up set with its base on a second downward-pointed pyramid.

The octahedron demonstrates the Universal Truth stated as "As above, so below."

The octahedron enables what is above to gain stability in what is below. This is Earth and Sky science; Earth and Heaven science.

Implicit in the eight sided octahedron is the hidden ninth. For the octahedron is made up of two pyramids joined at the base.

This hidden ninth symbolizes completion of a cycle. The number eight symbolizes value. Eight symbolizes the permanent value that is added to the whole Self from gaining stability in the inner Self and outer Self. Such a one must discipline the conscious mind through concentration, meditation, breath work and imaging. Then the conscious mind is aligned with one's subconscious mind in preparation for attunement to superconscious mind.

The inner and outer value gained leads to completion of a cycle as symbolized by the number nine. Nine may also be symbolized by the pyramid atop the cube.

The number ten is made up of the number one plus the space and placement of zero.

Ten indicates the understanding gained within the disciplined individual by completing the cycle of learning symbolized by the progression through the numbers one through nine.

The number ten can be seen in one cube set on top of another. Ten is then seen as the number of exterior sides of these two cubes.

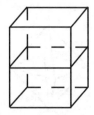

The number eleven is implicit in this double cube form as the side in which the two cubes come together. Thus eleven is a master number. A master number symbolizes the higher use of the previous numbers one through nine in order to teach and aid others to enlightenment.

Eleven symbolizes mastery of the aggressive quality.

The number twelve is indicated in the Platonic solid known as the dodecahedron.

The dodecahedron consists of 12, pentagon-shaped sides. The pentagon has five sides. Thus, the dodecahedron shows that mastery of the aggressive and receptive principles of creation is gained by the one that masters and fully uses reasoning to build permanent understandings of Self and Creation. The number five symbolizes reasoning. Five times 12 equals sixty. Sixty indicates the understanding of service to all humanity has been completed. This is the highest reasoning.

The number thirteen is the one who masters all 12 major aspects of Self and combines them into the one knowing Self. The one knowing Self is the Christ, the Christ consciousness.

The true nature of reality is connectedness. Connectedness is known as the still mind with no thought that can then receive all Creation. The still and empty mind can receive all of mind including superconscious mind.

Thus, according to the Platonic solids, creation is built of triangles, squares and pentagons.

Tetrahedron	= 4 regular triangles
Cube	= 6 regular squares
Octahedron	= 8 regular triangles
Icosahedron	= 20 regular triangles
Dodecahedron	= 12 regular pentagons

The triangle is the simplest straight lined, 2-dimensional, self enclosed figure.

Therefore, the first of the Platonic solids makes use of triangles. Four to be exact which anticipates the four sided squares used in the cube.

The easiest way for creation to build up from a cube is to use triangles again. Therefore, the next shape, the third of the Platonic solids, is an octahedron.

An octahedron is made up of eight triangles. The eight triangles in the octahedron anticipate or prepare the way for the dodecahedron, the 12 sided figure.

The octahedron has eight faces and 12 edges. The 12 edges anticipate or prepare the way for the 12 sided dodecahedron.

The 12 sided dodecahedron creates a stability at a new level of form. The dodecahedron indicates mastery of all 12 major aspects of Self.

The dodecahedron having 24 edges indicates mastery of the four and twenty elders (24) given in Revelation, chapter 4, verse 10.

The dodecahedron is made up of 12 regular sided pentagons. Thus the number five is brought into play at this level of creation.

Five is the number of reasoning. Through high reasoning we can master the 12 major aspects of the outer Self and the 12 major aspects of the inner Self.

Creation and nature then take the easiest and simplest way to create the next Platonic form, the 20 sided icosahedron. The icosahedron is made up of 20 regular triangles. Thus creation is made up of triangles, squares and pentagons.

The icosahedron has 12 vertexes showing its connection with the previous form of the 12 sided dodecahedron.

The twenty triangular faces of the icosahedron multiplied by the 12 edges give a sum of 144. The number 144 with 3 zeros indicating the power of complete understanding give us 144,000. One hundred forty-four thousand is the total of all the tribes of Israel given in Revelation 7:4. One hundred forty-four thousand is also the number of those having the name of the Father of the Lamb written on their brows as given in Revelation 14:1. There are 144,000 aspects of Self. This was anticipated in the octahedron which has a total of 1,440 degrees in all its eight triangles.

Thus, Creation in our physical universe is built up of three sided triangles, four sided squares and five sided pentagons. All of the higher numbers build on these numbers.

The five so called "Platonic Solids" are the basic geometrical building blocks of Creation. They are named Platonic because Plato taught them. However, Pythagoras taught these basic building blocks of Creation before Plato and the Egyptians taught them before Pythagoras.

Five basic structures of creation are the :

	Faces or Sides	Vertices or Corners	Edges
1. Tetrahedron	4	4	6
2. Cube	6	8	12
3. Octahedron	8	6	12
4. Icosahedron	20	12	30
5. Dodecahedron	12	14	24

The following is a list of the chakras and their corresponding Platonic figure.

The chakras are energy wheels or vortices in the body that enable one to mature as an enlightened being.

These energy wheels, called in Sanskrit, Chakras, recycle used mental energy back into Mind from the physical existence and conscious mind of the individual.

Platonic Solids

4 sided figure
Tetrahedron

= *Root chakra*
4 rays or undulation

6 sided figure
Cube

= *Spleen chakra*
6 rays

8 sided figure or 10 sided
figure if the bases of both
pyramids are counted
Octahedron

= *Solar Plexus chakra*
10 rays

Dodecahedron
12 sided figure, 24 edges

= *Heart chakra*
12 rays

2 octahedrons
2 x 8 = 16 sides
As above, so below.
12 sided dodecahedron
plus 4 sided tetrahedron

= *Throat chakra*
16 rays

12 sided dodecahedron times
8 sided octahedron

= *Brow chakra*
96 rays

The power of 10
The power of zero
10 times 96 = 960

= *Crown chakra*
960 rays or the thousand
petaled lotus

4 and 20 elders

= the tetrahedron-4 sides
plus the icosahedron-20
sides also the 24 edges of
the dodecahedron

The crown chakra, when brought into full activation is a large dome with 960 rays or petals. Rising out of this dome of 960 petals is a small dome of 12 petals or rays. This center group of 12 rays connects the crown chakra with the 12 rays of the heart chakra. The two together form the 4 and 20 (24) elders given in Revelation. Thus the crown chakra has the 12 sided dodecahedron within its makeup times the eight sided octahedron. Additionally the crown chakra with the smaller dome of 12 rays emphasizes or uses the power of the dodecahedron twice.

The chakras and their petals or rays:	
Chakras	Rays
1. root	4
2. spleen	6
3. solar plexus	10
4. heart	12
5. throat	16
6. brow	96
7. crown	960 + 12 = 972

The root chakra with its 4 rays can be added to the spleen chakra's 6 rays to achieve 10 rays. The solar plexus chakra contains 10 rays. Thus, the solar plexus chakra can be seen to rule the root and spleen chakras unless the discipline done with a still mind and a life of service overcomes this.

The root, spleen and solar plexus chakras total 20 rays or petals. 4+6+10 = 20. This coincides with the 20 sides or faces of the icosahedron.

The heart and throat chakra's rays added together total 28, which added together equal 10 indicating a higher form of the root and spleen chakras.

The 16 rays of the throat chakra multiplied times the 6 rays of the spleen chakra equal 96 which is the number of rays of the brow chakra. This correct perception-brow chakra is achieved by the correct use of the will-throat chakra through service-6.

The tetrahedron's number of 4 faces, 4 corners and 6 edges suggest the beginning of understanding the stability that service offers the individual. Service to humanity and the individual reveals the true nature of reality that is connectedness.

The cube's numbers of six edges, eight vertices or corners and 12 edges present the value gained and understood concerning service as it enables one to achieve to mastery of the 12 major aspects of Self.

The octahedron uses the same numbers as the cube but in a different order: 8, 6, 12. The octahedron, because it points both up and down, thereby signifies the use of service to gain permanent and lasting value of knowing Self.

The dodecahedron having both the number 12 and its multiple of 24 shows the one who is willing to still the mind and know the inner and outer Self and consciousness.

The icosahedron with its higher numbers of 20, 12, and 30 presents the one who is mastering and coming to know Self, the aggressive and receptive principles of Mind, Creation, reasoning and all aspects of Self.

Explanation of the Reception of Truth and Understanding

Having brought a certain understanding of the language of pictures or images into this lifetime, I have honed this ability through mental discipline and teaching.

From this mental discipline and the giving of teaching - service, the following has occurred - developed in me. I have received the following:

1. I noticed my mind - thoughts slowing down until I could observe my thoughts.

2. I developed the capacity to use my mind to observe my brain thoughts.

3. I began to consciously choose to be in a still mind state where no thoughts were present.

4. My mind became empty, and I experienced the empty mind state of consciousness.

5. In the empty mind I experienced the formless, that is the state or condition beyond form.

6. In the still and empty mind I received the high consciousness.

7. My Kundalini was - is raised, and I experience the up and down, inner to outer, outer to inner movement in consciousness.

8. All becomes connected as the separation between conscious, subconscious, and superconscious minds is removed.

From this movement in consciousness, I have been able to decipher, decode and distill the essence, the depth of the secret or inner meaning of the Book of Revelation, the last book of the **Bible**.

The **Bible** is the Book of: The Whole Structure of Mind.

The Book of Revelation is the Book of :
The Whole Structure of the Preparation to Receive the Plan of Creation.

Daniel R. Condron

About the Author

Throughout this lifetime, Daniel R. Condron has
strived to understand the secrets of life and to explain them in a form that is understandable to all.
He first accomplished this as a young boy when
he gained a connectedness with nature being in
the woods and pastures while growing up on the
family farm in northwest Missouri. In his boyhood,
Daniel discovered that the Bible was written in a
code of pictures. Since that time he has developed
his understanding and awareness of this picture
language, this Universal Language of Truth, of
Mind, of Laws. He has devoted his life to understanding what is permanent, lasting, knowing the
true reality, and the purpose of life. This he teaches
to others through the understanding of the still
mind. He resides with his wife Barbara and son
Hezekiah on the campus of the College of Metaphysics.

Additional titles available from SOM Publishing include:

The Purpose of Life by Dr. Daniel R. Condron
ISBN: 0944386-35-0 $15.00

Master Living by Dr. Barbara Condron
ISBN 0-944386-36-9 $18.00

Dharma: Finding Your Soul's Purpose by Dr. Laurel Clark
ISBN: 0944386-34-2 $10.00

The Wisdom of Solomon by Dr. Barbara Condron
ISBN: 094438633-4 $15.00

Every Dream is about the Dreamer by Dr. Barbara Condron
ISBN: 0944386-27-X $13.00

Peacemaking: 9 Lessons for Changing Yourself, Relationships, & World
Dr. Barbara Condron   ISBN: 0944386-31-8 $12.00

The Tao Te Ching Interpreted & Explained
Dr. Daniel R. Condron ISBN: 0944385-30-x $15.00

How to Raise an Indigo Child
Dr. Barbara Condron   ISBN: 0944386-29-6 $14.00

Atlantis: The History of the World Vol. 1
Drs. Daniel & Barbara Condron ISBN: 0944386-28-8 $15.00

Karmic Healing by Dr. Laurel Clark ISBN: 0944386-26-1 $15.00

The Bible Interpreted in Dream Symbols - Drs. Condron, Condron,
Matthes, Rothermel   ISBN: 0944386-23-7 $18.00

Spiritual Renaissance
Elevating Your Consciousness for the Common Good
Dr. Barbara Condron   ISBN: 0944386-22-9 $15.00

Superconscious Meditation
Kundalini & Understanding the Whole Mind
Dr. Daniel R. Condron ISBN 0944386-21-0 $13.00

First Opinion: Wholistic Health Care in the 21st Century
Dr. Barbara Condron ISBN 0944386-18-0 $15.00

The Dreamer's Dictionary by Dr. Barbara Condron
ISBN 0944386-16-4 $15.00

The Work of the Soul
Dr. Barbara Condron, ed. ISBN 0944386-17-2 $13.00

Uncommon Knowledge: Past Life & Health Readings
Dr. Barbara Condron, ed. ISBN 0944386-19-9 $13.00

The Universal Language of Mind
The Book of Matthew Interpreted by Dr. Daniel R. Condron
ISBN 0944386-15-6 $13.00

Dreams of the Soul - The Yogi Sutras of Patanjali
Dr. Daniel R. Condron   ISBN 0944386-11-3 $9.95

Kundalini Rising: Mastering Your Creative Energies
Dr. Barbara Condron   ISBN 0944386-13-X $13.00

Permanent Healing by Dr. Daniel Condron
ISBN 0-944386-12-1 $9.95

To order write:
                    School of Metaphysics
                    World Headquarters
                    163 Moon Valley Road
                    Windyville, Missouri 65783   U.S.A.

Enclose a check or money order payable in U.S. funds to SOM with any order. Please include $5.00 for postage and handling of books, $10 for international orders.

A complete catalogue of all book titles, audio lectures and courses, and videos is available upon request.

Visit us on the Internet at http://www.som.org
e-mail: som@som.org

About the School of Metaphysics

We invite you to become a special part of our efforts to aid in enhancing and quickening the process of spiritual growth and mental evolution of the people of the world. The School of Metaphysics, a not-for-profit educational and service organization, has been in existence for three decades. During that time, we have taught tens of thousands directly through our course of study in applied metaphysics. We have elevated the awareness of millions through the many services we offer. If you would like to pursue the study of mind and the transformation of Self to a higher level of being and consciousness, you are invited to write to us at the School of Metaphysics World Headquarters in Windyville, Missouri 65783.

The heart of the School of Metaphysics is a four-tiered course of study in understanding the mind in order to know the Self. Lessons introduce you to the Universal Laws and Truths which guide spiritual and physical evolution. Consciousness is explored and developed through mental and spiritual disciplines which enhance your physical life and enrich your soul progression. For every concept there is a means to employ it through developing your own potential. Level One includes concentration, visualization (focused imagery), meditation, and control of life force and creative energies, all foundations for exploring the multidimensional Self.

As experts in the Universal Language of Mind, we teach how to remember and understand the inner communication received through dreams. We are the sponsors of the National Dream Hotline®, an annual educational service offered the last weekend in April. Study centers are located throughout the Midwestern United States. If there is not a center near you, you can receive the first series of lessons through correspondence with a teacher at our headquarters.

For those desiring spiritual renewal, weekends at our Moon Valley Ranch on the College of Metaphysics campus in the Midwest U.S. offer calmness and clarity. Each weekend focuses on intuitive research done specifically for you in your presence. More than a traditional class or seminar, these gatherings are experiences in multidimensional awareness of who you are, why you are here, where you came from, and where you are going.

The Universal Hour of Peace was initiated by the School of Metaphysics on October 24, 1995 in conjunction with the 50th anniversary of the United Nations. We believe that peace on earth is an idea whose time has come. To realize this dream, we invite you to join with others throughout the world in reading a document written by over two dozen spiritual teachers – the Universal Peace Covenant – as you welcome the new year. During this time, students and faculty at the College of Metaphysics hold a 24 hour peace vigil in the world's Peace Dome. For more information visit www.peacedome.org .

There is the opportunity to aid in the growth and fulfillment of our work. Donations supporting the expansion of the School of Metaphysics' efforts are a valuable way for you to aid humanity. As a not-for-profit publishing house, SOM Publishing is dedicated to the continuing publication of research findings that promote peace, understanding and good will for all of Mankind. It is dependent upon the kindness and generosity of sponsors to do so. Authors donate their work and receive no royalties. We have many excellent manuscripts awaiting a benefactor.

One hundred percent of the donations made to the School of Metaphysics are used to expand our services. The world's first Peace Dome located on our college campus was funded entirely by individual contributions. Presently, donations are being received for the Octagon, an international center on the college campus that will serve as our headquarters building. Donations to the School of Metaphysics are tax-exempt under 501(c)(3) of the Internal Revenue Code. We appreciate your generosity. With the help of people like you, our dream of a place where anyone desiring Self awareness can receive education in mastering the mind, consciousness, and the Self will become a reality.

We send you our Circle of Love.

The Universal Peace Covenant

Peace is the breath of our spirit.
It wells up from within the depths of our being to refresh, to heal, to
inspire.

Peace is our birthright.
Its eternal presence exists within us as a memory of where we have
come from and as a vision of where we yearn to go.

Our world is in the midst of change.
For millennia, we have contemplated, reasoned, and practiced the idea
of peace. Yet the capacity to sustain peace eludes us. To transcend the
limits of our own thinking we must acknowledge that peace is more
than the cessation of conflict. For peace to move across the face of the
earth we must realize, as the great philosophers and leaders before us,
that all people desire peace. We hereby acknowledge this truth that is
universal. Now humanity must desire those things that make for
peace.

We affirm that peace is an idea whose time has come. We call upon
humanity to stand united, responding to the need for peace. We call
upon each individual to create and foster a personal vision for peace.
We call upon each family to generate and nurture peace within the
home. We call upon each nation to encourage and support peace
among its citizens. We call upon each leader, be they in the private
home, house of worship or place of labor, to be a living example of
peace for only in this way can we expect peace to move across the face
of the earth.

World Peace begins within ourselves. Arising from the spirit peace
seeks expression through the mind, heart, and body of each individual.
Government and laws cannot heal the heart. We must transcend
whatever separates us. Through giving love and respect, dignity and
comfort, we come to know peace. We learn to love our neighbors as we
love ourselves bringing peace into the world. We hereby commit
ourselves to this noble endeavor.

Peace is first a state of mind.
Peace affords the greatest opportunity for growth and learning
which leads to personal happiness. Self-direction promotes inner
peace and therefore leads to outer peace. We vow to heal ourselves
through forgiveness, gratitude, and prayer. We commit to causing
each and every day to be a fulfillment of our potential, both human
and divine.

Peace is active, the motion of silence, of faith, of accord, of service. It
is not made in documents but in the minds and hearts of men and
women. Peace is built through communication. The open exchange
of ideas is necessary for discovery, for well-being, for growth, for
progress whether within one person or among many. We vow to
speak with sagacity, listen with equanimity, both free of prejudice,
thus we will come to know that peace is liberty in tranquillity.

Peace is achieved by those who fulfill their part of a greater plan.
Peace and security are attained by those societies where the indi-
viduals work closely to serve the common good of the whole. Peace-
ful coexistence between nations is the reflection of man's inner
tranquillity magnified. Enlightened service to our fellowman brings
peace to the one serving, and to the one receiving. We vow to live in
peace by embracing truths that apply to us all.

Living peaceably begins by thinking peacefully.
We stand on the threshold of peace-filled understanding. We come
together, all of humanity, young and old of all cultures from all
nations. We vow to stand together as citizens of the Earth knowing
that every question has an answer, every issue a resolution. As we
stand, united in common purpose, we hereby commit ourselves in
thought and action so we might know the power of peace in our
lifetimes.

Peace be with us all ways. May Peace Prevail On Earth.

Created in 1996-97 by faculty & students of the School of Metaphysics